THE HOLOCAUST

Jack R. Fischel

Greenwood Press Guides to
Historic Events of the Twentieth Century
Randall M. Miller, Series Editor

Greenwood Press
Westport, Connecticut • London

Library of Congress Cataloging-in-Publication Data

Fischel, Jack.
　　The Holocaust / Jack R. Fischel.
　　　　p.　cm.—(Greenwood Press guides to historic events of the
　　twentieth century, ISSN 1092–177X)
　　　　Includes bibliographical references and index.
　　　　ISBN 0–313–29879–3 (alk. paper)
　　　　1. Holocaust, Jewish (1939–1945)　2. World War, 1939–1945—Jewish
　　resistance.　I. Title.　II. Series.
　　D804.3.F58　1998
　　940.53′18—DC21　　　97–29972

British Library Cataloguing in Publication Data is available.

Library of Congress Catalog Card Number: 97–29972
ISBN: 0–313–29879–3
ISSN: 1092–177X

First published in 1998

Greenwood Press, 88 Post Road West, Westport, CT 06881
An imprint of Greenwood Publishing Group, Inc.

Printed in the United States of America

The paper used in this book complies with the
Permanent Paper Standard issued by the National
Information Standards Organization (Z39.48–1984).

10 9 8 7 6 5 4

Front cover photo: A young boy in the Warsaw ghetto. Main Commission for the Investigation of Nazi War Crimes, courtesy of USHMM Photo Archives.

Back cover photo: A street in the Warsaw ghetto. Courtesy of Yad Vashem.

To Julie

Contents

A photo essay follows page 88

Series Foreword

As the twenty-first century approaches, it is time to take stock of the political, social, economic, intellectual, and cultural forces and factors that have made the twentieth century the most dramatic period of change in history. To that end, the Greenwood Press Guides to Historic Events of the Twentieth Century presents interpretive histories of the most significant events of the century. Each book in the series combines narrative history and analysis with primary documents and biographical sketches, with an eye to providing both a reference guide to the principal persons, ideas, and experiences defining each historic event, and a reliable, readable overview of that event. Each book further provides analyses and discussions, grounded in both primary and secondary sources, of the causes and consequences, in thought and action, that give meaning to the historic event under review. By assuming a historical perspective, drawing on the latest and best writing on each subject, and offering fresh insights, each book promises to explain how and why a particular event defined the twentieth century. No consensus about the meaning of the twentieth century emerges from the series, but, collectively, the books identify the most salient concerns of the century. In so doing, the series reminds us of the many ways those historic events continue to affect our lives.

Each book follows a similar format designed to encourage readers to consult it both as a reference and a history in its own right. Each volume opens with a chronology of the historic event, followed by a narrative overview, which also serves to introduce and examine briefly the main themes and issues related to that event. The next set of chapters is composed of topical essays, each analyzing closely an issue or problem of interpretation introduced in the opening chapter. A concluding chapter suggesting the long-term implications and meanings of the historic event brings the strands of the preceding chapters together while placing the event in the larger historical context. Each book also includes a section of short biographies of the principal persons related to the event, followed by a section introducing and reprinting key historical documents illustrative of and pertinent to the event. A glossary of selected terms adds to the utility of each book. An annotated bibliography—of significant books, films, and CD-ROMs—and an index conclude each volume.

The editors made no attempt to impose any theoretical model or historical perspective on the individual authors. Rather, in developing the series, an advisory board of noted historians and informed high school history teachers and public and school librarians identified the topics needful of exploration and the scholars eminently qualified to examine those events with intelligence and sensitivity. The common commitment throughout the series is to provide accurate, informative, and readable books, free of jargon and up to date in evidence and analysis.

Each book stands as a complete historical analysis and reference guide to a particular historic event. Each book also has many uses, from understanding contemporary perspectives on critical historical issues, to providing biographical treatments of key figures related to each event, to offering excerpts and complete texts of essential documents about the event, to suggesting and describing books and media materials for further study and presentation of the event, and more. The combination of historical narrative and individual topical chapters addressing significant issues and problems encourages students and teachers to approach each historic event from multiple perspectives and with a critical eye. The arrangement and content of each book thus invite students and teachers, through classroom discussions and position papers, to debate the character and significance of great historic events and to discover for themselves how and why history matters.

The series emphasizes the main currents that have shaped the modern world. Much of that focus necessarily looks at the West, especially Europe and the United States. The political, commercial, and cultural expansion of the West wrought largely, though not wholly, the most fundamental changes of the century. Taken together, however, books in the series reveal the interactions between Western and non-Western peoples and society, and also the tensions between modern and traditional cultures. They also point to the ways in which non-Western peoples have adapted Western ideas and technology and, in turn, influenced Western life and thought. Several books examine such increasingly powerful global forces as the rise of Islamic fundamental-ism, the emergence of modern Japan, the Communist revolution in China, and the collapse of communism in eastern Europe and the former Soviet Union. American interests and experiences receive special attention in the series, not only in deference to the primary readership of the books but also in recognition that the United States emerged as the dominant political, economic, social, and cultural force during the twentieth century. By looking at the century through the lens of American events and experiences, it is possible to see why the age has come to be known as "The American Century."

Assessing the history of the twentieth century is a formidable prospect. It has been a period of remarkable transformation. The world broadened and narrowed at the same time. Frontiers shifted from the interiors of Africa and Latin America to the moon and beyond; communication spread from mass circulation newspapers and magazines to radio, television, and now the Internet; skyscrapers reached upward and suburbs stretched outward; energy switched from steam, to electric, to atomic power. Many changes did not lead to a complete abandonment of established patterns and practices so much as a synthesis of old and new, as, for example, the increased use of (even reliance on) the telephone in the age of the computer. The automo-bile and the truck, the airplane, and telecommunications closed distances, and people in unprecedented numbers migrated from rural to urban, indus-trial, and ever more ethnically diverse areas. Tractors and chemical fertil-izers made it possible for fewer people to grow more, but the environmental and demographic costs of an exploding global population threatened to outstrip natural resources and human innovation. Disparities in wealth increased, with developed nations prospering and underdeveloped nations starving. Amid the crumbling of former European colonial empires, West-ern technology, goods, and culture increasingly enveloped the globe, seep-ing into, and undermining, non-Western cultures—a process that contributed to a surge of religious fundamentalism and ethno-nationalism in the Middle East, Asia, and Africa. As people became more alike, they also became more aware of their differences. Ethnic and religious rivalries grew in intensity everywhere as the century closed.

The political changes during the twentieth century have been no less profound than the social, economic, and cultural ones. Many of the books in the series focus on political events, broadly defined, but no books are confined to politics alone. Political ideas and events have social effects, just as they spring from a complex interplay of non-political forces in culture, society, and economy. Thus, for example, the modern civil rights and woman's rights movements were at once social and political events in cause and consequence.

Likewise, the Cold War created the geopolitical framework for dealing with competing ideologies and nations abroad and served as the touchstone for political and cultural identities at home. The books treating political events do so within their social, cultural, and economic contexts.

Several books in the series examine particular wars in depth. Wars are defining moments for people and eras. During the twentieth century war became more widespread and terrible than ever before, encouraging new efforts to end war through strategies and organizations of international cooperation and disarmament while also fueling new ideologies and instruments of mass persuasion that fostered distrust and festered old national rivalries. Two world wars during the century redrew the political map, slaughtered or uprooted two generations of people, and introduced and hastened the development of new technologies and weapons of mass destruction. The First World War spelled the end of the old European order and spurred communist revolution in Russia and fascism in Italy, Germany, and elsewhere. The Second World War killed fascism and inspired the final push for freedom from European colonial rule in Asia and Africa. It also led to the Cold War that suffocated much of the world for almost half a century. Large wars begat small ones, and brutal totalitarian regimes cropped up across the globe. After (and in some ways because of) the fall of communism in eastern Europe and the former Soviet Union, wars of competing cultures, national interests, and political systems persisted in the struggle to make a new world order. Continuing, too, has been the belief that military technology can achieve political ends, whether in the superior American firepower that failed to "win" in Vietnam or in the American "smart bombs" and other military wizardry that "won" in the Persian Gulf.

Another theme evident in the series is that throughout the century nationalism has continued to drive events. Whether in the Balkans in 1914 triggering World War I or in the Balkans in the 1990s threatening the post–Cold War peace—or in many other places—nationalist ambitions and forces would not die. The persistence of nationalism is yet another reminder of the many ways that the past becomes prologue.

We thus offer the series as a modern guide to and interpretation of the historic events of the twentieth century and as an invitation to consider how and why those events have defined not only the past and present but also charted the political, social, intellectual, cultural, and economic routes into the next century.

Randall M. Miller
Saint Joseph's University, Philadelphia

Preface

Between 1933 and 1945 Germany was ruled by the National Socialist Party. Its leader, Adolf Hitler, was an antisemite who espoused an Aryan racial supremacist ideology that argued for the destruction of Jews if Germany was ever to redeem its former greatness. Hitler blamed Jews for the decay and turmoil that afflicted Western society and for the humiliating defeat that Germany had suffered during World War I. He initially proposed that the Jews be driven from Germany, and when the Nazi Party came to power in 1933, it initiated legislation that pressured Germany's Jews to leave the country. As a consequence of its conquest of Poland in September 1939, Germany occupied territory that included millions of Jews. After Germany's invasion of the Soviet Union in June 1941, the number of Jews under German occupation increased dramatically. At this point, the Hitler regime turned to more drastic solutions.

The form of genocide known as the Holocaust marked Hitler's "final solution" to the "Jewish problem." From the outbreak of the war in September 1939 to Germany's surrender in 1945, almost a third of the world's Jewish population was murdered by the Nazis and their collaborators. Germany introduced unprecedented means of mass murder to attain its objective of making Europe *Judenrein* (free of Jews). Techniques associated with industry were applied to the mass murder of Jews in death factories, such as Auschwitz, Treblinka, and others detailed in the pages that follow.

Although millions of Europeans were killed by the Nazis, the term "Holocaust" is generally associated with the intentions of the Germans and their collaborators to rid the earth of its Jewish population. It is not my intention to minimize the brutality and mass murder of the Slavs, gypsies, and other victims of the Nazi genocide, but I want to emphasize that Hitler's war against the Jews was as much a priority as was the more traditional conflict against the Allies. Hitler was determined to win World War II, but it is arguable that had he been successful in annihilating the world's Jewish population but defeated in the conventional war, he would still have considered himself victorious. The purpose of murdering and enslaving millions of the Slavic people and others whom the Nazis viewed as racially inferior was to remove those obstacles to the fulfillment of their territorial and ideological objectives. The annihilation of the Jews, however, was a different matter.

Aside from the wealth that Germany expropriated from the Jews, there were no strategic or territorial benefits that the Germans gained from the destruction of European Jewry. Rather, the Nazi animus toward the Jews derived from racial ideology and also from the culmination of more than a thousand years of anti-Jewish church teaching that the Nazis secularized in racial terms. If the medieval Catholic church, as well as Martin Luther, taught that the Jews were in league with the devil, Nazi antisemitism caricatured them as the fomenters of bolshevism. If Christians blamed the Jews for the Great Plague of 1350, Hitler was convinced that the hidden hand of Jewry was behind not only the international communist movement but also international finance. The Nazis operated on the premise that the late nineteenth-century czarist forgery known as the *Protocols of the Elders of Zion* was the blueprint for Jewish world conquest and that it was Germany's role to save humanity from this threat by eliminating every trace of their existence.

This book provides a history and a reference guide to the Holocaust for general readers, with a focus on the destruction of European Jewry. Although there is virtually a cottage industry in books dealing with the Holocaust, few are written specifically for a general audience. This book meets that need by addressing a broader audience of readers and students with a general interest in history rather than the specialists. What follows is a history whose purpose is not so much to challenge current interpretations of the *Shoah*, the Hebrew word for the Holocaust, as it is to recount the tragedy of European Jewry and to analyze the key issues and historical problems relating to the Holocaust.

The book begins with a brief historical overview, followed by chapters on various important issues about the Holocaust. The conclusion evaluates the historical importance of the Holocaust from a contemporary perspective.

The book includes a chronology of events, biographies of major figures in the Holocaust, a selection of primary documents of some of the significant events described in the book, and a glossary. An annotated bibliography points to important works on the Holocaust and invites readers to consider further the many meanings of this historic event.

In this task, I have received much advice. Reynold Koppel, professor emeritus of history at Millersville University, read every word and challenged the text where my conclusions exceeded the evidence. My wife, Julie, was indispensable inasmuch as she read the text from the perspective of the general reader. I will always be appreciative for her time and astute observations regarding the material. Michael Berenbaum of the Holocaust Museum in Washington, D.C., was part of the vetting process, and I thank him for his time and many valuable suggestions. Randall Miller of St. Joseph's University proved to be a patient editor and a good listener. Barbara Rader of Greenwood Publishing Group was always helpful with advice. Millersville University provided support for the project and made possible my employment of Wendy Reynolds, a student, who took on assignments that made the completion of the book possible. I especially thank Maggie Eichler for the assistance that only a competent secretary can provide. I also thank Donald Yeager for his contributions. Finally, I relied heavily on four sources for the organization of this book: Raul Hilberg's indispensable *The Destruction of European Jewry*; Lucy Dawidowicz's *The War against the Jews*; Leni Yahil's *The Holocaust*; and the four-volume *Encyclopedia of the Holocaust*, edited by Israel Gutman. Despite all of the help, I assume full responsibility for the content included in the volume.

Chronology of Events

1919
January 5   The German Worker's Party (DAP), the forerunner of the Nazi Party, is founded in Munich by Anton Drexler and Karl Harrar.

September 16   Hitler joins the German Worker's Party.

1920
February 24   The DAP platform is written and a week later the party changes its name to the National Socialist German Worker's Party (NSDAP).

1921
July   Hitler becomes chairman of the NSDAP.

November   Hitler is recognized as party führer.

1923
November 9   In Munich, the Nazis, led by Adolf Hitler, fail to overthrow the government of Bavaria, in what is known as the beer hall putsch.

1933
January 30   Hitler becomes chancellor of Germany after the Nazi Party receives approximately 33 percent of the vote in the Reichstag election.

February 27   The Reichstag building is set afire, and the government declares a national emergency the next day.

March 20	The first Nazi concentration camp is established at Dachau.
March 24	The Reichstag passes the Enabling Act, which becomes the basis for Hitler's dictatorship.
April 1	A one-day nationwide boycott is instituted by the German government against Jewish businesses.
April 7	Quotas are applied to the number of Jewish students allowed in higher education, and laws are passed not allowing Jews to work in government offices.
May 10	Books are publicly burned throughout Germany. Thousands of students gather and put to the torch approximately 20,000 books written by Jews and other "undesirables."
August 25	Jewish leaders from Palestine and Nazi authorities sign the Haavara agreement, which allowed the immigration of Jews and the transfer of their capital to Palestine.
September 22	Jews are removed from literature, music, art, broadcasting, theater, and the press in Germany.

1934

June 30	Hitler orders the SS, under Heinrich Himmler, to purge SA leadership. In what is known as the "Night of the Long Knives," many are murdered, including Ernst Röhm, chief of staff of the SA.
August 2	Paul von Hindenburg, the German president, dies, giving Hitler the opportunity to establish a dictatorship.

1935

September 15	The Nuremberg Laws are decreed, defining who may be a German citizen and banning marriage and other forms of contact between Jews and Germans.
December 31	Jews are dismissed from civil service in Germany.
Late 1930s	Euthanasia programs—"mercy" killings of those the Nazis deemed incurably insane or biologically inferior—culminate. Begun as the first laboratories for mass murder, in the 1940s the programs were used as training centers for the death camps. Between 80,000 and 100,000 people died this way.

1937

March 21	Pope Pius XI issues *Mit Brennender Sorge* ("With Great Anxiety") a statement against racism and nationalism.

July 16	A concentration camp is established at Buchenwald.
1938	
March 13	The *Anschluss*, the German annexation of Austria, begins.
April 24	An announcement is made in Germany that all Jewish property must be registered.
April 26	Orders are issued in Austria for the expropriation of Jewish property.
May 29	The First Anti-Jewish Law is announced in Hungary, restricting to 20 percent the Jewish role in the economy.
June 25	German Jewish physicians are permitted to treat only Jewish patients.
July 6–15	A conference is held at Evian-les-Bains, in which representatives from thirty-two nations attended, to discuss the refugee problem. Little action toward solving the problem is taken.
August 17	All Jewish men in Germany are required to add "Israel" to their name, and all Jewish women "Sarah."
August 26	The Central Office for Jewish Emigration (Zentralstelle for Jüdische Auswanderung) is set up in Vienna under Adolf Eichmann.
September 27	Jews are banned from practicing law in Germany.
October 5	Passports of German Jews are marked with the letter *J*, for *Jude*.
October 28	Between 15,000 and 17,000 stateless Jews are expelled from Germany to Poland; most are interned in Zbaszyn.
November 9–10	The *Kristallnacht* pogrom takes place in Germany and Austria, when 30,000 Jews are interned in concentration camps.
November 12	In the wake of the *Kristallnacht* pogrom, German Jews are fined 1 billion reichsmarks.
1939	
January 1	The Measure for the Elimination of Jews from the German Economy is invoked, banning Jews from working with Germans.
March 2	Eugencio Pacelli becomes Pope Pius XII.
May 17	The MacDonald White Paper is issued by the British government, severely restricting Jewish immigration to Palestine.

July 4	The Reichsvereinigung der Juden in Deutschland (Reich Association of Jews in Germany), a Nazi-appointed organization of Jewish leaders, replaces the Reichsvertretung der Juden in Deutschland (Reich Representation of Jews in Germany).
August 23	The Nazi-Soviet Pact is signed.
September 1	Nazi Germany invades Poland.
September 1	A curfew forbidding Jews throughout Germany from being out of doors after 8 P.M. is imposed.
September 3	France and Great Britain declare war on Germany.
September 21	After meeting with *Einsatzgrüppen* commanders and Adolf Eichmann, Reinhard Heydrich orders the establishment of *Judenräte* (Jewish councils) in Poland, the concentration of Polish Jews and a census of them, and a survey of the Jewish workforce and Jewish property throughout Poland.
September 27	The Reichssicherheitshauptamt (Reich Security Main Office, RSHA) is established.
September 28	Poland is partitioned by Germany and the Soviet Union; German forces occupy Warsaw.
October 1	The Polish government in exile is formed in France. Later it moves to London.
October 8	The Nazis establish the first ghetto in Piotrkow Trybunalski in Poland.
October 16	Krakow becomes the capital of the *Generalgouvernment*.
November 9	Lodz is annexed to the German Reich.
November 12	The deportation of Jews from Lodz to other parts of Poland begins.
November 23	Hans Frank orders that by December 1, 1939, Jews in the *Generalgouvernment* must wear a yellow badge.
November 28	A regulation establishing *Judenräte* in the *Generalgouvernment* is ordered.

1940

February 8	The establishment of a ghetto in Lodz is ordered.
April 12	Hans Frank declares that Krakow must be *Judenfrei* ("free of Jews") by November. By March 1941, 40,000 of 60,000 Jews had been deported from Krakow.

April 27	Himmler orders the establishment of a concentration camp at Auschwitz. In June, the first prisoners, mostly Poles, are brought there.
May 16	Hans Frank orders the launching of the *AB-Aktion*, in which thousands of Polish leaders and intellectuals are killed.
June 22	Germany and France sign an armistice.
July 16	The expulsion of Jews from Alsace and Lorraine to southern France is begun.
July 19	Telephones are confiscated from Jews in Germany.
September 6	Michael I becomes the king of Romania, after his father, Carol II, flees the country, and a National Legionary Government is set up under Ion Antonescu.
October 3	The first *Statut des Juifs* is announced in Vichy France.
October 7	The Law for the Protection of Nations is issued in Bulgaria, curbing the rights of Jews.
October 22	Jewish businesses are registered throughout the Netherlands.
November 4	Jewish civil servants are dismissed throughout the Netherlands.
November 15	The Warsaw ghetto is sealed.
1941	Nazis, with the support of Ukranian militia men, shoot and bury over 100,000 Jews in one mass grave in a ravine near Kiev, inside the Soviet border, in what is known as Babi Yar.
January 21–23	The Iron Guard unsuccessfully attempts a coup in Romania, accompanied by riots against the Jews.
February 5	The Law for the Protection of the State is passed in Romania, making Romanian Jews subject to double the punishment for crimes committed.
February 22	Three hundred eighty-nine Jewish males from the Jewish quarter of Amsterdam are sent to Buchenwald.
February 25	A general anti-Nazi strike is held in Amsterdam.
March 1	Bulgaria joins the Tripartite Pact.
	Himmler orders the construction of a camp at Birkenau (Auschwitz II).
May 15	A law is passed in Romania permitting Jews to be drafted for forced labor.

June 2	The second *Statut des Juifs* is promulgated in Vichy France.
June 6	The *Kommissarbefehl* (Commissar Order), stating that political officers in the Soviet army must be singled out and killed, is issued in preparation for the invasion of the Soviet Union.
June 22	Operation "Barbarossa" is launched by the Germans, invading the Soviet Union.
June 23	The *Einsatzgrüppen* begin their killings in the Soviet Union and submit reports of their activities almost daily.
June 24	German forces occupy Vilna.
June 27	Hungary enters the war on the Axis side.
July 1–August 31	*Einsatzgrüppe* D, Wehrmacht forces, and Escalon Special, a Romanian unit, kill between 150,000 and 160,000 Jews in Bessarabia.
July 4	Latvians serving in German units set fire to the central synagogue in Riga.
	A *Judenräte* is established in Vilna. About 5,000 Vilna Jews are killed during the month of July by *Einsatzkommando* 9 and local collaborators.
July 21	Hermann Goering signs an order giving Heydrich the authority to prepare a "total solution" to the "Jewish question" in Europe.
August 1	The Bialystok ghetto is established in Poland.
August 21, 1941–August 17, 1944	Seventy thousand Jews pass through the Drancy transit camp.
September 1	The euthanasia program is officially ended; approximately 100,000 people have been killed in the German Reich during the course of the program.
September 3	The first experimental gassing at Auschwitz is conducted on Soviet prisoners of war.
September 19	Jews in the Reich are required to wear the yellow badge in public.
	Kiev is captured by Germans; 10,000 Jews are killed in Zhitomir.
September 29–30	33,771 of Kiev Jews are killed by *Einsatzkommando* 4a.

October 1– December 22	In *Aktionen* in Vilna, 33,500 Jews are killed.
October 19, 1941– September 28, 1943	Luxembourg Jews are deported to Lodz September 28, 1943 in eight transports.
October 28	Nine thousand Jews are killed in an *Aktion* outside Kovno at the Ninth Fort; 17,412 Jews remain in the Kovno ghetto.
November 8	The establishment of a ghetto in Lvov is ordered.
November 10	The Nazis finalize their plans for the creation of the Theresienstadt ghetto in Czechoslovakia.
November 29	The Union Générale des Israelites de France (Union of French Jews), the organization of French Jewry, is formed.
December 8	The first transport of Jews arrives at the Chelmno extermination camp; transports continue to arrive until March 1943. The camp reopened for operation in April 1944. About 320,000 Jews were killed at Chelmno.

1942

January 16	Deportations from Lodz to Chelmno begin and continue until September 1942.
January 20	The Wannsee Conference is presided over by Heydrich and attended by top Nazi officials, in order to coordinate the Final Solution.
February 1	The SS Wirtschafts-Verwaltungshauptamt (Economic-Administrative Main Office, WVHA) is established under Oswald Pohl.
February 8	The first transport of Jews from Salonika, Greece, is sent to Auschwitz.
February 23	The *Sturma*, a ship loaded with Jewish refugees, is refused entry to Palestine and sinks off the coast of Turkey; 768 passengers drown, and 1 survives.
March 1	Construction of the Sobibor extermination camp begins in Poland; Jews are first killed there in May 1942.
March 12–April 20	Thirty thousand Jews are deported from Lublin to Belzec.
March 17	Killings begin at the Belzec extermination camp, the first of the *Aktion Reinhard* (code name for the extermination of the Jews in the *Generalgouvernement* named for Reinhard Heydrich) camps put into operation.

March 26	The first transport of Jews sent by Adolf Eichmann's office goes to Auschwitz.
March 26– October 20	More than 57,000 Slovak Jews are deported.
March 28	The first transport of French Jews is sent to Auschwitz.
May 27	In Belgium, the wearing of the yellow badge is decreed and goes into effect on June 3.
June 7	The Jews in occupied France are required to wear the yellow badge.
June 11	Eichmann's office orders the deportation of Jews from the Netherlands, Belgium, and France to begin in a few weeks.
June 22	The first transport from the Drancy camp in France leaves for Auschwitz.
July 14	The systematic transfer of Dutch Jewry to Westerbork camp in the Netherlands begins.
July 15	The first transport leaves Westerbork for Auschwitz.
July 16–17	12,887 Jews of Paris are rounded up and sent to Drancy. About 42,500 Jews are sent to Drancy from all over France during this *Aktion*.
July 19	Himmler orders that the extermination of the Jews of the *Generalgouvernment* be completed by the end of the year.
July 22	The Treblinka extermination center is completed; by August 1943 about 870,000 Jews have been killed there.
July 22– September 12	During mass deportation from Warsaw, some 300,000 Jews are deported, 265,000 of them to Treblinka. About 60,000 Jews remain in the Warsaw ghetto.
July 23	The head of the Warsaw *Judenräte*, Adam Czerniakow, commits suicide rather than assist the Nazis in deporting the Warsaw Jews.
August 6, 1942– December 29, 1943	Jewish inmates from the Gurs camp in France are deported to Auschwitz and Sobibor.
August 8	In Geneva, Gerhart Riegner cables Rabbi Stephen S. Wise in New York and Sidney Silverman in London about Nazi plans for the extermination of European Jewry. The U.S. Department of State holds up delivery of the message to Wise, who receives it from Silverman on August 28.

August 12	Churchill, Stalin, and Averell Harriman meet in Moscow and affirm their goal of destroying Nazism.
August 13–20	The majority of Croatian Jews are deported to Auschwitz.
November 1	The deportation of Jews from the Bialystok district of Poland to Treblinka begins.
November 24	Rabbi Stephen S. Wise releases to the press the news contained in the Riegner cable.
December 4	Zegota (Council for Aid to Jews) is established in Poland.
December 10	The Polish government in exile asks the Allies to retaliate for the Nazi killing of civilians, especially Jews.
December 17	An Allied declaration is made condemning the Nazis' "bestial policy of cold-blooded extermination."

1943

January 14–24	Churchill and Roosevelt meet at Casablanca and proclaim that Germany's unconditional surrender is to be a central war aim.
January 18–22	Over 5,000 Jews are deported from Warsaw and are killed. The first Warsaw ghetto uprising breaks out.
February 5–12	In Bialystok, 2,000 Jews are killed and 10,000 deported to Treblinka; Jews offer armed resistance.
February 26	The first transport of gypsies reaches Auschwitz, where they are placed in a special section of the camp called Gypsy Camp.
March 20– August 18	Transports from Salonika arrive at Auschwitz.
April 13	Mass graves are discovered at Katyn, Poland, the site of a massacre of Polish officers by the Soviets.
May 8	Mordecai Anielewicz and other leaders of the Warsaw ghetto uprising are killed in a bunker at 18 Milna Street during the fighting.
May 12	Samuel Zygelbom, a Jewish representative of the Polish government in exile in London, commits suicide as an expression of solidarity with the Jewish fighters in Warsaw and in protest against the world's silence regarding the fate of the Jews in Nazi-occupied Europe.
June 1	The final liquidation of the Lvov ghetto begins. When the Jews resist, 3,000 are killed; 7,000 are sent to the Janowska camp.

July 5   Himmler orders that Sobibor, an extermination camp, be
                       made a concentration camp.

August 2   The uprising at Treblinka takes place.

August 15–20   Nazi forces under Odilo Globocnik surround the Bialystok
                       ghetto, and its 30,000 remaining Jews are ordered to appear
                       for evacuation. A Jewish uprising breaks out in the ghetto.

August 18–21   The final deportation of Bialystok Jewry takes place.

September 1   An uprising is attempted in the Vilna ghetto but is aborted.
                       During the rest of September, the fighters escape to the
                       partisans.

September 23–24   The Vilna ghetto is liquidated. Thirty-seven hundred Jews
                       are sent to labor camps in Estonia, and 4,000 are deported to
                       Sobibor.

October 1–2   German police begin rounding up Jews in Denmark for
                       deportation. The Danish population begins the rescue of
                       7,200 Danish Jews.

October 2–3   Throughout the Netherlands, families of Jewish men are
                       drafted for forced labor and sent to Westerbork.

October 14   The Sobibor uprising takes place.

October 18   In Rome, 1,035 Jews are deported to Auschwitz.

1944

April 5   Jews in Hungary begin wearing the yellow badge.

April 7   Alfred Wetzler and Rudolf Vrba escape from Auschwitz and
                       reach Slovakia with detailed information about the killing of
                       Jews in Auschwitz. Their report, which reaches the free
                       world in June, becomes known as the Auschwitz Protocols.

May 15   Between May 15 and July 9, 437,000 primarily Hungarian
                       Jews are deported to Auschwitz. Most of those sent to
                       Auschwitz are gassed soon after their arrival.

June 6   D-Day. Allied forces land in Normandy with the largest
                       seaborne force in history.

June 23–   Transports from Lodz reach Chelmno.
July 14

July 9   Miklos Horthy, Hungarian regent, orders an end to the de-
                       portations from Hungary. Two days later, they cease.

July 21–25	Children's homes in France operated by the Union Générale des Israélites de France are raided. Three hundred Jewish children, in addition to adult staff, are sent to Drancy and then to Auschwitz.
July 23	A delegation of the International Red Cross visits Theresienstadt.
July 28	The first major death march begins, with the evacuation of the Gesia Street camp in Warsaw. Thirty-six hundred prisoners set out on foot for Kutno; 1,000 are killed on the 81-mile journey.
October 6–7	In the *Sonderkommando* uprising at Auschwitz, one of the gas chambers is destroyed before the uprising is quelled.
November 8	Deportations from Budapest are resumed.

1945

January 17	The SS is ordered to evacuate Auschwitz and on the following day begins leaving. Sixty-six thousand prisoners are marched on foot toward Wodzislaw, to be sent from there to other camps; 15,000 die on the way. Forty-eight thousand men and 18,000 women prisoners are still in Auschwitz and its satellite camps.
January 19	Lodz is liberated by the Soviet army.
April 5–6	More than 28,250 inmates are evacuated from Buchenwald, and from 7,000 to 8,000 others are killed.
April 9	The evacuation of Mauthausen begins.
April 11	The Buchenwald concentration camp is liberated by American forces.
April 15	Danish Jews in the Protectorate are transferred to Sweden with the help of the International Red Cross.
April 29	Dachau is liberated by the American Seventh Army.
April 29–30	Ravensbrück is liberated; in the camp are 3,500 sick women.
April 30	Hitler and Eva Braun commit suicide in Hitler's bunker in Berlin.
May 3	The Nazis hand over Theresienstadt, with 17,247 Jewish inmates, to the International Red Cross.
May 7	The Germans surrender to the Allies.

August   The Nuremberg Trial, an international military tribunal, is
                         established to punish those who had planned or waged
                         aggressive war or acted criminally against humanity. Great
                         Britain, the United States, the Soviet Union, and France act
                         on behalf of the United Nations for the twenty-six countries
                         that had fought Germany. The evidence taken by the tribunal
                         exposes to the world the genocidal fury that had fueled the
                         Nazi movement.

Introduction

The unimaginable horror of the Holocaust was an unprecedented event in the history of civilization. Although genocidal behavior had occurred prior to the Holocaust, such as the Turkish atrocities against the Armenians in 1915 and America's brutal treatment of the Native American population, never before had an entire people been marked for death because of the accident of their birth. After the German invasion of the Soviet Union in June 1941, the objective of the Nazis was to murder every last man, woman, and child of Jewish ancestry, which the Nazis defined as anyone with a trace of Jewish "blood" dating back two to three generations. Prior to the outbreak of World War II in 1939, Germany legally segregated Jews from the rest of society and justified this action by representing the Jews as a threat to the collective health of the German nation.

Germany under Nazi rule (1933–1945) emphasized the primacy of racial ideology. Hitler's close confidant Rudolf Hess made this clear when he defined National Socialism as applied biology. The genocide against the Jews derived from the view that Jews were one large, diseased, and alien entity and therefore must be separated from the rest of the German people. Although the Nazis also targeted other groups, such as the disabled, gypsies, and Slavs, they placed Jews in a special category.

Nazi racial ideology stressed the descent of the German people from the Aryan race, an Indo-European language group. They described the history of civilization as the struggle between the superior Aryan race and the inferior but powerful Semites. Because the semitic Jews had attained positions of prominence not only in Germany but throughout the Western world, they were deemed a threat to the Aryan race. In their efforts to reassert the primacy of the Aryan peoples over everyone else, the Nazis believed that the removal, if not the destruction, of the Jews was the necessary condition for the attainment of their ideological objective. So compelling was this belief that Adolf Hitler compromised the German war effort to achieve it. The construction of the death camps and the rerouting of trains to camps such as Auschwitz in times of severe wartime shortages testify to the priority that the Germans placed on the murder of European Jewry.

The application of genocidal policies did not start with the Jews. From the moment the Nazis took power in 1933, they introduced racial hygiene programs to weed out those deemed "unfit" for German society. Nazi propaganda—educational curriculum used in the Hitler Youth, school-books, articles, and films—mobilized the population behind its far-reaching racial hygiene policies. New schoolbooks, for example, introduced the cost of racial hygiene in mathematical problems that asked, for example, how many new houses at 15,000 marks apiece can be built for the construction of an asylum that costs 6 million marks. The implication, of course, was that Germany would be better off using its capital to build homes for those who contributed to society than for expenditures on the unproductive elements that utilized limited resources. Through such lessons, German youth were subtly indoctrinated to accept the premises behind the genocidal euthanasia program that Germany introduced at the start of World War II.

German scientists and physicians were in the forefront of the eugenics movement (the study of racial differences), which was popular on both sides of the Atlantic. In the 1920s the Rockefeller Foundation played a major role in establishing and sponsoring major eugenics institutions in Germany. In 1935 Adolf Hitler thanked Leon Whitney of the American Eugenics Society for sending him a copy of his book, *The Case for Sterilization* (1934). Support for racial hygiene courts and programs of sterilization reached a climax in 1939 when Hitler secretly authorized a euthanasia program for the purpose of eliminating from Germany "life unworthy of living": the physically deformed, the mentally retarded, alcoholics, and those labeled as "social undesirables." The euthanasia program was perpetrated in secret inasmuch as Hitler feared that the public would not approve such killings and that they would spark public unrest.

Despite the efforts at secrecy, the euthanasia killings became widely known. Part of the problem was that the killings were on such a large scale that they could not be kept a secret. In addition, despite the efforts of the Nazis to stigmatize the disabled as "life unworthy of living," they could not break the bonds between patients and relatives. When, in August 1941, Hitler ordered an end to the euthanasia program, he did so because he realized that the program had become public knowledge and was arousing public disquiet. Church protest developed only after the full extent of the euthanasia killings had become public knowledge by the summer of 1940. The euthanasia program, however, continued sub rosa until the end of the war, and by 1945 more than 100,000 "patients" had been legally murdered with the consent of medical doctors who actively took the role of killers in pursuit of the Third Reich's war against social and physical undesirables. Both the machinery and the technicians of the euthanasia program were later transferred to the death camps in eastern Europe.

Holocaust historians are divided on the question as to whether the plan to murder the Jews of Europe was Hitler's objective from the moment he became the leader of the National Socialist movement or whether the opportunity to implement the Final Solution presented itself as a functional response to the exigency of World War II. Over the course of the war, the Germans ruled over more than 5 million Jews, about one-third of all Jews at that time. It was impossible during wartime to continue the policy of crowding Jews in ghettos in preparation for resettling them on "reservations" such as the 1939 proposal to move Jews to the Lublin district in Poland (Nisko Plan) or the 1940 plan to move them to the French colony of Madagascar. Unable to remove Jews from Europe, Germany turned to mass murder to solve its "Jewish problem."

The turn to genocide prompted few reservations among the German leadership. The reluctance of the rest of the world to absorb Jewish refugees who were fleeing Nazi persecution persuaded the Nazis that they could deal with the Jews as they wished. As evinced by the failure of both the American-initiated Evian Conference in 1938 and the Bermuda Conference in 1943 to alleviate the plight of Europe's Jews, Hitler was convinced that the democratic nations cared little for Jews. He concluded that the application of the euthanasia program to the Jewish problem probably would not elicit more than the normal reaction that wartime atrocities stories usually generated. Hitler was right. Questions of mobilizing armies rather than saving the victims of Nazi atrocities dominated Allied policy. Nevertheless, Germany cloaked the language of the plan to murder Europe's Jews in euphemisms in order not to panic the victims or to prevent a repetition of the reaction that had occurred in Germany when news of the euthanasia program had filtered out.

When Hitler came to power in 1933, Jews composed about 1 percent of the German population of 55 million people. Beginning with the boycott of

Jewish stores on April 1, 1933, the Nazis incrementally passed laws that segregated German Jews from the rest of the nation. Between 1933 and 1938, the policy of social and political ostracism was accompanied by intense pressure that encouraged Jews to emigrate from Germany. This policy failed for a number of reasons, including the reluctance of many German Jews, especially among the elderly, to leave their homeland. German Jews accompanied this refusal to emigrate with the belief that conditions would not deteriorate further and that having withstood the worst of the Nazi excesses, they would be able to maintain their life in Germany as second-class citizens. This attitude changed after *Kristallnacht* ("The Night of Broken Glass") on November 9, 1938, when the German government orchestrated a pogrom (riot) in Germany and Austria in which mobs attacked Jews, sacked synagogues, and looted property. Those who chose to emigrate after *Kristallnacht*, however, found obstacles in their path, including the reluctance of the United States, Canada, and other countries to alter their restrictive immigration laws. By 1939 this included limited immigration to the British Mandate of Palestine, where the British imposed a quota of 75,000 Jews for each of the following five years.

The German invasion of Poland in September 1939 marked the beginning of World War II. The war against Poland, however, would not have been possible had it not been for the treaty between the Soviet Union and Germany signed in August 1939. As a result of this pact between the former enemies, Germany annexed the territory in western Poland and used the central part of the country, which it called the *Generalgouvernment*, as an area of resettlement for Poles and Jews. The Soviets, in turn, sent their troops into eastern Poland and the Baltic states. The Germans, however, considered their own invasion not as an act of aggression but as one of restoration. As the Germans viewed it, their policy of *lebensraum* or "living space" was one in which they would recover land that Poland had acquired at Germany's expense as a result of World War I. Nazi Germany hoped to resettle some 10 million ethnic Germans living in eastern Europe and in the Baltic states on the reconquered German land in western Poland in order to create a utopia of pure-bred Aryan men and women who would help to restore Germany's greatness through their work on the soil. As for the Poles and Jews who lived on the conquered territory, they were to be resettled in the *Generalgouvernment*, with the Poles reduced to the status of serfs and the Jews temporarily placed in ghettos until plans were finalized regarding their future.

One of the occupied territories was Oswiecim, located in Upper Silesia, which the Germans claimed had at one time been an integral part of

Germany. Upon the occupation of the town, the Germans changed its name to Auschwitz. Initially the idea was to resettle Germans in the area, but it had few resources to sustain a large population. On April 27, 1940, Heinrich Himmler, Reichsführer-SS, head of the Gestapo, and the Waffen-SS, the militarized units of the SS, ordered the establishment of a concentration camp near the town of Auschwitz. In order to make the area economically attractive, Himmler invited I. G. Farben to build a factory to produce vitally needed synthetic rubber. Himmler guaranteed the corporation that it would receive an unlimited pool of slave labor, which initially consisted of Polish workers. The camp was also used for the punishment of political prisoners. It did not take long before the camp acquired the reputation as one of the cruelest of the Nazi concentration camps, where torture and executions became a daily occurrence.

In March 1941, Himmler ordered the erection of a second camp, which was known as Auschwitz II or Birkenau. In March 1942 a third camp was constructed in nearby Monowitz and was known as Auschwitz III. Both Auschwitz I and Monowitz were primarily labor camps. In Birkenau, the Nazis built gas chambers and crematoriums for the extermination of prisoners. Those who worked at forced labor at Auschwitz survived until the Germans determined otherwise. Once the Final Solution was implemented, Soviet prisoners of war and Jews were sent to Auschwitz, where those deemed unfit for labor were immediately put to death. It is estimated that between 1.1 and 1.3 million Jews and more than 1 million non-Jews were ultimately gassed at Auschwitz.

Hitler believed that both bolshevism and democracy were Jewish inventions. Following the German invasion of Russia in June 1941, Hitler considered himself at war with the Jews through their proxies the United States, Great Britain, and the Soviet Union. With war a reality, the Nazis wasted little time in organizing their killing machine against the disabled and shortly after against the Jews, gypsies, and Slavic elites. Most historians agree that the Holocaust began with the German invasion of the Soviet Union in June 1941. Squads of special commando forces known as *Einsatzgrüppen* accompanied the German army into Russia with the objective of killing captured Soviet political commissars, communist functionaries of all ranks, agitators, and all Jews. The German military and the *Einsatzgrüppen* acted under the authority of the Guidelines for the Treatment of Political Commissars (June 6, 1941), also known as the Commissar Order, which abolished the rules of war as established by custom and formulated in international law. The actions of the *Einsatzgrüppen* in the Soviet Union were not the first instance of civilians being killed by these units. As they accompanied the army in the invasion of Poland in 1939, the *Einsatzgrüppen* performed similar actions against Jews.

The decision to pursue a "Final Solution to the Jewish Problem" followed Germany's failure to resettle the Jews outside German-occupied Europe. The unwillingness of the Allied governments to liberalize their immigration laws hastened the Nazis' move to a policy of extermination. During the German invasion of the Soviet Union, the *Einsatzgrüppen* killed Jews through mass shootings and even employed mobile vans as gas chambers using carbon monoxide to kill their victims. But given the large number of Jews targeted for annihilation, such methods of killing were too expensive and inefficient to achieve the desired result. The killing process also had a psychologically traumatizing effect on the perpetrators. Efficiently murdering large numbers of Jews required expertise and techniques found in industrial factories. Annihilation camps such as at Auschwitz, Treblinka, Belzec, and Sobibor became factories of death where the techniques of industrial engineering were applied to genocide.

The Wannsee Conference, held in a suburb of Berlin in January 1942, coordinated the major German bureaucracies that were necessary to implement the Final Solution. The meeting was chaired by Reinhard Heydrich, the head of the Reich Main Security Office and Himmler's closest aide. The assembled Nazi bureaucrats were informed of the high priority the annihilation of Europe's Jews had among the German leadership, especially Adolf Hitler. The conference participants were told that they were expected to cooperate in all facets of the process that would eventually make Europe *Judenrein.*

Following the conference, the plan to annihilate the Jews of Europe intensified. The ghettos, which the Germans had viewed as a temporary location for Jews until they could be resettled to the Nisko region or Madagascar, now became warehouses for a different kind of resettlement. The Germans appointed Jewish councils in each ghetto to maintain law and order and fill the daily quota of Jews who were to be sent by train to the death camps. Historians such as Raul Hilberg and the late Hannah Arendt have accused the Jewish councils of complicity in the annihilation of European Jewry because of their cooperation with the Germans. Others have argued that the councils had little choice; had they not undertaken this responsibility, the Germans would have made life even more brutal for the Jews trapped in the ghettos. Whatever the case, the ghettos expedited the process of mass murder.

The Germans used the ghettos as the primary reservoir for the camps and, for Himmler, as a source of slave labor. Until 1943, he believed that "there was no reason not to use the labor potential of Jews as an integral part of the Final Solution." In January 1943, however, Himmler realized that Germany would not win the war. At this point, his dream of resettling millions of Germans evaporated, and cleansing Europe of Jews became an end in itself. Auschwitz once again became an object of his concern, only this time it was not to supply labor for I. G. Farben but to expand the operating facilities of the crematoriums. Although Jews continued to work as slave laborers at the synthetic rubber plant and "productive work" was performed by the mostly Jewish inmates of Auschwitz, their labor ceased to be important to Himmler. Only the "special squads" mattered. It was their task to maintain order among those selected to be killed, to extract gold teeth and cut the women's hair, to burn the corpses, and to prepare the belongings of the dead for transport to the Reich. Each squad, which consisted primarily of Jews, lasted for a short period of time; after a few months, they too were killed.

It would be impossible to calculate with accuracy the number of those killed by the Germans in the death camps. Various historians have given different estimates of the number of Jews killed by the Nazis in the Holocaust, which range between 4 million and 7 millon. One study of the Nazi genocide estimates that of the 9,797,840 Jews in German-dominated Europe, the Germans massacred approximately 5,291,000 or 54 percent of the Jews within their reach, including more than 1.5 million children under the age of eighteen.[1] For any Jews living in 1939 in soon-to-be-German-occupied Europe, there was a better than even chance that they would die a violent death. Jews were not the only targets of the Germans. They also killed an estimated 10,547,000 Slavs, which included millions of Poles, Ukrainians, Byelorussians and Soviet prisoners of war. Others whom the Nazis marked for death included the gypsies, and about 5,000 homosexuals of an estimated million Himmler believed resided in Germany. These numbers suggest that the Nazi genocide was far-reaching in its preoccupation with the creation of a master race and that although the Jews composed the primary category of people designated by the Nazis for extermination, there were many such categories. From the perspective of the sheer numbers of those killed as a consequence of German policy, this was certainly the result of the regime's racial ideology.

An additional factor must be considered in order to comprehend the uniqueness of the Holocaust. Nazi propaganda depicted the Jews in the same way as the devil was imagined during the Middle Ages. Just as witches were construed as minions of Satan and were burned at the stake, the Nazis viewed Jews as agents of bolshevism and international finance and were burned in crematoriums. Slavs, like the Jews, were considered inferior by the Nazis, and it is probable that eventually most would be killed. But during the war years, the Nazis called for physically removing millions of Slavs in eastern Europe for the purpose of resettling Baltic Germans and others of Aryan stock in their place. The policy also called for the execution of the Slavic elites, including the professional classes, the political leadership, and intellectuals. The majority of Slavs were to be consigned to forced labor characterized by starvation rations, lack of medical care, and the deportation of millions to Siberia once the Soviet Union was conquered. That millions would eventually die as a result of this policy was consistent with the Nazi goal of creating vast spaces in eastern Europe that would serve as the new home for a growing German population. By 1940, the Nazi plan called for the resettlement of 100 million slaves in Poland, the Ukraine, and Russia, for the purpose of slave labor, and the elimination of everyone else. The Slavic peoples were viewed as inferior but not as devils, and their immediate fate was not driven by the same ideology as that of the Jews.

The often used and inaccurate definition of the Holocaust as the murder of 6 million Jews and 5 million others is not meant to imply that Jewish life was somehow more valuable than that of the Slavs and other victims of the Nazi terror. Rather, it is to suggest that the Nazi objective in regard to the Jews was different from that directed toward other groups and that the purpose for killing Jews was unprecedented in history. Auschwitz, Treblinka, and the other extermination camps were built primarily to murder Jews. They would not have been built for the purpose of annihilating Poles, gypsies (their numbers were too small to warrant an infrastructure committed to mass murder, although gypsies were killed in large numbers in Auschwitz), or any of the other targeted groups, and it is the creation of these factories of death that gives the Holocaust its unique characteristic.

The following chapters trace the evolution of the Holocaust. Chapter 1 concerns Hitler's antisemitism within the context of racial nationalism and its radical fringe, which advocated the annihilation of the Jews as the solution to Germany's "Jewish problem." The chapter also deals with the position of the Jews in the Weimar Republic and their response to the rise of the Nazis. Chapter 2 traces the evolution of the racial state and the translation of Nazi antisemitism into public policy. The Nazis passed hundreds of laws that resulted in the removal of Jews from German society. Under the circumstances, why did so many Jews remain in Germany, and what was the reaction of the rest of the world to the persecution of the Jews? The chapter also raises questions about the role of the German churches and the indifference of the public to the fate of the Jews. Chapter 3 discusses genocide as it evolved under the cover of World War II. Chapter 4 discusses the murder of millions of Jews as a problem of management, which included matters relating to bureaucracy, the availability of manpower, and psychological and moral considerations that affected those involved in the killing process. The chapter also traces the implementation of the Final Solution in German-occupied Europe and discusses the varied responses of different countries to the deportation of Jews to the death camps. Why did countries such as Italy and Bulgaria refuse to cooperate with German demands for deportation, whereas Vichy France and Croatia cooperated with Germany in this matter?

Chapter 5 discusses the controversy concerning Jewish resistance during the Holocaust. Did Jews go like sheep to the slaughter, or did they resist where it was possible? The chapter considers the argument advanced by both Raul Hilberg and Hannah Arendt that had the Jewish councils not cooperated, it would have been more difficult for the Germans to empty the ghettos and send the Jews to the death camps. The failure to resist the Germans is also discussed, with emphasis on the response of the Allies and the churches to news of the Holocaust. Could they have done more to save the Jews of Europe? Why didn't the Allies bomb Auschwitz and thus put the killing apparatus out of commission? Under the circumstances, could the churches have done more to speak out against genocide? In the case of the Catholic church, information about the Final Solution was known early in the process, yet there was relative silence. Given the immoral nature of the Nazi regime, was it the moral duty of the churches to confront the German government? Could more have been done to hide Jews? The conclusion discusses the implications of the Holocaust for both Jewish and German identity. "Ethnic cleansing" in Bosnia and genocidal atrocities in Rwanda and Zaire during the 1990s raises anew the question as to whether the world has learned anything from the lessons of the Holocaust. The long-term meaning and implications of the Holocaust haunt us still and remind us why, as Nobel prize-winner Elie Wiesel insists, "we must never forget."

NOTE

1. Deborah Dwork, *Children with a Star* (New Haven: Yale University Press, 1991), p. xi.

THE HOLOCAUST EXPLAINED

I

Hitler and the Jews

The founding of the Nazi Party in 1920 transformed the German *völkisch* or radical nationalist antisemites into a political movement, which had as its primary objective the removal of the Jews from Germany. Although the Nazis were not the only antisemitic party to emerge in Germany after World War I, it quickly evolved into the most important of the right-wing groups because of the charismatic leadership of Adolf Hitler. If Hitler's antisemitism included a genocidal agenda, throughout the 1920s he kept it carefully hidden from both the Jews and the rest of the German people. Only in his autobiography, *Mein Kampf*, did he reveal thoughts that were later translated into the Final Solution. During the era of the Weimar Republic (1919–1935), Hitler's rhetorical outbursts against the Jews were calculated to feed on the antisemitism of millions of Germans, but he fell short of calling for their annihilation. Hitler's anti-Jewish beliefs were more extreme than those of the average German, but he cloaked his radicalism by appealing to the more traditional forms of antisemitism. Many Germans harbored antisemitic feelings and likely would not have objected to the removal of Jewish citizenship rights or their segregation from the rest of the population. But outside of Nazi Party ranks, there was no massive popular agitation to expel Jews from Germany or to unleash violence against them.

JEWS IN THE WEIMAR REPUBLIC

Since their emancipation in 1871, Jews had considered themselves full citizens of the Reich. They took pride in describing themselves as German by nationality and Jewish by religion. During the years of the Weimar Republic, Jews attained a measure of achievement unparalleled in their thousand-year history in Germany. Despite the efforts of right-wing antisemitic political parties to associate all Jews with bolshevism, the majority of Jews were strong supporters of the democratic Weimar government. Prominent in government, business, the professions, and the world of Weimar culture, Jews were confident that they could counter the growing virulent antisemitism of the right-wing political parties. The rise of the Nazis in the early 1920s did not immediately threaten the Jewish community, and there was a tendency not to take Hitler too seriously.

EARLY INFLUENCES ON NAZI IDEOLOGY

The German Worker's Party was founded on January 5, 1919, by a small right-wing group led by Anton Drexler, a locksmith, and Karl Harrer, a member of the *völkischer*-occult Thule society, which was founded in 1918 for the purpose of advancing nationalistic and antisemitic ideas. When Adolf Hitler joined the party on September 12, 1919, it had already incorporated the *völkisch* antisemitism of Paul de Lagarde, a well-known biblical and near-Eastern scholar, and the pan-Germanic ideas of Georg von Schonerer, leader of the Pan German nationalist movement, into its platform. The works of de Lagarde, in particular, played an important role in the formation of the party's ideology, especially his ideas about blood and soil, the "master race," and his militant utopian vision of *lebensraum* ("living space") in the east and the resettlement of Germans in the conquered area. In 1920 the party was transformed into the National Socialist Worker's Party (NSDAP, or Nazi Party).

In September 1919, Hitler had been assigned by his commander in the List Regiment of the German army to monitor meetings of the German Worker's Party. Shortly after, he discovered his affinity with much of the party's program and joined the organization. Hitler's extraordinary oratorical ability quickly propelled him to the leadership of the party in July 1921, where he moved his comrades to a more militant position in regard to the Jews. Hitler's earliest extant political statement, in response to a question regarding the "Jewish question," advocated that Jewish emancipation should be legally revoked, but that the final objective must be the complete removal of Jews from German soil. Hitler's remark mirrored Article 4 of the NSDAP program, which called for a Greater Germany in which only "those with German blood, regardless of creed, can be countrymen. Hence no Jew can be a countryman." Article 24 also foreshadowed the later Nazi effort to "Aryanize" the German churches, when it called for the restoration of a positive Christianity, that is, a Christianity devoid of Jewish influences, which necessitated fighting against "the Jewish materialist spirit within and without."

HITLER'S ANTISEMITISM DURING THE WEIMAR DECADE

Hitler transformed the party into an instrument of his political will. He attacked the Weimar Republic and disseminated stereotypical images of the Jews as the power behind the government. In speeches he contrasted the building of a *volksgeimeinschaft* ("people's community") with references to the "Jew-republic," "Jewish Marxism," and Jewish-directed "culture-bolshevism." Hitler's attack on both the Weimar Republic and the Jews resonated with Germans who found themselves not only suffering the humiliation of wartime defeat but also of having reparations and a govern-ment imposed on them by the victorious Allies. The spread of bolshevism also bred fears of "invasion" among many Germans. The postwar Weimar government, whose constitution was written by Hugo Preuss, a Jew, was portrayed in the *völkisch* newspapers as a Jewish creation. The rabidly nationalist writers also claimed that Jews dominated both the new govern-ment and the communist movement in Germany. Many Germans, who sought an explanation for their defeat in the war, found it in the propaganda of the many nationalist and *völkisch* groups that blamed the Jews for the nation's humiliation.

Hitler also began to disseminate in his speeches the "stab in the back" accusation that held Jews responsible for Germany's defeat in World War I and the country's subsequent economic and political ills. The phrase "stab in the back" was first used by General Paul von Hindenburg when he was summoned by the Reichstag to explain Germany's defeat, but at the time he did not use it as a condemnation of the Jews. Hitler used the phrase exclusively against the Jews for purposes of political propaganda. Through-out the rest of the life of the Weimar Republic, Hitler made antisemitism his primary focus in building his political movement. In speech after speech, he identified Jews with bolshevism and the Weimar government. Certainly those who joined the Nazi Party may have done so for many reasons, but no one could have become a Nazi without being aware of the centrality of antisemitism in the party's program.

MEIN KAMPF

Historians who argue that the idea of solving Germany's "Jewish problem" through extermination was at the core of Hitler's thinking point to the virulent antisemitic passages in *Mein Kampf*, a compendium of Hitler's autobiography and reflections. In 1923, in the so-called beer hall putsch, Hitler staged a revolt against the government of Bavaria as the first step leading to the overthrow of the Weimar Republic. The failure of the putsch led to his imprisonment in Landsberg prison in 1924, where he wrote his book. *Mein Kampf* brims with anti-Jewish invective, and a comparison of the book with Hitler's speeches and writings on the eve of World War II shows a consistency in regard to his hatred of the Jews. The autobiography remains an uncanny record of Hitler's obsession with the Jews and provides insight into the origin of the Nazi racial laws of the 1930s and the subsequent ideas that propelled the Nazis to murder the Jews of Europe.

Invoking Christian imagery, Hitler identified himself with Christian anti-*Judentum* and portrayed himself as a medieval knight defending Germany against the forces of evil as personified by the Jews. He wrote, "By keeping the Jews at bay, I fight for the Good Lord's way." Hitler shrewdly linked the language of traditional Christian animus against the Jews with racial antisemitism. He cast the struggle between the Aryan and the Jew in apocalyptic terms and warned that should the Jews conquer, "[the Jew's] crown will become the funeral wreath of humanity, and once again this planet, empty of mankind, will move through the ether as it did thousands of years ago."[1]

For Hitler, Jews represented evil incarnate. Wherever Jews settled, he wrote, they strove for mastery over the host population. In his assault, Hitler accused Jews of an extensive catalog of sins. By Hitler's rendering, they were responsible for Marxism, democracy, the outbreak of World War I, and Germany's collapse in 1918, as well as being the invisible hand behind the Weimar Republic. Hitler found the Jewish menace lurking everywhere, and he asserted that Jews controlled countries such as the United States through their influence over world finance. The influence of the czarist forgery, *Protocols of the Elders of Zion*, which "exposed" the Jewish "conspiracy" to rule the world, is evident in Hitler's ability to connect the Jews as responsible for both the bolshevik revolution in Russia and their grip over world finance. In Hitler's mind, both communism and finance capitalism were means by which Jews furthered their plans for world domination.

In *Mein Kampf*, Hitler devoted more than twenty pages to prostitution and syphilis. He blamed the spread of both on the Jews' effort to corrupt the "racial purity" of the German people. The Jews were accused not only of attempting to subvert the nation politically but also of undermining its racial foundation. As the authors of *The Racial State* suggest,

The language [Hitler] used to describe "the Jew" suggests one of the means he had in mind. They were "Bacilli," "spongers," "parasites," "poisonous mushrooms," "rats," "leeches," and so forth.[2]

Although one may argue that these metaphors were used as a rhetorical device, the terms employed implied extermination as one possible fate for the Jews.

VÖLKISCH (NATIONALIST) ANTISEMITISM

Hitler's language of annihilation was not simply the ranting of an angry and violent personality. Rather, he borrowed and adapted the writings of *völkisch* antisemites who were proponents of exterminating Jews as the final solution to Germany's "Jewish problem." Both Paul de Lagarde and Julius Langbehn, a cultural scholar a generation younger than de Largarde, for example, described the Jews in a fashion similar to Hitler's in *Mein Kampf*. De Lagarde called the Jews a "bacillus, the carrier of decay . . . who pollute every national culture . . . and destroy all faith with their materialistic liberalism. . . . Already the German press had been 'Palestinized' so too the literature, medicine, law and the economy."[3] He called for the destruction of these "usurious vermin" before it was too late. "With trichinae and bacilli one does not negotiate . . . they are exterminated as quickly and thoroughly as possible." Langbehn called for a war of annihilation against the Jews and, according to historian John Weiss, both de Lagarde's and Langbehn's genocidal solutions were published in many versions by the Nazis and distributed to soldiers at the front during World War II.[4] There is little that both of these late nineteenth-century *völkisch* intellectuals wrote that is not found in *Mein Kampf* or in Nazi propaganda and ideology. But they were not unique. A study of twenty-eight prominent antisemitic writers from 1861 to 1895 who proposed solutions to the "Jewish problem" found nineteen calling for the extermination of the Jews.[5] The significance of *Mein Kampf* therefore is that Hitler's thoughts about Jews mark the nexus between nineteenth-century exterminationist antisemitism and its links to the ideology of National Socialism.

THE SA

Although Hitler turned from a reliance on force following the failed Munich fiasco to working within the political process, violence was always present in the Nazi movement. The SA, or *Sturmabteilung* (storm troopers), was founded in 1923 as the Nazi Party's main instrument in its attempt to undermine the Weimar Republic. The SA caused turmoil in Germany throughout the remaining years of the ill-fated democracy. Engaging in street brawls with the communists and attacking Jews, the SA brought terror to those it identified as supporters of the "Jewish and corrupt" government. By 1932 the SA membership, under the leadership of Ernst Röhm, exceeded 2 million, and even after Hitler violently purged its upper ranks in 1934, the SA remained as a threat that could be unleashed at any time against the Jews and others opposed to the Nazi leadership.

THE SS

Also formed in 1923 was the SS (*Schutzstaffel*, or Protection Squad). At first as Hitler's personal bodyguard, the organization was eventually to replace the SA as the weapon of terror in the Third Reich. Under the leadership of Heinrich Himmler, who was appointed Reich leader of the SS in 1929, the organization broadened its responsibilities and became synonymous with the terrorist state. The SS opened the first concentration camp in Dachau in 1933, and it provided the *Einsatzgrüppen*, or special commando units, with recruits to murder Jews during the German invasion of the Soviet Union in June 1941. Himmler was also in charge of the death camps and the implementation of the Final Solution. Like Hitler, Himmler viewed the war against the Jews as a racial struggle in which the SS was given primary responsibility for making German-conquered territories free of Jews. Consequently, racial ideology was institutionalized in the SS, and racial characteristics were a primary criterion for admittance into the organization. For example, SS officers had to prove their own and their wives' "racial purity" back to the year 1700 as a condition of membership. The SS objective toward the Jews was exemplified by Theodore Eicke, the first commandant of Dachau, who in a speech to fellow concentration camp commandants stated that "the obligation to destroy an internal enemy of the state is in no way different from the obligation to kill your adversary on the battlefield."[6]

NAZI VIOLENCE AGAINST THE JEWS

Throughout the Weimar Republic, Hitler's violent language against the Jews was implemented in deed by both the SA and the SS. Jews were an easy target because, although constituting only 1 percent of the population, they were visible in all aspects of German life. Their most obvious presence was in politics, where the Nazis were able to connect Jews with bolshevism.

In the war's aftermath, the radical communist Sparticist League sparked a revolution in Berlin in 1919 that had as its objective the creation of soviets modeled on the bolshevik example in Russia. The insurrection, however, was brutally crushed by the Free Corps, one of the paramilitary groups consisting of war veterans that offered to protect Germany from the "Reds." Rosa Luxemburg and Karl Liebknecht, both nominal Jews, were the leaders of the revolt. Right-wing propagandists made the point of connecting these two Jews with all Jews as being supportive of a bolshevik Germany. In Bavaria, the minister president, Kurt Eisner, a Jew, was assassinated by Count Arco-Valley because admission to the right-wing Thule Society, which helped fund the fledgling Nazi Party, demanded that he perform an act that would prove his worthiness to the group.

The German right-wing hatred of Jews was not limited to Jews on the Left. It was all Jews. Max Warburg, one of Germany's leading bankers, was accused by General Erich Ludendorff, the army's chief of staff, of consorting with the enemy after the banker returned from a mission authorized by Chancellor Georg von Hertling to make overtures to the United States to end the war. Later, a reluctant Warburg would be persuaded to join the German delegation at Versailles. Warburg's role in politics near the end of the war added grist to the Nazi charges that "Jews had stabbed Germany in the back." In 1922 Walter Rathenau, the minister of foreign affairs and a nationalist, was gunned down by right-wing terrorists. Despite his impeccable conservative credentials and his total alienation from any identification with the German Jewish community, Rathenau was universally despised by the Right, who manifested their hatred in a popular couplet: "Shoot down that Walter Rathenau / That cursed, goddamned Jewish sow."[7]

THE JEWISH PRESENCE IN WEIMAR GERMANY

It was not only politics that made Jews visible in Germany. Jews were largely found in the major cities such as Berlin, where in 1925 they numbered approximately 173,000, or 5 percent, of the city's population. The next largest concentration was in Frankfurt, with close to 29,000 Jews. The cities also were the centers of banking and commerce, and Jews were prominent as bankers in Weimar Germany. Almost half of all private banks, the number and importance of which declined after 1920, were owned by such Jewish banking families as the Mendelssohns, Bleichroders, and Schlesingers. Although Jews were not owners of the increasingly important credit banks, some of the largest of these banks employed Jewish managers. Arthur Salomonsohn directed the Disconto-Gesellschaft and engineered its merger with the Deutsche Bank before his death in 1930, thus creating the important DD Bank. In commerce, Jews were identified with huge department stores, such as Wertheim, Tietz, and Kaufhaus Israel. In 1932 department stores owned by Jews accounted for 79 percent of all business done by such enterprises.[8] One of Berlin's most influential publishing houses, Ullstein and Mosse, was owned by Jews. Jews were also important in the professions. Jews constituted 11 percent of all doctors in Germany in 1933 and more than 16 percent of its lawyers and notaries public. In Berlin during the 1920s, more Jews than non-Jews practiced law.

Jewish visibility was most pronounced in the unique artistic and intellectual flowering known as Weimar culture. Jews were proud that a quarter of all the Nobel prizes won by Germans by 1933 were won by German Jews. The spectacular culture of Berlin in the 1920s was dominated by such artists and intellectuals as Max Reinhardt, Bruno Walter, Richard Willstatter, Kurt Weil, and Albert Einstein, to name several. If one adds Austrian Jews such as Sigmund Freud, the list becomes even more impressive. Jews were involved in all aspects of cultural innovation, as exemplified in the Bauhaus school, founded by Walter Gropius (a non-Jew) in 1919, which revolutionized the teaching of fine arts, architecture, and design.

Finally, Jews had every reason to be proud of their military record during World War I, despite charges made by right-wing groups that Jews had evaded military service. Jews flocked to the front and contributed 100,000 soldiers, or nearly 18 percent of the German Jewish population. Four-fifths of these volunteers served on the front lines. Of the 100,000 Jews who served in the German military, 35,000 were decorated, and 12,000, or 12 percent, were killed in battle. The participation of Jews in the war entitled them to believe that through the crucible of battle, they had proved their loyalty beyond question.

This was not to be. Hitler, in particular, accused the Jews of betraying the German war and Jewish soldiers of lacking ability and courage in battle. Hitler knew better, but his antisemitism prevented him from acknowledging that his Jewish regimental adjutant, Hugo Gutmann, recommended him for one of the two Iron Crosses he received for bravery under fire during the war. The lies spread by the Nazis and other right-wing groups, and the unwillingness of the military to clarify the record of German Jews in the armed services, fueled antisemitism both during and after the war.

NAZI PROPAGANDA AGAINST THE JEWS

After the war, Nazi propaganda made much of the presence of Jews in public life. The Nazis capitalized on the fear and insecurity of the German people and intensified their efforts to identify bolshevism with the Jews. In the 1920s Alfred Rosenberg, a White Russian emigré and a convert to Nazism, disseminated the infamous forgery, *Protocols of the Elders of Zion*, and the ideas of a Judeo-Masonic conspiracy were highlighted in the *Völkischer Beobachter*, the Nazi Party newspaper. The Nazis hammered home the theme that Jews controlled all aspects of German life and were responsible for its political and moral decline. The number of Jews in publishing, law, medicine, and in other professions was attributed not to their merit or "fitness" but to the worldwide Jewish conspiracy described in the *Protocols*. Nazi propaganda repeatedly voiced the argument that if the nation was to be protected from "these predators," the Jews must be driven from German society.

THE ASCENDANCE OF THE NAZI PARTY

Starting with the economic downturn caused by the depression of 1929 and the inability of the Weimar Republic to come to grips with the problem of unemployment and the general insecurity precipitated by hard times, a series of political crises occurred that eventually led to the appointment of Adolf Hitler as chancellor of Germany on January 30, 1933. The question that remains inconclusively answered by historians is why the German people supported the Nazis to the extent that by 1933 Hitler was deemed acceptable as chancellor. Most Germans tacitly accepted antisemitism, but it was not high on their priority list. The German people were more concerned about political stabilization, the dismantling of the Left, economic improvement, and national revival. The issue of the Jews, although central to the Nazis, was not what attracted millions to vote for the party. The Nazis promised radical solutions for difficult times, including the promise of millions of jobs to a desperate people, and this prospect of change made many Germans believe that the Nazis represented the best hope for the future.

That antisemitism was not the major issue that propelled Germans to vote for the Nazis is illustrated in the Reichstag elections in 1932. In the July election, the Nazis won 230 seats in the Reichstag, and became its largest party but received only 37 percent of the vote. This was a benchmark election for the Nazis, but if one counted the votes of the Left, the Social Democrats, and the Communists, they equaled that of the Nazis. Add on another 10 percent for other parties that did not press the Jewish issue, and one must conclude that on the eve of Hitler's appointment as chancellor, a majority of Germans voted for parties that did not promote antisemitism.

In fact, in the last free election in Germany on November 6, 1932, the Nazis lost 2 million votes and saw their representation in the Reichstag reduced from 230 to 196. Thousands of Germans were revolted by the excesses of the Nazis when it was reported that SA storm troopers had trampled to death a young Communist in plain sight of his horrified mother. When the Nazi Party later condoned the murder, many former Nazi voters had second thoughts about the prospect that the violence-oriented Nazis stood a real chance of running the government. The Nazis lost further public backing when they supported a crippling strike by transport workers in Berlin on the eve of the November election.

The reasons for Hitler's popularity may have included his virulent attack against the Jews, but this alone was not what drove millions of Germans to vote for the Nazis. Although Nazi propaganda stressed the language of violence as it related to the future of the Jew in Germany, it is not at all clear that most ordinary Germans paid attention to this aspect of the party's ideology. Most Germans seemingly had relegated antisemitism to the periphery of their daily lives, and it sufficed for them to know that Hitler would do something about the Jews. Hitler's obsession with the Jews and his belief that Germany was locked in an apocalyptic struggle against the Jews were concerns not shared by most other Germans. There is little evidence to suggest that the great majority of Germans foresaw that his resolution of the "Jewish problem" would terminate in the death camps.

On the eve of Hitler's becoming chancellor of Germany, the response of many Jews was to urge patience. They reasoned that the responsibility of power would mitigate both the rhetoric and violence of Nazi antisemitism. They believed that the influence of the conservatives who surrounded Hitler would temper his anti-Jewish passion. German Jews also believed that a watchful outside world would exercise a moderating influence on any Nazi tendency to excess. German Jewry erred in all of these assumptions.

NOTES

1. Adolf Hitler, *Mein Kampf* (Boston: Houghton Mifflin, 1943), pp. 225, 235.

2. Michael Burleigh and Wolfgang Wippermann, *The Racial State: Germany 1933–1945* (New York: Cambridge University Press, 1991), p. 42.

3. John Weiss, *The Ideology of Death* (Chicago: Ivan R. Dee, 1986), p. 138.

4. Ibid., pp. 138–139.

5. Daniel Jonah Goldhagen, *Hitler's Willing Executioners: Ordinary Germans and the Holocaust* (New York: Alfred A. Knopf, 1996), p. 71.

6. Tzvetan Todorov, *Facing the Extreme: Moral Life in the Concentration Camps* (New York: Henry Holt and Company, 1966), p. 127.

7 Klaus P. Fischer, *Nazi Germany: A New History* (New York: Continuum, 1995), p. 69.

8. Donald L. Niewyk, *The Jews in Weimar Germany* (Baton Rouge: Louisiana State University Press, 1980), p. 14.

2

The Nazi Racial State

In January 1933, Adolf Hitler was appointed chancellor of Germany by President Paul von Hindenburg. Within months, the new German government had issued a series of laws that converted its racial ideology into public policy. The creation of the Nazi racial state was established at the expense of the Jews and those others whom the Nazis disapproved of. Between 1933 and 1935, the German government enacted laws that removed Jews from public life and revoked their rights as citizens. Concurrent with the passage of anti-Jewish legislation, on July 14, 1933, the government issued the Law for the Prevention of Genetically Diseased Offspring, allowing for the sterilization of anyone recognized as suffering from hereditary diseases, including manic-depressive disease, genetic blindness, genetic deafness, and other chronic diseases.

Both the passage of anti-Jewish racial laws and the assault on the disabled derived from Nazi racial ideology, which held that the German community derived its strength from the purity of its blood and its roots in the soil. If Germany were to become a powerful state again, it must root out the unhealthy organisms that weakened the nation. Toward this end, the Hitler government developed policies for the purging of the disabled and the mentally ill simultaneously with laws governing the place of Jews in German society. The policies for each group, however, had different objectives. Sterilization and, later, euthanasia were aimed at improving the health of the national community through a program of "negative eugenics," or the elimination of the unfit from society. The laws directed toward the Jews had a different intent. Jews were characterized as an active and dangerous enemy that endangered the very existence of the nation. Like traditional antisemitism, which portrayed Jews as enemies of Christendom, the Nazis viewed themselves in an apocalyptic struggle with consequences that would determine the fate of the Aryan race.

THE PATH TO DICTATORSHIP

Following the Reichstag fire, the mysterious fire that destroyed the German "Parliament," in February 1933, which the Nazis blamed on the Communists, President Paul von Hindenburg signed a series of emergency decrees allowing the government to suspend the constitutional right of free speech. These decrees, "for the protection of the people and the state against the betrayal of the German people and treasonous machinations," plus the Enabling Act, or Law for the Removal of the Distress of the People and Reich, would allow Hitler to annul the right of habeus corpus and rule Germany as a dictator. Together these measures became the basis for Nazi rule until 1945.

Accompanying these decrees was a campaign of violence directed against Jews. In some cities, department stores owned by Jews were looted, and Jewish lawyers were forcibly barred from the courts. In addition, Jews who were identified as Communists or Social Democrats were rounded up by the SA and taken to "wild" (the absence of any legal protection for incarcerated victims of the Nazis) concentration camps, located in former barracks, factories, breweries, water towers, and other makeshift facilities. Jews and other enemies of the Nazis incarcerated there were brutally beaten, tortured, and sometimes murdered. In Berlin alone, there were about 100 of these camps. Within three weeks after the Reichstag fire, these make-shift "pens" gave way to a "more orderly process" when the Nazis opened the first concentration camp at Dachau where political opponents of the Reich were held and brutalized. The international press reported the SA violence toward Jews, and the threat by leaders of the American Jewish community of a boycott of German goods in retaliation for Nazi excesses gave the Nazi Party the excuse to organize a boycott against the Jews.

THE PERSECUTION OF JEWS

The boycott took place on April 1, 1933, and lasted one day because of fears that prolonging it would harm the government's image in the international community as well as its economy. The boycott, however, did signal that everyday life for Germany's Jews had changed for the worse. Practi-

cally every business in Germany was affected by the boycott. Posters—
"Germans, defend yourselves, don't buy from Jews!" or "Jews out, beware
Itzig, go to Palestine"—were placed in front of Jewish establishments.
("Itzig" was pejorative German slang for a male Jew.) Similar posters
appeared outside the offices and chambers of Jewish physicians and lawyers. Many people nevertheless ignored the boycott and continued to
patronize Jewish businesses. Overall, the German public displayed a lack
of enthusiasm for the boycott, and this indifference confirmed Hitler's
concern that there was little popular support for a crackdown on the Jews.
Yet this too was an illusion. As historian Richard Miller notes, despite the
failure to gain the public's backing for the boycott, there did exist a residue
of support for anti-Jewish measures, especially for those decrees that
removed Jews from competition with non-Jews or those that permitted
non-Jews to profit at the expense of Jews.[1]

Nazi antisemitism went unabated once the party took power. If anything
did change in the first years of Hitler's rule, it was the decision to curtail
the violence against Jews in favor of legal measures that would effectively
segregate them from the rest of the German population. Toward this end,
the Nazi Party embarked on a propaganda campaign against the Jews with
the objective of winning public support for its measures. The *Völkischer
Beobachter*, the Nazi Party newspaper, consistently displayed its hatred of
the Jews and identified them with Marxism as well as prostitution, pornography, and other vices. Nazi antisemitic propaganda also included *Der
Stürmer*, a journal founded by Julius Streicher in 1923 and continued under
his hand until 1945. This weekly became the world's best-known antisemitic newspaper. It included stories about ritual murder, Jewish pornography,
excerpts from the *Protocols of the Elders of Zion*, and repellent porno-
graphic photographs of Jews. In 1938 the Stürmer Publishing House published *The Poisonous Mushroom* in the form of a book for children. Among
the vile antisemitic passages found in this primer is the couplet, "From a
Jew's appearance, Evil Satan speaks to us. The Devil, who in every land is
known as a terrible plague." The Nazis were determined through texts such
as this to indoctrinate the next generation of Germans to recognize Jews as
the nation's enemy.

After the Nazi takeover, propaganda about the Jews was officially
invested in the office of the Reich's minister for public enlightenment and
propaganda, Joseph Goebbels. From 1933 to 1945, Goebbels presided over
all aspects of the German media and was primarily responsible for its
antisemitic propaganda. For example, Goebbels assigned Fritz Hippler to
produce the 1940 motion picture *The Eternal Jew*, a film of hate that invited

its audience to compare Jews with rats attacking the nation's food supply. This incendiary film attacked all aspects of Jewish life, including lurid staged scenes of kosher meat-slaughtering practices.

The Nazis also removed from public life every trace of "Jewish culture." In this aspect of their war against the Jews, the Nazis rejected all forms of modern art, which they labeled degenerate or "Jewish art" as an expression of "cultural bolshevism," a product of Jewish racial sensibilities. In 1937, works of art including those of cubists, futurists, expressionists, and dadaists were purged from museums and galleries and put on display in Munich in a separate exhibition of "degenerate art." In that same year, the works of Marc Chagall were ordered removed from German museums. It is apparent from these examples that the Nazis were determined to use the power of the government to erase all aspects of the Jewish contribution to German culture while magnifying negative images of the Jews. Inasmuch as many Germans were receptive to negative Jewish stereotypes and those who might have protested were fearful of finding themselves in concentration camps, the Jewish community in Germany found itself bereft of allies in the first years of the Nazi regime.

If the failure of the April 1, 1933, boycott had less to do with sympathy for Jews than an abhorrence of the bullying tactics of the SA, then it is not surprising that the Nazis intensified the pressure against the Jews in other ways. As organized violence against the Jews gradually receded as public policy, it was replaced by laws that isolated them from the rest of society, without any public outcry or protest in their behalf. But violence did not end. Commenting on his return from a visit to Nazi Germany in 1933, theologian Reinhold Niebuhr wrote, "With unexampled and primitive ferocity, Jews were beaten and murdered with no public protest." He pointed to the silence of the German churches, both Protestant and Catholic, to Nazism and antisemitism.[2]

ELIMINATING JEWS FROM PUBLIC LIFE

It was under these circumstances that the German government promulgated the Law for the Restoration of the Professional Civil Service on April 7, 1933, barring anyone not of Aryan descent from public employment and establishing in law the principle of racial differences between Jews and all other Germans (although there were exceptions, as a result of President von Hindenburg's intervention in behalf of Jewish war veterans). The 1933 law represented the link between Nazi ideology and public policy. Inasmuch as the Nazi vision was one of creating a utopia based on racial purity, the law effectively excluded Jews from all key areas of German life. The Civil Service Law removed the Jews from the state structure, and subsequent laws regulated Jewish physicians to "protect" the biological health of the nation. The disbarment of lawyers had the objective of protecting the social fabric of society, and the laws regarding schools, universities, the press, and the cultural professions aimed at restoring the primacy of Aryan culture. Only the Civil Service Law was fully implemented in 1933, but subsequently all of the other mentioned professions fell subject to Nazi racial law.

THE RESPONSE OF THE GERMAN CHURCHES

The objective of creating a racial utopia required removing Jews from all institutions of German life, including the churches. With their advent to power in 1933, the Nazis attempted to transform Christianity by eliminating its Jewish roots. In the Nazi version of Christianity, Jesus was transformed into an Aryan, and the teachings of the "rabbi" Paul were eliminated from the church service along with other Jewish elements from the Christian liturgy and practice. The Nazis also attempted to monitor what was taught in the churches, as well as expel converted Jews from church offices or membership. This manifested itself in the so-called Aryan paragraph, which demanded the removal of all Christian pastors with Jewish ancestry from their posts. These excesses were condemned by clergy from the Confessing churches (Protestant Evangelical churches) who fought all efforts of the Nazis to control German Protestantism. But these same ministers and pastors remained silent when it came to opposing the persecution of the Jews.

The indifference of the churches to Jewish suffering stemmed principally from the antisemitism of the Protestant clergy. During the Weimar period, between 70 and 80 percent of Protestant pastors had allied themselves with antisemitic political parties.[3] Despite their opposition to the Nazi effort to create an Aryan church and the Confessing churches' refusal to abandon Jewish scripture as a source of revelation, some major figures, including Martin Niemoller, a Protestant pastor and leader of the anti-Nazi confessing church; Karl Barth, a Swiss Protestant theologian; and Otto Dibelius, a Protestant bishop and member of the German church resistance to the Nazis, harbored the traditional Lutheran contempt toward Jews on both theological and social grounds. Their lack of protest regarding passage of the Nuremberg Laws of 1935 and the later excesses of *Kristallnacht* indicate that their opposition to the Nazis was motivated by parochial concerns as they defended church autonomy and resisted the efforts to expel Jewish converts.

Dietrich Bonhoffer, the young theologian who was executed in July 1944 for joining the anti-Hitler resistance, was virtually alone in recognizing that the persecution of the Jews was a theological concern for all Christians. Ultimately, he helped a small number of German Jews to escape into exile. Bonhoffer, however, was the exception to the rule among the Protestant pastors. By the time Protestant ministers, such as Niemoller, realized that the persecution of the Jews marked the first step in the creation of one of history's most oppressive dictatorships, it was too late. When members of the Confessing church went on record in 1935 in rejecting Nazi racial practices, the Nazi regime arrested seven hundred ministers and severely restricted the civil liberties of the clergy. By the late 1930s the Protestant churches had been subdued by the government, and resistance to Hitler's dictatorship all but disappeared.

Unlike German Protestants, German Catholics were part of an international religious movement. In 1933 the Vatican negotiated a concordat with the new German government, believing that the latter would not interfere in the internal affairs of the church. But it soon became evident that Hitler would not tolerate the influence of any organization other than the Nazi Party within Germany. It also became apparent that as long as German Catholics kept to matters of religion, the government would not interfere with the church. This policy did not last as the German government began to subvert the influence of the Roman Catholic church in Germany almost from the moment the Nazis took power. In 1937 Pope Pius XI issued the encyclical *Mit Brennender Sorge* (With Burning Anxiety), attacking the regime's racial theories and condemning the Nazi attack on the church, though remaining silent on the suffering of the Jews. When the encyclical was read throughout Germany from church pulpits, the Nazis retaliated by arresting priests and nuns on trumped-up charges ranging from financial malfeasance to sexual aberrations. Hundreds of nuns and priests were convicted and sent to concentration camps. Nevertheless, despite the Nazi attack on Catholics, many priests joined the Protestant clergy in protesting against the euthanasia program in 1941.

The government's attempt to control the Catholic church in Germany occurred almost simultaneously with the Nazi efforts to exorcize Jews from German society. Attempts to speak out on behalf of the Jews would have resulted in a further deterioration of the status of Catholics in Germany. But it is also true that traditional religious prejudices toward Jews were as ingrained among the Catholic clergy in Germany as were the rabid anti-Judaic diatribes of Martin Luther among their Protestant counterparts. The prevalence of anti-Jewish sentiments in Christian theology, coupled with state-sponsored xenophobia and racial ethnocentricity, mitigated against Christianity's being a strong deterrent against the escalating ostracism and violence against the Jews.

Yet before his death in 1939, Pius XI had prepared a draft of an encyclical, *Humani Generis Unitas,* that would have condemned antisemitism. Although the pope had previously condemned the "pernicious errors" of the Nazi regime, in *Mit Brennender Sorge* he had not explicitly condemned Germany's victimization of the Jews. He had censured the Declaration of Race issued by the Italian government in 1938, which stated that the Jews did not belong to the "Italian race." But as the conditions of the Jews in Germany continued to deteriorate, the pope was determined to speak out on their behalf. *Humani Generis Unitas* was never published. As the pope grew weaker from heart disease, the encyclical became a casualty of bureaucratic inertia. According to one participant in drafting the encyclical, the document was delayed by those in the Vatican who were fearful that "the encyclical against racism might alienate rich, powerful industrialists who applauded Nazi Germany's regimentation of workers."

The encyclical included a condemnation of the Nuremberg Laws, which changed the status of German Jews to that of aliens and rebuked the Nazis for excluding Jews from the community because of race. But the document also called for the quarantine of Jews from Christians "lest their profaneness infect good Christians. The church has always recognized the historic mission of the Jewish people, and its ardent prayers for their conversion, do not make it lose sight of the spiritual dangers to which contact with Jews can expose souls." Elsewhere, the encyclical includes the following warning:

So long as the Jewish people persist in their unbelief and maintain their hostility to Christianity, the Church must exert itself by every means to avert the perils that this unbelief and hostility might create for the faith and mores of its flock.[4]

The "hidden encyclical" remained largely unknown until 1972. One can concur with the observation of Johannes Nota, a Dutch Jesuit, that "when one imagines these sentences made public in the context of the racist legislation in Germany . . . one can only say today: Thank God this project remained a project."[5]

It is conceivable that had his health not failed him, Pius XI might have changed the language hostile to the Jews. Yet the document does indicate that even among clergy, ostensibly sympathetic to the plight of the Jews, traditional negative attitudes toward the Jews continued to exist within the Vatican.

THE RESPONSE OF THE GERMAN JEWISH COMMUNITY

The first few months of Hitler's rule were a disappointment to those who believed that the responsibility of power would moderate his antisemitism. The effort to drive Jews from German life intensified throughout 1933 and 1934. In July 1933, *Newsweek* reported the arrest of 200 Jewish merchants on the charge of profiteering in Nuremberg, the beating of several American Jews in Berlin, and the closing of the Jewish Telegraphic Agency. A 1933 directive ordering companies to fire Jewish employees said, "It is not religion but race that is decisive. Christianized Jews are thus equally affected."[6] Although this was only partially enforced until 1938, this definition increased the number of those considered Jews from approximately 540,000 by religious profession to a pool of possibly 700,000 by genealogy. By 1934 Jews were prohibited from taking the bar examination, the medical or the apothecary examination, or the test to become a university professor. As the vise tightened, Jews began to reevaluate their future. By the end of 1934, more than 50,000 of the approximately 540,000 Jews emigrated from Germany.

This migration of German Jews consisted primarily of the young. The Jewish community was an aging one, and many of its older members were reluctant to leave their homeland. Many who stayed believed that conditions would get better, and others were fearful of starting life anew in an alien culture. By the end of 1938, 73.7 percent of the Jews left in Germany would be forty years or older.[7] The overall migration of Jews would average about 24,000 a year after 1933. The exodus was aided by the so-called Transfer (Haavara) Agreement of August 1933, which allowed Jews to transfer some of their assets to Palestine in the form of currency.

The transfer arrangement was popular with the Nazi regime because it promoted Jewish emigration and German trade at the same time. Jewish funds were placed in blocked accounts of the Reichsbank and then used as credit for the purchase of German goods. The Transfer Agreement was criticized by Jewish groups outside Germany because it was seen as forging an unholy alliance with the Nazi regime. The Yishuv or Jewish community in Palestine, however, was pleased with the arrangement because it promoted migration to *Erez Israel*. In 1934 alone, a third of the approximately

23,000 emigrants from Germany elected to go to Palestine, taking advantage of the Haavara pact.[8]

THE NUREMBERG LAWS

In a plebiscite that took place in 1934, 88 percent of the voters confirmed Adolf Hitler in his new role as chancellor and president of Germany following the death of President Paul von Hindenburg in August of that year. While in office, Hindenburg had insisted that Jewish war veterans be exempted from the increasing civil disabilities that were affecting Jews throughout Germany. His death removed the last barrier to Hitler's objective of making life so unbearable for the Jews that they would migrate from Germany. Failing that, Jews who remained would have to accept the loss of their citizenship and a segregated status within the Reich.

The problem arising from these objectives was to determine who was a Jew and what constituted membership in that group. One of the first Nazi definitions of a Jew came from Alfred Rosenberg, head of the Nazi Party's foreign-policy department, who stated, "A Jew is he whose parents on either side are nationally Jews. Anyone who has a Jewish husband or wife is henceforth a Jew."[9] In April 1933, a government decree designated as non-Aryan anyone who had a Jewish parent or a Jewish grandparent; the parent or grandparent was presumed to be Jewish if he or she belonged to the Jewish religion. This definition remained operative until September 15, 1935, when the Nuremberg Laws were proclaimed at a special session of the Reichstag summoned to Nuremberg during the annual Nazi Party rally in that city.

This session of the Reichstag produced two laws that became the basis for the exclusion of Jews from German life. The Reich Citizenship Law stated that only Germans or people "of related blood" could be citizens of the Reich. As a result, Jews lost their political rights and were relegated to the status of subjects of the state. The Law for the Protection of German Blood and Honor prohibited marriage and extramarital intercourse between Jews and Germans. It also prohibited the employment of German maids under the age of forty-five in Jewish households (this provision was unpopular among servants who worked for Jews and therefore lost their positions). Although haphazardly enforced until 1938, Jews were also forbidden to raise the German flag. The exceptions made in earlier anti-Jewish legislation for Jewish World War I veterans and state officials who held posts before 1914 were now voided.

The law defined a Jew as

anyone who had descended from at least three Jewish grandparents or from two Jewish grandparents and belonged to the Jewish religious community on September 15, 1935, or joined the community on a subsequent date or was married to a Jewish person on September 15, 1935, or married a Jew on a subsequent date or was the offspring of a marriage contracted with a three-quarter or a full Jew after the Law for the Protection of German Blood and Honor had come into force or was the offspring of an extramarital relationship with a three-quarter or full Jew and was born out of wedlock after July 31, 1936.[10]

Not defined as a Jew but counted as a *Mischling*, or of mixed Jewish blood, was "any person who descended from two Jewish grandparents but who did not adhere to the Jewish religion on September 15, 1935 and who did not join it at any subsequent time and was not married to a Jewish person on the September 15 date and who did not marry such a person at any subsequent time." Such persons were designated as *Mischlinge* of the first degree. Any person descended from one Jewish grandparent was designated as a *Mischling* of the second degree. Thus the non-Aryans were split into two groups, Jews and *Mischlinge*, with the latter exempt from the subsequent destruction process. However, the *Mischling* was excluded from the civil service and the Nazi Party, and was restricted to the rank of a common soldier in the army. *Mischlinge* also could not marry Germans without official consent.

The definition of who was a Jew was determined after a prolonged debate between the antisemitic zealots in the Nazi Party, who saw the *Mischling* as a carrier of the "Jewish influence," and the civil service, which wanted to protect "that part which is German."[11] The victory of those who would protect the part-Jew, however, was no solace for the Jewish community. After the promulgation of the Nuremberg Laws, Jews now found themselves not only socially ostracized but also denied access to German law and the courts for protection. In fact, the position of Jews in Germany had reverted back to their status prior to the nineteenth century. There was little in the Nuremberg Laws of 1935 that could not be found in the restrictions affecting Jews during the Middle Ages. The Nuremberg Laws also acted as levelers of differences between the some 500,000 German Jews and the almost 100,000 Jews of Russian and eastern European descent living in the Reich. Thinking that Hitler's animus toward Jews was directed at Jews from the East who were living in Germany, German Jews found that under the Nuremberg Laws, the Nazis would not distinguish among Jews in enforcing their racial policy.

JEWISH REACTION TO THE NUREMBERG LAWS

The reaction of the German Jewish community to the Nazi racial state was hampered by division. Responses to anti-Jewish legislation on the eve of the Nuremberg Laws ranged from those who believed that the worst was behind German Jewry, to Zionists who urged that the Jews migrate to Palestine. Jewish nationalists such as Max Naumann, the head of the Union of National German Jews, and Hans Joachim Schoeps, who founded the German Vanguard, an organization that rejected the tenets of liberalism and fostered soldierly virtues, tried to make their peace with the new government. In early 1933 the German Vanguard joined with Naumann's group to form the short-lived Action Committee of Jewish Germans, with the objective of opening a dialogue with the Nazis inasmuch as they shared many of the same nationalistic, but not racial, values and policies. The regime flatly rejected their offer. Despite the difficulties, the Reichsvertretung der Deutschen Juden (Reich Representation of German Jews) was founded in 1933. Its name was changed to the Reichsvereinigung der Juden in Deutschland (Reich Association of Jews in Germany) in 1939. The organization elected Rabbi Leo Baeck as its president, and it organized a communal response to the serious problems facing German Jewry. The Reichsvertretung sought to retrain the large number of Jews who had lost their positions as a result of Nazi measures and to offer vocational training for those who sought emigration. When Bernhard Rust, the Nazi minister of education, announced in September 1935 that all German public elementary schools were to be racially "cleansed," the Reichsvertretung expanded its support for Jewish schools. The organization also served as the spokesman for the Jewish community as Nazi excesses intensified. It protested the Nuremberg Laws, the mass arrests that took place in the summer of 1938, and even the first deportations in 1940. The Reichsvertretung did not have a legal status, but the Nazis recognized it de facto. From 1939 until its demise in July 1943 the Reichsvereinigung, the successor to the Reichsvertretung, was the only organization in Germany dealing with Jewish survival.

There were limits as to what the organization could do in the face of the escalating measures that the Nazis took against the Jews prior to and after the Nuremberg Laws. Between 1933 and 1939, the Nazi government issued more than 400 laws and decrees, with the cumulative effect of leaving the Jews of Germany socially and politically dead. Included among these laws and decrees were the installation of yellow benches in Berlin parks that were designated only for Jews, the exclusion of Jews from military service, and the revocation of licenses for Jewish pharmacists and physicians. Jews were deprived of their homes and businesses, which were then placed under Aryan ownership, and in 1938 German Jews were ordered to use Jewish first names; those with Aryan first names had to add "Israel" or "Sarah" to their names. In the promulgation of these measures, the Nazis were aided by local authorities who issued their own regulations against the Jews. In one decree, a village municipal council forbade Jews the use of the communal bull for their cows, and even the goats owned by Jews were off-limits for the communal billy goat. Still another decree prohibited veterinarians from treating dogs belonging to Jews.

All of this should not have come as a surprise even to the optimists within the German Jewish community, who believed that some accommodation could be found with the Hitler regime. In late 1931, the Frankfurt police made public the so-called Boxheim papers, in which the Nazi party described the "ruthless measures" it would take against its political opponents once it took power. The documents also called for barring Jews from economic activities and plans for slowly starving them to death.[12] German Jews found that the Nazis, once in power, were determined to carry out their plans toward them as described in the Boxheim papers. Under these circumstances, the Reichsvertretung found the situation hopeless and recognized that no number of appeals would help. As this tragedy unfolded, many Jews focused on maintaining pride by displaying the Jewish colors of blue and white. Others turned to Zionism, studied Hebrew, and prepared to emigrate to Palestine. Thus German Jews found themselves faced with two choices: accept a pariah status in their own country or emigrate. Twenty-five thousand had left in the first part of 1933, 50,000 between July 1, 1933, and September 15, 1935, and 100,000 during the following two years. After *Kristallnacht*, November 9–10, 1938, a great many more would seek to leave Germany, but complications barred their exodus.

KRISTALLNACHT

Kristallnacht marked a turning point for Germany's Jews and, by extension, for all Jews who would be victims of the Holocaust. These events witnessed the government's legitimizing violence and brutality against the Jews. The events leading to *Kristallnacht*, or Night of the Broken Glass, began on October 7, 1938, when the Nazis decreed that the letter "J" be stamped on all Jewish passports and identity papers. On the same day, the Polish government announced that their nationals living abroad would require the purchase of a stamp on their passports or lose their Polish nationality. Polish consulates had also been instructed not to renew the passports of Jews who had lived abroad for more than five years. More than 20,000 Polish Jews who had lived in Germany for at least five years now found themselves stateless. The German government retaliated at the end of the month by ordering the immediate arrest and expulsion of most Polish Jews living in Germany. The Polish government, in turn, refused to allow these Jews to enter Polish territory. The result was that thousands of Jews found themselves in a no-man's-land along the border town of Zbaszyn, in freezing weather with limited food. Eventually world opinion forced the Polish government to relent and take back most of these Jews, but others were returned to Germany, where many of them were sent to concentration camps.

It was under these circumstances that Herschel Grynszpan, a seventeen-year-old Jewish refugee residing in France, shot a German diplomat in the German embassy in Paris. Having learned of the deportation of his parents to the German-Polish frontier and feeling helpless to aid them, he vented his rage on Ernst vom Rath, the third secretary of the German embassy, although his original target was the German ambassador. This was not the first time that a German diplomat had been the target of assassination by an outraged victim of Nazi persecution. In February 1936, David Frankfurter, a twenty-five-year-old Jewish medical student from Yugoslavia, shot Wilhelm Gustloff, Hitler's personal representative to Switzerland, in protest against the persecution of the Jews in Germany. Perhaps it was because the Olympics were to be held in Berlin that year that the Nazis did not overreact to the shooting. But 1938 was different. The Nazis retaliated in full force against the German Jewish community.

Calling for "the sharpest measures against the Jews," Joseph Goebbels orchestrated the first state-organized pogrom against the Jews under the Hitler regime. Sporadic anti-Jewish rioting broke out in various cities in revenge for the shooting. When vom Rath died from his wounds, the retaliation began in full force. Led by SA groups, a loosely coordinated orgy of violence spread through the country, with the police instructed not to interfere. Starting in Munich, about 500 synagogues were burned throughout Germany. On the night of November 9, windows of hundreds of Jewish shops were shattered, with looters hauling away what jewelry, furs, and other items they could carry. Offices of Jewish organizations and apartments and houses owned by Jews were forcibly entered, and many were ransacked. Before it was over, ninety Jews were killed and about 30,000 Jewish men were imprisoned in concentration camps or Gestapo prisons for "protective custody." In Berlin, despite the prohibition of racial mixing, a number of Jewish women were raped.[13]

On November 10, Goebbels announced over the radio that the anti-Jewish action was over, after having accomplished its "desired and expected purpose." Nevertheless, the rioting and looting continued into the next day, as did the arrest of Jews. On November 12, Hermann Goering laid out a series of measures designed to reduce the Jewish community to poverty. Jews were prohibited from owning retail stores as well as working as independent craftsmen. Jews working for Aryans were to be fired. Jews were banned from going to concerts, the cinema, or other forms of public entertainment. They were prohibited from driving automobiles. Prevented from earning a living, Jews were denied public assistance. The final blow was the announcement that German insurance companies were released from their obligation to cover the damage done to Jewish property. Instead, the Jews themselves would have to pay for both the losses they had suffered at the hands of Nazi mobs and the clean-up. The total bill charged to the Jewish community was 1 billion reichsmarks or $400 million, approximately 3,000 marks for every living Jew in the Reich.[14]

There was virtual silence from the German people and the churches as the orgy of destruction spread. If not glee, the response of Germans to *Kristallnacht* certainly took the form of a general indifference to the suffering of the Jews. As Herman Rauschning, a Nazi politician who broke with Hitler, wrote, "The reaction of the German people to the pogroms of the fall of 1938 shows how far Hitler has led them in five years and how much he has degraded them."[15] If the intention of the Nazis was to coerce its Jews to leave Germany, then the events of November 9–10 served the purpose. In the ten months after *Kristallnacht*, between 100,000 and 150,000 German Jews departed, as many as had left the Reich during the first six years of Nazi rule.

THE POLICY OF FORCED EMIGRATION

As Hitler became increasingly preoccupied with foreign affairs after the annexation of Austria in March 1938, he wanted the Jewish problem resolved quickly. He anticipated the coming of a European war and feared that Jewish enclaves within the Reich could act as a "fifth column" in league with Germany's enemies. In this respect, *Kristallnacht* marked the most dramatic turn in the Nazi objective of forcing Jews to leave Germany. Prior to 1938, the strategy was to make life so intolerable that Jews would leave voluntarily. But as the Jewish community organized and adapted to its increasing isolation, the Nazis embarked on a policy of forced emigration in June 1938, signaled by the roundup of Jews and their placement in concentration camps. By the end of the month the number of Jews incarcerated reached 2,000, with 1,500 of them branded "antisocial" and coerced into emigrating directly from their cells.[16]

BARRIERS TO IMMIGRATION

The shift in policy was more easily stated than accomplished. At the moment that Jews became convinced that life for them in Germany was hopeless, the doors overseas were beginning to close. In Palestine, a logical place of refuge, British policy wavered in its commitment to the Balfour Declaration. Against the background of Arab violence and protest against Jewish immigration into Palestine, British policy, as reflected in its visa quota, began to tilt toward limiting Jewish immigration. By 1939 the British limited the number of Jews allowed to enter Palestine to 75,000 over a five-year period. One country after another with sizable Jewish populations began to restrict entry to Jewish immigrants. South Africa refused visas to 93 percent of the German Jews who applied for entry. Canada and Australia raised similar barriers to Jewish immigration. Great Britain, perhaps because of the embarrassment of its Palestine policy, did not restrict its immigration laws, becoming one of the few islands of sanctuary for Jews but with the proviso that Jews would not seek employment or public assistance in the United Kingdom. In response to the *Anschluss* in March 1938, the German occupation of the Sudetenland in October, and *Kristallnacht*, Britain liberalized its regulations governing the entry of refugees. Britain's response was unique among other countries of potential refuge on the eve of World War II. With the outbreak of war in September 1939, however, all immigration into Britain and the British Empire was banned, and young adult Jewish immigrants were interned and sent to British overseas territories together with German nationals.

Because of the rigid enforcement of its immigration laws, the United States took in fewer refugees than it was capable of absorbing. Many reasons have been offered to explain why the United States did not become a sanctuary for European refugees fleeing political persecution. As Hitler's persecution of the Jews intensified, President Franklin D. Roosevelt found himself caught between those who demanded help for Hitler's victims and those who warned against liberalizing the immigration laws. One poll taken in April 1938 revealed that 60 percent of the American people believed that the persecution of European Jews was entirely or partly their own fault. The president also was aware that strong currents of antisemitism were being fanned by individuals such as Father

Charles Coughlin, who linked isolationism and antisemitism in his defense of Germany. Most scholars agree that between the outbreak of the Great Depression and the end of World War II, antisemitism reached its highest point in American history. Politically, it also made little sense to liberalize the immigration laws when unemployment was still a national problem. The economic factor was complicated by a policy in which those who sought a visa had to prove that they had "adequate means of support." Many American Jews lacked the requisite financial resources to sponsor their European brethren. Those Jews granted visas during this period were among the fortunate minority who had relatives able to provide the necessary support. This financial requirement limited the number of German Jews who were admitted into the United States at less than a third of the openings set aside for German immigrants.

Additional considerations that prevented the modification of the U.S. immigration laws included the fear that Nazi spies would enter the country in the guise of refugees or that Jewish refugees would be forced to spy for Germany for fear that harm would befall the relatives whom they had left behind. The attitude of the State Department also was directly responsible for shaping refugee policy. The personal antisemitism of those in charge of implementing the immigration laws may have played a role in obstructing efforts at finding a refuge for Jews in the United States. Specifically, much has been written about the antisemitism of Under Secretary of State Breckenridge Long and the rigid manner in which he carried out the immigration laws.[17]

THE EVIAN CONFERENCE

President Roosevelt did make several speeches that demonstrated concern for Nazi victims, but he was careful never to identify them as Jews. Roosevelt was concerned by the growth of antisemitism in the United States, which was advanced by not only Father Coughlin but also by bigots such as Gerald L. K. Smith, Gerald Winrod, and the militant neo-Nazi German American Bund. Thus any sympathetic display of support for Jews would confirm the arguments of antisemites that Roosevelt was being unduly swayed by them.

Prior to the outbreak of World War II, Roosevelt attempted to deal with the Jewish refugee crisis when he convened the Evian Conference in July 1938, precipitated by the chaos that followed Germany's annexation of Austria in March 1938 and the subsequent expulsion of most of its Jews. Roosevelt made it clear from the beginning that no country would be expected to change its immigration policies, nor did the United States contemplate an increase in its immigration quotas, although the Austrian and German quotas would soon be opened for full use. The British insisted, as a condition for their attendance, that Palestine be excluded entirely from the conference agenda. In all, the thirty-two nations attending the conference accomplished little. The remarks of the Australian delegate were perhaps indicative of the state of mind of many of the delegates: "It will no doubt be appreciated that as we have no racial problem, we are not desirous of importing one."[18]

In retrospect, the Evian Conference exposed the low priority that the Western democracies gave to the rescue of Jews in their hour of need. Thus, for many historians, 1939 was the crucial year in the coming of the Holocaust. After *Kristallnacht*, it became even more apparent that Jews could not remain in Germany and that the Nazis were determined to force them to emigrate. Yet the nations of the free world affirmed that their immigration quotas would not be liberalized. This indifference was brought home in May 1939 when more than 900 German Jewish refugees arrived at the port of Havana on the passenger ship *St. Louis* and were refused entry on the grounds that their permits were invalid. Jewish-American organizations appealed to the U.S. State Department to allow the passengers entry into the United States, but to no avail. Ultimately the refugees returned to Europe, where they were admitted to England, Belgium, Holland, and France. Many of those refugees would eventually be sent to concentration camps as a result of the Nazi conquest of Europe. The failure to provide sanctuary to Jewish refugees was not lost on the Nazis. One conclusion they logically drew was that the rest of the world cared little about Jews and that they now had a green light for solving their "Jewish problem."

On the eve of World War II, Hitler had fulfilled many of his promises to the German people. He had restored the national economy, rearmed Germany, and reversed much of the humiliation associated with the Treaty of Versailles. The success of Hitler's policies enabled him to proceed with his agenda regarding the Jews without opposition. In the process of creating a state based on Aryan racial supremacy, Hitler had also become a very popular leader. There is little doubt that had a free election been held in Germany in September 1939, Hitler would have been overwhelmingly elected chancellor. Whether by compulsion or conviction, the German people accepted the creation of concentration camps, the elimination of political parties, the emergence of a police state, and the brutalization of Jews for the pride and prosperity associated with Hitler's new order.

NOTES

1. Richard Lawrence Miller, *Nazi Justiz: Law of the Holocaust* (Westport, Conn.: Praeger, 1995), p. 54

2. Cited in Judah Gribetz, Edward L. Greenstein, and Regina Stein, *The Timetables of Jewish History* (New York: Simon & Schuster, 1993), p. 404.

3. Daniel Goldhagen, *Hitler's Willing Executioners* (New York: Knopf, 1996), p. 107.

4. Frederick Brown, "The Hidden Encyclical," *New Republic*, April 15, 1996, pp. 27–29.

5. Ibid.

6. Miller, *Nazi Justiz*, p. 18.

7. John V. H. Dippel, *Bound upon a Wheel of Fire: Why So Many German Jews Made the Decision to Remain in Nazi Germany* (New York: Basic Books, 1996), p. 247.

8. Ibid., p. 160.

9. Miller, *Nazi Justiz*, p. 11.

10. Raul Hilberg, *The Destruction of the European Jews* (Chicago: Quadrangle Books, 1961), p. 48.

11. Ibid., p. 47.

12. Dipple, *Bound upon a Wheel of Fire*, p. 54.

13. Ibid., p. 245.

14. Ibid., p. 246.

15. Leon Poliakov, *Harvest of Hate: The Nazi Program for the Destruction of the Jews of Europe* (New York: Holocaust Library, 1979), p. 7.

16. Dipple, *Bound upon a Wheel of Fire*, p. 219.

17. Jack Fischel, "American Response to the Holocaust, 1933–1945," in Saul S. Friedman, ed., *Holocaust Literature: A Handbook of Critical, Historical and Literary Writings* (Westport, Conn.: Greenwood Press, 1993), pp. 470–477.

18. David Wyman, "Evian Conference," in Israel Gutman, ed., *Encyclopedia of the Holocaust* (New York: Macmillan, 1990), 2:454–456.

3

Genocide

When World War II erupted in September 1939 with the German invasion of Poland, the term "genocide" had not yet been coined, nor was the use of the term "Holocaust" associated with the murder of millions of innocent people. Few outside of Nazi circles could imagine that the war would lead to the destruction of European Jewry. The German invasion of Poland brought a new dimension to the history of warfare. The large number of casualties in World War I had diminished the value of human life, as evidenced by the soldiers who perished in battles at Verdun and the Somme. But these were soldiers, and the application of modern technology to war could explain the large numbers of those killed on both sides. What World War I had not prepared the world for was the application of the technology that had killed millions of soldiers in World War I to the murder of millions of civilians in World War II.

THE EUTHANASIA PROGRAM

The turn to genocide began in Germany under the cover of war. After many years of sterilizing entire categories of people deemed unworthy of life, the Nazis turned to euthanasia as a means of eliminating the "unfit" from Germany. The euthanasia program coincided with the outbreak of war, when Hitler authorized doctors and medical aides to participate in the murder of their incurably ill patients. The operation, known in code as the T-4 program (T-4 refers to the street address—4 Tiergarten Strasse—where the headquarters of the euthanasia program was located), gassed its victims in rooms camouflaged as shower chambers. The bodies were then cremated. The estimate is that approximately 100,000 people were killed in this manner.[1] A large number of those who participated in the implementation of the euthanasia program were members of the SS, and these veterans of the T-4 program would later bring their experience to the death camps: their familiarity with the operation of the gas chambers and crematoriums and the techniques of subterfuge in luring unsuspecting victims into the shower-like chambers. The participating doctors, led by Karl Brandt and his team, did not appear disturbed by their involvement in the euthanasia program. As doctors, they believed that they were "cleansing the Fatherland" of disease, much as one operates on a cancer, and consequently were not bothered by legal or moral niceties concerning their activities. Collectively, the healers who became killers have been described as career minded, venal, and unscrupulous.[2]

The euthanasia program ostensibly came to a halt after relatives of many of the victims protested the deaths of their loved ones. This protest was joined by clergy of both the Protestant and Catholic churches, and as a consequence, Hitler, bowing to public pressure, ended the program in September 1941. In practice, however, the killings continued under a more effective disguise until the end of the war.

POLAND AND THE TURN TO GENOCIDE

The invasion of Poland, which started out as a conventional war, was quickly transformed into a genocidal struggle against the entire population. Ostensibly a war to redeem lost territory in the east, the Nazi objective of acquiring *lebensraum*, or living space, was combined with a racial ideology that viewed the Slavic peoples as inferior to the Aryan race. Once Poland was conquered, a process of "ethnic cleansing" occurred in which Poles were displaced from their homes, and ethnic Germans were resettled in their place. Along with this objective, the Germans anticipated the elimination of all traces of Polish ethnic identity. Heinrich Himmler foresaw the future of Poland as one in which all traces of Polish national consciousness would disappear and be replaced by total obedience to Germany. Polish children would receive severely limited primary education and become a source of cheap labor for the Reich.

Not all inhabitants of Poland were subject to this dismal future. Himmler theorized that in times past, ethnic Germans had ruled in the east and had intermarried with the Slavic population, thus creating a population of mixed blood. Over time, this element, and even Germans of pure blood, had come to view themselves as Poles. Himmler believed that the Nordic traits among the Slavs made them dangerous to the Reich, because it was their German blood that gave them their leadership skills. Thus Germany's mission was either to reincorporate this remnant of Aryan blood or eliminate it. Toward this end, Himmler ordered the SS to search for this valued racial stock in Poland, and later in the Soviet Union. Writing to *Gauleiter*, or Nazi Party district leader, Arthur Greiser, Himmler declared: "Racially pure children of Poles should be brought up by us in special kindergartens or children's homes."[3] Himmler used the Lebensborn ("Life Spring") organization in this project. Lebensborn homes in Germany took in Polish and Russian children of Nordic or Aryan appearance, some orphaned but many brutally taken from their parents. Under the code name Haymaking, thousands of children were kidnaped and sent to Germany. Himmler maintained that once the war was over, there would be a further effort to sift out those with the desired traits, whereas those Slavs lacking the racial criteria would be sent to the *Generalgouvernment*, the conquered area of Poland unincorporated into the Reich.

THE MADAGASCAR PLAN

For Jews, there was to be no sorting out. The Nazi objective for Poland's Jews destined them for a precarious existence in the *Generalgouvernment*. The Jews were crowded in ghettos throughout Poland under the supervision of Jewish councils appointed by the Germans for the purpose of implementing their orders. Initially the German plan was to remove the Jews to the Lublin district, located on the border of the German and Soviet zone, and resettle them in the transit camp near the Nisko River. This scheme failed when Germany was unable to defeat Great Britain and thus control the sea lanes to Africa. The resettlement of the Jews then focused on the French colony of Madagascar after the Nazi victory over France in 1940. The Madagascar plan, however, was contingent on German control of the seaway leading to the colony, which required the conquest of Great Britain. This plan was aborted with Germany's failure to defeat England. However, the plan to resettle Jews to a remote region with little in the form of resources was in itself a prescription for genocide, albeit a slow process.

THE BUREAUCRACY OF GENOCIDE

Following the German invasion of the Soviet Union in June 1941, the Nazis decided to annihilate the Jewish people. As the Nazis implemented their policy of resettling ethnic Germans from throughout eastern Europe, Jews were uprooted and forced into ghettos in the *Generalgouvernment*. Initially the ghettos were established to serve as temporary areas of Jewish settlement until the establishment of a reservation in the east, or in Madagascar, was feasible. When these plans failed, Germany turned to more radical measures to solve the "Jewish question." From the introduction of both forced sterilization and the murderous euthanasia program to the mass killings of Polish Jews and Gentiles perpetrated by the *Einsatzgrüppen*, under the code name Tannenberg, Germany exhibited few inhibitions in using mass murder to realize its racial objectives.

Germany created a bureaucracy to carry out the murder of the Jews. The entire responsibility for the resettlement of the Jews was placed under the supervision of Reinhard Heydrich, head of the Main Office for the Security of the Reich (RSHA). In September 1939, the Nazis subordinated the party intelligence apparatus, the security services of the SS (SD), the security police (Sipo), and the state security and the criminal police (Gestapo and Kripo, respectively) to the RSHA under the command of Heydrich, who in turn reported to Heinrich Himmler, Reichsführer (Reich leader) of the SS. Prior to this step, the SD had created a special unit of mobile killing units known as the *Einsatzgrüppen*, who made their initial appearance during the *Anschluss*. They accompanied the regular German army in the Nazi invasion of Czechoslovakia in March 1939 and Poland in September. On the eve of the Polish invasion, six of these mobile units were formed, and five traveled with the German army into Poland. During the invasion of Poland, 16,000 Polish and Jewish civilians and prisoners of war were killed in mass executions by the *Wehrmacht* (the German army) and the *Einsatzgrüppen*. Now merged under the RSHA, they took their orders from Heydrich, who in September 1939 told his *Einsatzgrüppen* chiefs that the priority of the "final aim" was to clear the Jews out of western Poland and concentrate them in ghettoes in larger cities, near railway junctions or along the railways so "that future measures may be accomplished more easily." Heydrich ordered that the mission be kept a "total secret."[4] Although historians agree that the implementation of the Final Solution commenced with the invasion of the Soviet Union in June 1941, it is evident that genocidal behavior had already become a fixed part of German policy following the invasion of Poland.

The upper echelons of the German political hierarchy had considered genocidal acts against the Jews as early as 1938. In the aftermath of *Kristallnacht* in November 1938, the SS publication *Das Schwarze Korps* published remarks by Reinhard Heydrich in which he called for the Jews to be driven out of Germany because Germany would not tolerate "hundreds of thousands of criminals." He accused the Jews of being a breeding ground for bolshevism and predicted "the final end of Jewry in Germany, its absolute annihilation."[5] In a speech given by Hitler to the commanders of the *Wehrmacht* on August 22, 1939, he told them,

Thus for the time being I have sent to the East only my "Death's Head Units" with the orders to kill without pity or mercy all men, women, and children of Polish race or language. Only in such a way will we win the vital space that we need. Who still talks nowadays about the Armenians?[6]

In his speech to the Reichstag on January 30, 1939, Hitler used the language of genocide when he warned the Jews that

if international finance Jewry in and outside Europe should succeed in thrusting the nations once again into a world war, then the result will not be the Bolshevization of the earth and with it the victory of Jewry, but the destruction of the Jewish race in Europe.[7]

In March 1939, Goebbels pressed for the total elimination of the Jews: "We cannot allow Jewry, as a seat of infection to exist any longer." He added that this could be accomplished humanely in peacetime but in a crueler way should there be war.

These random examples of the language of genocide are not meant to suggest that the murder of European Jewry was already being planned in the late 1930s. Rather, the passages indicate that the mass murder of Jews was always an option among other plans, such as resettlement in the Lublin region or Madagascar. In fact, the Germans were engaged in a dress rehearsal for the Holocaust in the murderous actions of the *Einsatzgrüppen* in Poland, which they replicated on a much larger scale during the invasion of the Soviet Union.

Similarly, although the decision to murder the Jews of Europe was made after the attack on the Soviet Union, the model for the extermination camps predated the decision to implement the Final Solution. In an effort to maintain secrecy regarding the brutal massacres of Poles and Jews by his *Einsatzgrüppen*, Heydrich in 1940 converted the medieval town of Soldau, located over the German side of the East Prussian–Polish border, into a concentration camp. It was at Soldau that perceived enemies of the Reich were secretly executed. Soldau was the prototype of the extermination camp and represented one of the earliest examples of how the euphemism of resettlement was used as a cover for the mass murder of Poles and Jews.

JEWS IN THE SOVIET ZONE

Not all of Poland's Jews came under Nazi rule. The Ribbentrop-Molotov pact of August 1939 had divided Poland between the Soviet Union and Germany, placing the regions of eastern Poland, the Baltic states, and eastern Romania (Moldavia) under Soviet control. This treaty also placed approximately 2 million Jews under the control of the Soviets, whose objective was to "Sovietize" the newly acquired population and make them as secularized as the Jews living in the Soviet Union. The great majority of the Jews in the newly acquired territories were proud of their Jewish heritage and, unlike their Soviet Jewish brethren, were marginally affected by assimilation. Thus the Jews in the new Soviet territories found themselves between the Soviets, who wanted to destroy their Jewish cultural heritage, and the Nazis, whose reputation for brutality and antisemitism preceded their occupation of Poland. Faced with these choices, thousands of Jewish refugees fled the German areas of occupation in western Poland to seek shelter in the Soviet zone.

At first the fear of the Germans was not shared by many of the ethnic groups in the areas under Soviet control who regarded the Soviet regime as the enemy. Jews, on the other hand, had mixed feelings. Many fondly remembered the benevolence of German soldiers during World War I and subsequently underestimated the terror of the German occupation. Others feared the Soviets as much as their Gentile countrymen. For those Jews who were aware of events in Poland, the German army was synonymous with terror, and they viewed the Soviet occupation as the lesser of the two evils. Relationships between the Jews and the non-Jewish populations became more strained when the Soviets placed Jewish communists in positions of authority in the annexed territories. A Jewish communist elite emerged in the territories and quickly replaced the older Gentile leadership. For example, Jews had not served in the internal security services in independent Lithuania; now Jewish policemen were mustered into service under Soviet rule. In areas of eastern Europe where antisemitism had become particularly strident in the years between the two world wars, the appearance of Jews in positions of authority under Soviet rule easily translated into an identification of all Jews with the enemy.

That the Soviets were bent on destroying traditional Jewish life as well as the national aspirations of all other groups was ignored by the non-Jewish population, and both Baltic and other eastern European antisemites were able to characterize Jews as disloyal members of their respective countries. When it came to the Jewish question, therefore, the Nazis found willing accomplices in their war against the Jews in the east. Many of those living in the Baltic states, the Ukraine, Romania, and Poland would greet the Nazis as liberators from Soviet rule, whereas the Jews were identified with the Soviet occupation. Thus the *Einsatzgrüppen* had little difficulty recruiting auxiliaries from these groups to help them in the massacre of Jews.

THE GERMAN INVASION OF THE SOVIET UNION

The German invasion of the Soviet Union in June 1941 effectively put an end to the plans for resettling the Jews in the Lublin region or in Madagascar. By virtue of their invasion of Soviet territory, the Nazis increased the number of Jews within their orbit by 3 million, with about half of them in the Ukraine. Combined with Poland's Jews, the Nazis now controlled approximately one-third of all of the world's Jewish population. Hitler signaled the stakes involved in the invasion when he referred to the war as not merely an armed conflict but a war of ideologies. For Hitler, the Jews were the ultimate ideological foe of the Nazi movement, and now that Germany was at war with the Soviet Union, all previous restraints regarding the Jews were removed. As a consequence, he viewed all Jews, including the elderly, women, and children, as bearers of bolshevism and therefore subject to liquidation.

In the months leading up to the attack on the Soviet Union, Hitler issued a series of instructions regarding the forthcoming war. He called for the elimination of the "Bolshevist-Jewish" intelligentsia and authorized Himmler to carry out "special tasks" in the operational areas independent of the army. In March 1941, Hitler told senior *Wehrmacht* officers that the coming eastern campaign would be the most barbaric of all time and reiterated his belief that "bolshevism was a sociological disease, and that we must abandon any thought of soldierly comradeship. . . . Commissars and OGPU (secret police) are criminals and must be treated as such." Two weeks before the invasion, Hitler again emphasized the need to act ruthlessly against the bearers of bolshevism and drew up guidelines to that effect. Issued on June 6, 1941, the Commissar Order called on German troops to hand over captured communist functionaries to the *Einsatzgrüppen* or, if that was not feasible, the *Wehrmacht* was to kill, without trial, all political commissars who fell into its hands. Guidelines for the army went beyond killing political commissars and ordered "merciless intervention" against Jews, bolshevist agitators, guerrillas, and saboteurs. Inasmuch as Nazi propaganda closely identified Jews with commissars and party functionaries, it is not surprising that a great many Jews were murdered as much for their ethnicity as for their suspected political activity. The Commissar Order was a clear violation of international convention regarding the treatment of prisoners of war and civilians during wartime and made the *Wehrmacht* an accomplice in genocide.

Although no signed order by Hitler for the annihilation of the Jews has surfaced, his wishes in regard to making Europe *Judenrein* were well known to close associates, such as Himmler and Goering, as well as through his speeches and directives. As in the case of the euthanasia program, the killing process was to be kept secret and not alluded to directly in correspondence. Instead, directives incorporated euphemisms that conveyed the unstated goal of murdering the Jews of Europe. In a letter dated July 31, 1941, for example, Hermann Goering requested that Heydrich "send me, as soon as possible, a draft setting up details of the preliminary measures taken in the organizational, technical and material needs for the achievement of the 'final solution' which we seek." In using the term "final solution," the letter discreetly revealed that not only had the decision been reached to liquidate the Jews of Europe, but that the objective was to entail a shared responsibility among Goering, Himmler, and Heydrich for implementing this continent-wide total solution of the Jewish problem. Unlike the euthanasia program, which took place on German soil, the need for written authorization, as a protection against future prosecution for engaging in criminal acts, was viewed as unnecessary in the new type of warfare that commenced in the Soviet Union. Himmler, who was directly responsible for implementing the Final Solution, invoked Hitler as the source of his authority in each of the stages that culminated in the murder of the bulk of European Jewry. The war against the Soviet Union was therefore marked by two different kinds of objectives: a genocidal racial war primarily against the Jews and others, such as the gypsies, who were viewed as racially expendable, and the more conventional objective of reducing the Soviet population by 30 million people in order to make room for German settlers.

During the two years of the pact between Germany and the Soviet Union (1939–1941), German objectives toward the Jews were limited to various resettlement plans as well as a policy of attrition, whereby Jews died through hunger and disease as a result of their enforced ghettoization. What is more, prior to June 1941, the large numbers of Jews under German control were also useful as hostages against Hitler's imagined Jewish conspiracy, which he believed was leading the United States into a war against Germany. In the United States, Charles Lindbergh, perhaps the most popular personality in American life, gave credence to these beliefs during a September 1941 speaking tour when he warned his audience that the Jews were using their influence to manipulate the country against Germany. Father Charles Coughlin contributed to the demonization of Jews in American life when he serialized the *Protocols of the Elders of Zion* in his weekly newspaper, *Social Justice*. Nazi antisemitic propaganda in its overseas radio broadcasts reiterated the theme of a Jewish conspiracy directed toward bringing about war against Germany.

THE *EINSATZGRÜPPEN* AND THE ORDER POLICE

The invasion of the Soviet Union in June 1941 removed all restraints on Nazi Germany regarding Jews. By the end of December 1941, with the United States allied with Great Britain and the Soviet Union in the war against Germany, Hitler was convinced that beneath the conflict was the guiding hand of the Jews. Given the conspiratorial nature of his beliefs, the war now provided Hitler with both a sense of urgency and an opportunity to deal with the Jewish question. If Jews were previously viewed as potential hostages stored away in Polish ghettos, the invasion of the Soviet Union now made every Jew a security risk. Jews were collectively accused of guiding the partisan resistance against the German invasion of the Soviet Union and were dealt with accordingly by *Einsatzgrüppen* units. In fact, the contention that all Jews were partisans allowed both the *Wehrmacht* and the *Einsatzgrüppen* to justify the mass murder of Jews as antipartisan warfare. In 1942 Himmler confided to Mussolini that "in Russia we had to shoot a considerable number of Jews, both men and women, since there even the women and the older children were working as couriers for the partisans." He went on to tell Mussolini that Jews everywhere were responsible for sabotage, espionage, and resistance and also for the formation of partisan bands.[8]

The Germans deployed four *Einsatzgrüppen* units to the Soviet Union under officers personally chosen by Himmler and Heydrich. *Einsatzgrüppe* A, headed by Dr. Franz Stahlecker, consisted of 1,000 men whose base of operations was primarily in the Baltic states. Arthur Nebe, the commander of *Einsatzgrüppe* B, had 655 men under his command and was responsible for operations in Belorussia and the Smolensk region, up to the outskirts of Moscow. *Einsatzgrüppe* C in the southern and central Ukraine was under the command of Dr. Emil Otto Rasch and had a complement of 700 men. Otto Ohlendorf commanded *Einsatzgrüppe* D and was responsible for the southern Ukraine, the Crimea, and Ciscaucasia. His unit consisted of 600 men. Each of the *Einsatzgrüppen* had subunits known as *Sonderkommandos* attached to it. In addition, units of the Order Police, the reorganized

Germany police, as well as native auxiliaries were part of the special forces that participated in the killing operations. Collectively, the officers of the *Einsatzgrüppen* were professionals, and their ranks included academics, ministerial officials, lawyers, a Protestant minister, and an opera singer. Averaging about thirty years of age, most of them could be described as intellectuals who did not actively seek an assignment to a *Kommando* but sought some measure of power and success and found in the *Einsatzgrüppen* a means of obtaining these personal objectives.

A problem faced by the *Einsatzgrüppen* was the vast size of the Soviet Union. The more than 3,000 *Einsatz* commandos comprising the four units sent to the Soviet Union and the Baltic states were insufficient to liquidate the large numbers of Jews under their control, which by July 1941 had increased to a pool of 5 million people. Nevertheless, the order to kill Jews was relayed to them in instructions sent by Heydrich to all *Einsatzgrüppen* commanders on July 2, 1941. Under part 4 of this communiqué, Jews in the Soviet party and state apparatus were singled out for execution. In practice, however, the *Einsatzgrüppen* took this directive as a license to murder all Jews whom they encountered. In Balti, for instance, Jews were shot for attacks on German troops; in Novoukrainka for encroachment; and in Kiev for arson and "a spirit of opposition."[9]

Of the many massacres perpetrated by the *Einsatzgrüppen*, perhaps the most infamous took place in late September 1941 at Babi Yar, located outside the city of Kiev in Ukraine. Under the command of Paul Blobel, *Sonderkommando* 4A, attached to *Einsatzgrüppe* C, murdered 33,771 Jews in cold blood during a two-day period :

They [the Jews] were forced to lie face down, and the executioners, also at the base of the ravine, equipped with Schmeisser automatic rifles, tried to shoot them in the back of the head, per instructions. Because of the mass of victims, some were shot several times over, others only wounded. Then the next batch came in and lay down on top of the first. According to one of the executioners, Blobel yelled frequently to his men below that the killings were not going fast enough. The killers worked in shifts, and they were supplied with ammunition and rum. At the end of the day lime chloride was spread on top of the layers of bodies.[10]

Himmler was concerned about the psychological repercussions on his men of so much killing and sought every opportunity to bolster the morale of his *Einsatzgrüppen*. In October 1943, he delivered a speech before a meeting of the SS-Gruppenführer in Posen where he praised the unselfish nature of the "special action" perpetrated by the *Einsatzgrüppen*:

Most of you will know what it means to see a hundred corpses—five hundred—a thousand—lying there. But seeing this thing through and nevertheless—apart from certain exceptions due to human infirmity—remaining decent, that is what has made us hard. This is a never-recorded and never-to-be recorded page of glory in our history.[11]

Operating in concert with the *Einsatzgrüppen* in the massacre of Jews were the regular German police units known as the Order Police (ORPO), who were commanded by Kurt Daluege. The approximately 100,000 members of the Order Police were used for the roundup or killing of Jews. In Amsterdam, for example, the ORPO rounded up Jews for deportation to the east. In eastern Europe, they were responsible for the supervision of the ghettos. Once the deportations to the camps began, the ORPO accompanied the special trains to their destination. In the invasion of the Soviet Union, ORPO units were found in all four of the *Einsatzgrüppen* formations and participated in the massacres of Jews and communists. Two units of the Order Police participated in the shootings at Babi Yar. Unlike the SS and its *Einsatzgrüppen* formations, Order Police units were not necessarily motivated by ideological or even antisemitic convictions as they participated in the killing process. Nor are there any recorded cases of members of the Order Police being imprisoned or shot for refusing to participate in the massacre of Jews.[12] Rather, they appeared to be ordinary Germans who, for a variety of reasons, found themselves participating in the "extraordinary tasks" that were a necessary precondition for the Final Solution.

In other parts of the Soviet Union, the *Einsatzgrüppen* were aided by Romanian forces who committed atrocities against Jews with such ferocity that German witnesses were disturbed. On the Black Sea coast, *Einsatzgrüppe* D was joined by local ethnic Germans who were extremely zealous about the shooting of Jews. One former chief of *Einsatzkommando* 6 commented after the war that "we were actually frightened by the bloodthirstiness of these people."[13] In the Baltic areas, Jews were subject to the same types of massacres. Jews in Vilna, Kovno, Riga, and many other towns and cities in Lithuania became victims of these death squads. In all of these actions, the *Einsatzgrüppen* were aided by local auxiliaries. This took the form of local communities' participating in pogroms organized or inspired by the *Einsatzgrüppen*. The Germans encouraged pogroms for two reasons: for every Jew murdered by anti-Jewish outbursts, there was one fewer for the *Einsatzgrüppen* to kill, and the Nazis wanted the population to share responsibility in the killing process. The commander of *Einsatzgrüppe* A, Franz Stahlecker, described his thinking regarding the participation of the local community in the killings as a way "to establish as an unquestionable fact that the liberated population had resorted to the most severe measures against the Bolshevist and Jewish enemy, on its own initiative without instructions from German authorities."[14] In Lithuania, many of those who were recruited for the pogroms were subsequently incorporated by the *Einsatzgrüppen* into police companies for the purpose of seizing and shooting Jews. According to Raul Hilberg, the total number of victims killed through mass shootings by *Einsatzkommando* 3, with Lithuanian help, was 46,692 Jews in less than three months. The *Einsatzgrüppen* set up similar types of auxiliary units for the purpose of killing Jews in Latvia and Estonia. The majority of the Baltic and Ukrainian populations were not engaged in the massacres, but they displayed indifference to the murder of their Jewish countrymen. In Lithuania, Bishop Vincentas Brizgys set the example when he forbade the clergy to aid the Jews. By the winter of 1941–1942, almost a half-million Jews had been killed by the *Einsatzgrüppen* formations and their auxiliaries. Conceivably more Jews would have been slain in these sweeps had it not been for the overwhelming number targeted for annihilation. The limited number of *Einsatzgrüppen* formations sent to murder 5 million people made it an almost impossible logistical task.

Himmler's concern about the psychological repercussions of the killings on the *Einsatzgrüppen* was reinforced by his field commanders. Erich Bach-Zelewski, general of the Higher SS and Police Leader Corps and responsible for antipartisan warfare in central Russia, complained to Himmler about the effect the killings were having on his men. Paul Blobel, leader of *Einsatzgrüppe* 4A, lamented that the real unfortunates were the perpetrators themselves: "The nervous strain was far heavier in the case of our men who carried out the executions than in that of their victims. From the psychological point of view they had a terrible time."[15] Himmler, aware of the psychological nature of the problem, concluded that shooting was not the most pragmatic way of dealing with the Reich's enemies because it placed too heavy a burden on the executioners. At one point, Himmler authorized experiments with explosives as a means of dealing with the problems of mass murder.

The turn to a more efficient way to implement the Final Solution came as a result of a combination of forces emanating from the killing process. Himmler was frustrated not only by the psychological problems but also by the technological limitations of a process that had as its objective the murder of millions of Jews. What Himmler wanted was a neater and less upsetting method of killing the victims and, at the same time, a more efficient means to increase the daily number of those to be killed. He eventually saw poison gas as the solution to the problem.

GAS CHAMBERS

The decision to introduce the gas chamber and the crematorium as the most efficient means of murder marks the unprecedented characteristic of the Holocaust. The technology, the chemicals, and the willingness of the Nazis to use both in behalf of their ideological objectives already had been demonstrated in the euthanasia program, as well as in the liquidation of the Polish leadership. The turn to genocide appears to have been made with little hesitation. The construction of the extermination camps resolved the technical problem presented by the addition of millions of Jews absorbed by Germany in the aftermath of the invasion of the Soviet Union.

HITLER AND THE FINAL SOLUTION

Jews were still able to emigrate from German-occupied territory until October 1941, but even under the best of circumstances, where could they go? Most nations retained the rigid quota systems of the 1930s and would admit only those who had guarantees that a job awaited them or the promise of private support so that they would not become public charges. The reality was that for most Jews, Nazi-occupied territory was a trap from which there was little chance of escape.

Given Hitler's disposition toward the Jews, it is not surprising that once the war started and he confronted the reality of millions of Jews under Nazi rule, he would turn to genocide. In a January 1939 speech, for example, his rhetoric was filled with genocidal threats against the Jews, and in 1944, after millions of Jews had already been killed in extermination camps, Hitler boasted, "I have gotten rid of the Jews." There can be little doubt that the decision to implement the Final Solution was his and was conveyed down the German bureaucracy on a need-to-know basis by Hermann Goering, Hitler's appointed successor, Heinrich Himmler, and his aide, Reinhard Heydrich, who was given the operational responsibility for making Germany and then the rest of Europe *Judenrein*. Each official in the chain of command understood that he was fulfilling the wishes of the Führer.[16]

GENOCIDE

In the aftermath of the German conquest of Poland, the *Einsatzgrüppen* introduced the use of gas to kill civilians. The euthanasia program in

Germany had six killing centers complete with gas chambers and crematoriums. The Germans now applied these techniques to Poland. The first use
of this method of mass murder was recorded in December 1939, when an
SS *Sonderkommando* unit used carbon monoxide to kill Polish mental
patients. Following the invasion of the Soviet Union, the Nazis introduced
gas chambers as a means of killing Jews. Under SS supervision, mobile
vans equipped for the purpose of mass murder were first used in December
1941 at the Chelmno camp (also referred to as the Kulmhof station).
Eventually the extermination camp was used to gas Jews from the Lodz
ghetto and from the Warthegau region. The method used by the SS was to
bring Jews to the vans, where they were made to strip under the pretense
that they were to shower. They were then packed into a van, and after the
doors were hermetically sealed, concealed pipes filtered exhaust gas fumes
among the victims. Normally, a special detachment of Jews were then
ordered to heave the bodies into waiting mass graves. Depending on the
truck's size, forty to sixty persons could be gassed at a time. The Nazis
constructed twenty of these mobile gas chambers for use in the Soviet
Union, and most of them were operated by the four *Einsatzgrüppen* deployed on Soviet territory.

This deadly process did not always work according to schedule. Liqui-
dations that were supposed to take fifteen minutes often lasted for hours,
and sometimes a few of the victims remained alive when the van doors were
reopened. The capacity to kill millions of Jews in gas vans also had technical
deficiencies, including the mental stress on the SS in those areas where they
had to unload the bodies themselves as well as the frequent van breakdowns
caused by the poor conditions of the Soviet roads. Nevertheless, the total
number of victims killed by gas vans was approximately 700,000, with half
of these in the Soviet Union and the other half in the Chelmno extermination
camp.

Despite the problems with the vans, the success at Chelmno convinced
Himmler that he was on the right track in using gas to solve the problem of
exterminating large numbers of Jews, and he proceeded to order the construction of a chain of extermination camps on Polish territory for this
purpose. In retrospect, aside from the euthanasia program in Germany,
neither the Nazis nor any other government had ever perpetrated mass
murder through gassing on the scale Himmler and Heydrich conceived for
the Final Solution. Himmler was also aware that such a massive undertaking
could no longer be kept a secret and that the Final Solution would require
the cooperation of other agencies of the German government.

THE WANNSEE CONFERENCE

With these considerations in mind, Reinhard Heydrich convened the Wannsee Conference. Although many people in and out of government were aware that Jews were being massacred in the Soviet Union, few knew that the objective was the total extermination of the Jews of Europe. On January 20, 1942, in a villa in Wannsee, a suburb of Berlin, Heydrich invited the state secretaries of the most important German government ministries to attend a meeting for the purpose of coordinating the Final Solution, as well as to inform them officially of Hitler's decision to solve the so-called Jewish question. In his address to the assembled government officials and SS leaders at the conference, Heydrich cited Goering's July 31, 1941, letter as the basis for his authority to coordinate the Final Solution. He then proceeded to discuss the implementation of the new policy:

The Jews would be utilized for labor in the east. Separated by sex, the Jews capable of work will be led into these areas in large labor columns to build roads, whereby a large part will doubtless fall away through natural diminution. The remnant that finally survives all this . . . will have to be treated accordingly, because this remnant, representing a natural selection, can be regarded as the germ cell of a new Jewish reconstruction if released.[17]

In stating that those Jews who survived the ordeal of slave labor would "have to be treated accordingly," Heydrich meant that the 11 million Jews living in continental Europe and in the British Isles were now targets for liquidation. Still to be resolved, however, was the fate of "mixed Jews." Were they also to be dealt with "accordingly"? It was this part of the meeting that resulted in much animated discussion. Heydrich's preference was to have half-Jews killed but to consider quarter-Jews as Germans, provided that their appearance or behavior did not betray Jewish characteristics. Dr. Wilhelm Stuckart of the Interior Ministry argued for the sterilization rather than the murder of half-Jews. Ultimately these issues remained unresolved and were deferred to later meetings.

Adolf Eichmann, who was present at Wannsee, shed light on the unrecorded parts of the meeting at his trial in Jerusalem in 1961. According to Eichmann, "During the conversation they minced no words about it all. . . . They spoke about methods of killing, about liquidation, about extermination."[18] Given the intense rivalries within the Nazi political system, Heydrich had every reason to anticipate difficulty in getting the assembled government and party officials to cooperate in the implementation of the Final Solution. To his surprise, he found that they were not only receptive to his briefing but committed and enthusiastic about doing their part in liquidating the Jews of Europe.

The Wannsee Conference was held at a time when the gas vans at Chelmno had been in operation for only six weeks and Belzec was still under construction. At the main camp at Auschwitz, experiments with Zyklon B—prussic acid, sold as an antivermin substance by the Degesch Company—had been initiated in autumn 1941. For Heydrich, the meeting was a success, and as chief planner for the Final Solution, he began preparations for the deportation of the Jews in the *Generalgouvernement* to the newly constructed extermination camps. He never lived to see the fulfillment of what would have been the high point of his career. On May 27, 1942, Heydrich was assassinated by members of the Czech underground. He was succeeded by Ernst Kaltenbrünner as head of the RSHA. Under Kaltenbrünner's ruthless prodding, the RSHA continued Heydrich's work in sending millions of Jews to their deaths.

AKTION REINHARD

The SS men in charge of the deportations of Jews from the *Generalgouvernment* coined the term *Aktion Reinhard* in memory of their fallen chief. The aim of *Aktion Reinhard* was to kill the more than 2.2 million Jews living in the five districts of the *Generalgouvernment*, and three extermination camps were designated for this purpose: Belzec, Sobibor, and Treblinka. All three were located near a railway and were remote from population centers.

The first Jews were brought to the stationary gas chambers, located in the Belzec camp near the Lublin-Lvov railway, in February 1942. After experimenting with different types of gas, exhaust gas was chosen for the liquidation process because it was cheap and did not require special supplies. The liquidation of 10,000 Jews a day began shortly after by means of six gas chambers, which were disguised as "inhalation and bath rooms," located in a single wooden barrack. The chief advocate of exterminating Jews by exhaust gasses from diesel engines was Christian Wirth, inspector of the exterminating squads at Belzec, Sobibor, and Treblinka.

Wirth's role in the extermination process attests to the significant role played by the personnel of the euthanasia program in the death camps. The "veterans" of the T-4 program brought to the extermination sites the technical skills and methods that were employed in the murder of the handicapped and mentally ill. This included not only their experience in the operation of the gas chambers and crematoriums but also the subterfuge that was used to lure their victims into the shower-like gas chambers. Even the gruesome practice of extracting gold from the teeth and bridgework of the dead bodies was copied from procedures first used in the euthanasia program. As historian Henry Friedlander notes, "there was little in the infrastructure of the killing process that did not have a precedent in the T-4 program."[19]

AUSCHWITZ

Wirth's reputation as the *Reich's* foremost expert on extermination did not go unchallenged. Competition came from the commandant of Auschwitz in Upper Silesia. On April 27, 1940, Himmler authorized the use of the military barracks near the town of Auschwitz as a concentration camp. Unlike the *Aktion Reinhard* camps, Auschwitz was initially designed to serve as a forced labor camp in order to attract the I. G. Farben Company to the area. Thus, the camp served two purposes: as a source of slave labor and a camp to punish enemies of the Reich. By March 1941, the camp held approximately 11,000 prisoners, most of them Poles. Before Auschwitz became synonymous with the gassing of Jews, it had already acquired a reputation for cruel punishment, which included executions that took place on a regular basis. In March 1941, Himmler called for the building of a second and much larger section of the camp, called Auschwitz II or Birkenau, where the gas chambers and the crematoriums of the Auschwitz killing center would operate. In May 1942, with Goering's approval, Auschwitz III at Monowitz was constructed for the purpose of providing forced labor for the I. G. Farben Buna synthetic rubber works. In Buna-Monowitz, inmates of the camp, primarily Jews, were shorn of their hair, numbers were tattooed on their arms, and, clad in striped pajamas, they were worked literally to death. Jews who could not keep up with the work were beaten or killed on the spot. Those too exhausted or too ill to work were sent to the nearby Auschwitz II camp at Birkenau to be put to death by gas. By the winter of 1942, Auschwitz would become the most infamous of the death camps.

ZYKLON B

It was Rudolf Hoess, commandant of Auschwitz, who concluded that Zyklon B was better than the gas used in the *Aktion Reinhard* camps. He found the gas to be infinitely more hygienic, safer, and efficient, for the operator, protected by a gas mask, had only to open the tin and scatter the contents through a grill in the roof of the chamber; within minutes, the victims were dead. Wirth's gas, contended Hoess, took much longer. In fact, Wirth's reputation as the preeminent expert on the use of gas in the extermination process suffered after SS leaders reviewed his operation at Belzec. In August 1942, SS-Obersturmbannführer Kurt Gerstein, who was in the prussic acid trade and was one of those who observed Wirth's methods at work, wrote of what he saw:

The train arrives. 200 Ukranians fling open the doors and hunt out the people out of the trucks with ox-hide whips. Instructions come through the loudspeaker: strip completely. . . . Then the women and girls go off to the barber [who] cuts off all their hair and stuffs it into a potato sack. . . . So they move down the alleyway, all naked men, women and children. . . . They mount the steps, hesitate, and enter the death chambers. . . . One Jewess, aged about 40, eyes blazing, calls down upon the murderers the blood which is being shed here. She gets five or six strokes of the whip across the face and disappears into the chamber like the rest. The chambers fill up tight—that's Wirth's order. People are treading on each other's toes . . . the victims are to be killed by the diesel's exhaust gas.[20]

Gerstein noted that the engines refused to fire, and at that point he took out a stopwatch and measured the time it would take for the engines to work. To Wirth's embarrassment, the engine would not start:

My stop-watch ticks faithfully on, 50 minutes 70 seconds and the diesel won't start! . . . The men in the gas chambers are waiting. . . . One can hear them sobbing. . . . After 2 hours and 49 minutes—measured exactly on the stop watch—the diesel starts. . . . A further 25 minutes pass. . . . One can look through the peephole. . . . A few are still alive after 28 minutes. Finally after 32 minutes they're all dead. Men of the labour detachment open the wooden doors. . . . Jammed in the chambers, the dead are still standing there like marble pillars. There's no room for them to fall or even bend over.[21]

News of Wirth's fiasco spread, and after additional study, those responsible for choosing the gas to be used at Auschwitz concluded that Hoess was right. Zyklon B was approved and immediately used to exterminate Jews at Birkenau. The decision was made to use prussic acid in Auschwitz. Wirth took it as a personal affront, and a state of hostility emerged between Auschwitz and Wirth's camps. As for Hoess, he would record in his autobiography, "I must admit that the gassing process had a calming effect upon me. I always had a horror of the shootings, thinking of the number of people, the women and children. I was relieved that we were all to be spared these blood-baths."[22] The rivalry over which gas would be the most efficient for the murder of European Jewry was not, however, the only battle that had to be overcome in the course of implementing the Final Solution.

SLAVE LABOR

The exterminationist ideology that made Auschwitz-Birkenau synonymous with the gassing of 1.1 to 1.3 million Jews was at cross purposes with the requirements of slave labor that prevailed at the Buna-Monowitz camp. The contradiction between targeting Jews for extermination and at the same time relying on them for labor can be seen in the policy used at the Gross-Rosen concentration camp in Silesia, which was opened in August 1940. At Gross-Rosen, Jews were used to dig canals, build roads, and work on river control projects. They labored under the most primitive conditions, and although the use of forced labor was profitable for the SS, the profit motive was not necessarily the dominant one behind the use of Jewish labor. At Gross-Rosen, the conditions of labor were so horrible that one could only conclude that the Nazis were attempting to work the Jews to death. As Richard Breitman points out, if the profit motive was the primary reason that the SS used Jewish forced labor, then the minimal food and clothing and exhausting labor, all day long, every day, could not have produced a productive labor force for any length of time.[23]

A comparison of Gross-Rosen and the Buna works at Auschwitz reveals the conflicting objectives among the Nazis regarding Jewish labor, once the decision had been made to implement the Final Solution. On one side of the argument were those who believed that Jewish labor was necessary for the production of materials for the war effort. Companies such as I. G. Farben, Öberschlesische Hydriewerke, Deutsche Gasrusswerke, Erdol Raffinerie, and Krupp worked Jews to total exhaustion at Auschwitz but required their labor, not their death. Himmler and Heydrich, however, saw labor by Jews as a temporary condition, with their destruction as the ultimate objective. Until it became clear to Himmler in January 1943 that Germany was not going to win the war, he took the position that "there was no reason not to use the labor potential of the Jews as an integral part of the Final Solution." But he viewed this as a concession to difficult circumstances, which was to be aborted at the first opportunity. As long as Himmler allowed Jews arriving at Auschwitz to work, the conflict between industry and the exterminationists was somewhat muted. Those who profited from forced labor therefore became less concerned about losing their workers or working them to death because Himmler had tacitly promised that they would be replaced. At Auschwitz, for example, Jews were worked to a state of collapse at the Krupp-owned fuse factory and then gassed. Systemic to the Final Solution in the long run was the objective of eliminating Europe's Jews regardless of their value to German industry. In the short run, work was encouraged as a means of survival for the prisoners in the extermination camps. This illusion was cynically reinforced in the sign that greeted the newly arrived victims: *"Arbeit Macht Frei"* ("Work Liberates"). The Nazis, however, worked their prisoners to such exhaustion that few could persevere for very long.

In 1944, Raphael Lemkin published *Axis Rule in Occupied Europe: Laws of Occupation-Analysis of Government, Proposals for Redress*, using for the first time the term "genocide," which refers to the systematic killing of a nation or people. It described the actions of the *Einsatzgrüppen* in Poland and the Soviet Union and, later, the extermination camps. The effort to annihilate the Jews and others deemed enemies of Germany was unprecedented in its intensity and objectives. The form of genocide known as the Final Solution had as its primary aim the elimination of the entire Jewish people. In its resolve to destroy European Jewry, Germany mobilized the full apparatus of the state. European civilization had never before experienced the calculated effort of a nation-state to exterminate an entire people, including its own citizens. The turn to genocide was possible because the state had access to the vast technological and managerial resources associated with the industrial process. The influence of the industrial plant played an important role for those bent on genocide, and the model of the factory system was not far from the minds of those who built the factories of death.

NOTES

1. The most comprehensive book on the euthanasia program is Henry Friedlander's *The Origins of Nazi Genocide: From Euthanasia to the Final Solution* (Chapel Hill: The University of North Carolina Press, 1995).

2. Hans-Heinrich Wilhelm, "Euthanasia Program," in Israel Gutman, ed., *Encyclopedia of the Holocaust* (New York: Macmillan, 1990), pp. 453–454.

3. Klaus Fischer, *Nazi Germany*, (New York: Continuum, 1995), p. 495.

4. Lucy S. Dawidowicz, *The War Against the Jews: 1933–1945* (New York: Holt, Rinehart and Winston, 1975), p. 116.

5. Richard Breitman, *The Architect of Genocide: Himmler and the Final Solution* (New York: Knopf, 1991), p. 58.

6. Ibid., p. 43.

7. Ibid., p. 63.

8. Heinz Hohne, *The Order of the Death Head: The Story of Hitler's SS* (New York: Coward-McCann, 1969), p. 367.

9. Ibid., p. 367.

10. Breitman, *Architect*, p. 212.

11. Hohne, *Order*, p. 365.

12. See the argument regarding the role of the Order Police and the issue of refusing an order to participate in the killing of Jews in Daniel Jonah Goldhagen's *Hitler's Willing Executioners: Ordinary Germans and the Holocaust* (New York: Knopf, 1996) and Christopher R. Browning, *Ordinary Men: Reserve Police Battalion 101 and the Final Solution in Poland* (New York: HarperCollins, 1992).

13. Raul Hilberg, *The Destruction of European Jewry* (Chicago: Quadrangle, 1961), p. 206.

14. Ibid., p. 203.

15. Hohne, *Order*, p. 364.

16. Benjamin B. Ferncz, *Less Than Slaves* (Cambridge, Mass.: Harvard University Press, 1979), p. 12.

17. Christopher R. Browning, "Wannsee Conference," in Gutman, *Encyclopedia*, 4:1593.

18. Ibid.

19. Henry Friedlander, *Origins of Nazi Genocide*. This is evident throughout Friedlander's book. See p. xiii.

20. Ibid., p. 377.

21. Ibid.

22. Ibid., p. 378.

23. Breitman, *Architect*, p. 137.

4

The Final Solution

The cooperation displayed by German government officials attending the Wannsee Conference was necessary for implementating the Final Solution. The killing process required the participation of the bureaucratic apparatus of the German state, and the consensus reached at the Wannsee Conference ensured this cooperation. German sociologist Max Weber wrote many years before the ascent of Nazism that when fully developed, bureaucracy stands for the principle of "without scorn and bias." Weber observed that to the degree that the modern bureaucracy eliminates from its duties love, hatred, and all other emotional and irrational elements, it fulfills its functions. "Precision, speed, unambiguity . . . strict subordination, reduction of friction and of material and personal costs—these are raised to the optimum point in the strictly bureaucratic organization."[1] Indeed, Weber may well have been describing the role of the Nazi bureaucracy in the Holocaust.

THE FINAL SOLUTION AS A COOPERATIVE EFFORT

The logistics required to murder millions of people necessitated that German bureaucrats implement directives that came from the architects of the Holocaust. German railway officials, for example, scheduled the trains that carried Jews to the extermination camps in Poland. The confiscation of Jewish property and personal belongings required assistance from the Finance Ministry. The armament inspectorates were concerned with forced labor. Christian ministers provided baptismal certificates that allowed the Nazis to determine Jewish ancestry under the Nuremberg Laws. The medical profession sanctioned the medical experiments carried out in the concentration camps. Architects and civil engineers designed and constructed the installations for efficient mass annihilation. The Degesh (Deutsche Gesellschaft fur Schdlingsbekampfung mbH, or German Vermin-combating Corporation), supplied the Zyklon B that made the gassing process possible. The planned murder of millions of Jews was a major government project that required the assistance of many segments of German society.

ADOLF EICHMANN

Hermann Goering's July 1941 letter to Heydrich, which authorized the head of the RSHA to organize the Final Solution, marked the official change of German policy from expulsion to annihilation. The genesis of the Final Solution had already begun in the Soviet Union, where the *Einsatzgrüppen* engaged in the mass killing of Jews. Europe's Jews were then deported from the ghettos to the newly constructed extermination camps in Poland. This authority to organize the mass deportations of Jews to the death camps was delegated to Adolf Eichmann, then a major in the SS and head of IV-B-4, the section of the RSHA dealing with Jewish affairs. In this capacity, Eichmann's duties included the task of creating extermination camps, monitoring the development of gassing techniques, and organizing the deportations to the death camps. Eichmann, like Himmler, was not sadistic or a fanatical antisemite. In fact, he claimed that personally he had nothing against Jews.[2] Rather, Eichmann, like Himmler, shared the bureaucratic ethos. Eichmann was a model of bureaucratic industriousness, driven by a determination to implement the Final Solution in an impersonal and efficient manner. In 1941, he visited Auschwitz on the first of his tours of the extermination camps, where he educated himself in every aspect of the killing process.

Eichmann and his operatives were responsible for the deportations of Jews to the extermination camps from every part of occupied Europe, with the exception of the Scandinavian countries. He was fastidious in ensuring that the rail schedules were followed, and he interceded to solve problems when delays threatened to halt the departure of trains to the death camps. He also organized the effort to hide the news of the extermination campaign from the world.

At one point, between November 1 and December 4, 1941, fifty transports were scheduled simultaneously with the advance of the German army in the Moscow area before the onslaught of the Russian winter. Yet supplies and reinforcements for the military campaign did not interfere with the movement of Jews to the camps. "Apparently," states Raul Hilberg, "military considerations also were not to be considered in the 'Final Solution' of the Jewish problem."[4]

To pay the cost of sending large numbers of people by train to the death camps, the Railway Administration devised a billing procedure whereby they charged the Jews for the transportation to the extermination camps. Train tickets were sold to Jews as if they traveled third class; children aged four to ten paid half the full fare, and those under the age of four were transported free. Half-fare was charged for organized groups of four hundred or more. The fare was billed to the Gestapo, who shifted the funding burden to authorities in foreign areas where Jewish property had been expropriated or to Jewish communities themselves. In Germany the Gestapo directed the Reichsvereingigung to collect cash contributions from the deportees to help defray the cost of the trip to the east. Bizarre as it may seem, Jews were forced to pay the fare for their deportation to the death camps! So complicated was this self-financing, because of the different currency zones that had to be calculated each time a border was crossed, that the Nazis considered the construction of a death camp in Germany for Jews from western countries.

Without the efficiency of the German rail system, the operation of the extermination camps would have been impossible since they depended on the regular delivery of victims. Despite breakdowns and the requirements of fighting a war, the trains continued to roll and deliver the passengers to their destination. There can be little doubt that those who routed the trains to the death camps knew the fate awaiting the Jews. Yet after the war, not a single official of the Railway Administration was put on trial for taking part in the Final Solution.

Railway depots for the "resettlement" of the Jews were in all of the major ghettos. *Aktion Reinhard*, the code name for the destruction of the Jews in the *Generalgouvernement*, witnessed the liquidation of the ghettos and the deportation of the Jews by train to the extermination centers. The operative decree for the *Aktion* was given by Himmler on July 19, 1942, when he ordered the physical destruction of the Jews in the *Generalgouvernement* by the end of the year. Between 1941 and 1942 approximately 112,000 Jews— 20 percent of the population—had died of starvation and disease in the Lodz and Warsaw ghettos. Thus, at the time of Himmler's decree, Jews were already perishing in large numbers. The construction of camps such as Auschwitz did not mark the beginning of the German-imposed death sentence on the Jews, but the exacerbation of a process that had already begun when Jews were forced into the ghettos.

GHETTOS AND THE FINAL SOLUTION

The policy was stated by Hans Frank, the head of the *Generalgouvernment* and an early advocate of exploiting skilled Jewish labor, when he said, "Clearly, we are sending 1.2 million Jews to death by starvation. . . . If they do not die from hunger, we will adopt other anti-Jewish measures."[5] At the time that the decision was made to exterminate the Jews, the Germans were determined to make the liquidation of the ghettos as efficient as possible. Euphemisms were introduced for the purpose of deceiving the Jews into believing that they were being sent for "resettlement work in the East," and the Germans encouraged this belief by allowing Jews to take personal belongings with them. Once the roundups for deportations began in the Polish ghettos, the Nazis enticed thousands of starving Jews to volunteer for resettlement with the offer of bread and marmalade. Little did the unsuspecting Jews know that "resettlement" was a euphemism for the gas chambers.

In spring 1941, the Nazis established the Lublin ghetto. At its peak, the ghetto population totaled 34,000 Jews. In March 1942, the process of liquidating the ghettos began in Lublin as its Jews were deported to Belzec. In his diary entry for March 27, 1942, Goebbels noted, "Beginning with Lublin, the Jews in the *Generalgouvernement* are now being evacuated eastward. The procedure is a pretty barbaric one and not to be described here more definitely. Not much will remain of the Jews."[6] Lublin, located in eastern Poland, initially was to be part of the ill-fated Lublin Reservation, but after the Lublin Plan was dropped, the area became the headquarters of Odilo Globocnik, head of *Aktion Reinhard*, and founder of the Majdanek, Belzec, Sobibor, and Treblinka death camps.

The deportation quota set by the Germans for the Lublin ghetto was 1,400 Jews per day, and by April, the deportations came to a close with approximately 30,000 Jews having been sent to their death at Belzec. The remaining 4,000 Jews were removed to a suburb of Lublin and interned in what was referred to as the "little ghetto." A small number, however, managed to escape and made their way to the Warsaw ghetto. Chaim Kaplan, who chronicled the events occurring in the Warsaw ghetto, noted the arrival of the refugees in his entry dated April 17, 1942: "We trembled when we heard of the Lublin events. Some refugees, risking their lives, fled the town of death and came to the Warsaw ghetto. Their tales freeze the blood in your veins. . . . Jewish Lublin, a city of sages and writers, a place of learning and piousness, is totally and utterly destroyed."[7]

The sorrow Chaim Kaplan expressed for the annihilation of Lublin Jewry could also be shared for the Jews of the Warsaw ghetto. Prior to the start of the deportations in July 1942, Warsaw's Jewish population numbered approximately 380,000. As was the case in the other ghettos, the Jews of Warsaw suffered from the spread of disease and starvation, but despite severe food shortages, they managed to feed refugees, such as those from Lublin, who came to the ghetto seeking shelter. Hunger and despair, however, took their toll, and toward the end, many of Warsaw's Jews reported to the *Ümschlagplatz* (the area near the railway where Jews reported for deportation to the extermination camps) in return for the promise of bread and jam. On July 20, 1942, the Judenrat (Jewish Council) received orders from the Germans to prepare for the deportations starting on July 22. Those affected by the decree were to report to the *Ümschlagplatz* where freight trains were waiting to take them to Treblinka. It was under these circumstances that Adam Czerniakow, the chairman of the Jewish Council, suspecting that the trains were taking Jews to their death, committed suicide rather than be a party to the murder of his own people.

By the end of July the ghetto's "nonproductive element" had been transported to Treblinka, and the SS accelerated the deportations with an additional category of formerly exempted Jews, which included the children of the ghetto orphanage headed by its Jewish director, Dr. Janusz Korczak (pen name of Henryk Goldszmit). On August 5, the Germans rounded up Korczak and his 200 orphans and deported them to Treblinka. Korczak had been offered asylum by friends on the Polish side, but he refused to save himself if it meant abandoning the children. Korczak and the children were killed at Treblinka upon their arrival.

The Lodz ghetto was the last to be liquidated by the Germans. As in Warsaw, the Jews endured overcrowding and insufferable hunger. Approximately 43,500 Jews, or 21 percent of the population, died from hunger and disease. The first stage of clearing Jews from the ghetto occurred between December 1940 and June 1942 when 7,200 Jews were sent to the forced labor camp in the Posen area, where many died because of deplorable working conditions. Concurrent with the removal of Jews to the labor camp was the first wave of deportations to Chelmno, where 55,000 Jews were gassed. The second deportation, during the summer of 1942, included the sick, children, and those too weak to work. They were brutally dragged from their homes, and about

20,000 Jews were gassed in Chelmno. The final series of *Aktions*, between September 1942 and May 1944, differed from the earlier deportations in that most Jews were not sent to extermination camps. Rather, the Germans turned the ghetto into a forced labor camp with 90 percent of the population employed in factories. By August 1944, the 77,000 Jews remaining in the Lodz ghetto were told the following by the Gestapo:

Thousands of German workers were going to the front. These workers would have to be replaced. Siemens and Schuckert needed workers, . . . the munitions plants need workers. . . . Everybody was satisfied with the Jews and the Gestapo is very satisfied with their output. After all, you want to live and eat and that you will have.[8]

Convinced that they were to be deported to Germany to work as replacements in factories, the remaining Jews of Lodz instead were sent to Auschwitz to be murdered.

DEPORTATIONS FROM GERMANY

The liquidation of the ghettos in eastern Europe occurred simultaneously with the deportation of Jews to the extermination camps from other areas of Nazi-occupied Europe. In Germany, the process that led to the liquidation of German Jewry began in October 1941, when transports of Jews were sent to the Lodz and Warsaw ghettos, as well as to Riga, Kovno, and Minsk in the German-occupied areas of the Soviet Union. In Riga and Minsk, the Jews were killed on arrival. Between 1942 and 1943, tens of thousands of German Jews were sent to Auschwitz, and approximately 42,000 mostly elderly and "privileged" Jews were sent to Theresienstadt.

In Germany, the Gestapo made use of the Jewish Council and the Jewish police to prepare lists and seize Jews for deportation. Rabbi Leo Baeck, the head of the Reichsvereinigung in Berlin, explained the decision to use Jewish police in the roundup of Jews:

I made it a principle to accept no appointments from the Nazis and to do nothing which might help them. But later, when the question arose whether Jewish orderlies should help pick up Jews for deportation, I took the position that it would be better for them to do it, because they could at least be more gentle and helpful than the Gestapo and make the ordeal easier. It was scarcely in our power to oppose the order effectively.[9]

The deportations were frequently resisted because Jews were aware of what awaited them. Goebbels complained in his diary that about 400 Jews had escaped the clutches of the Gestapo and now represented a danger to society.[10] According to Hilberg, about a few hundred Jews were able to succeed in hiding from the Gestapo for any length of time, although Peter Weydn estimates that there were 6,800 Jews living an underground existence.[11] These hidden Jews came to be known as U-Boote (submarines or U-boats), were hunted down by the Gestapo, who were assisted by paid Jewish informers known as *Greifers* or "catchers, who ultimately were responsible for the deportation of hundreds of Berlin's Jews."[12] By December 1942, more than 150,000 Jews from Germany and Austria had been deported from the Greater Reich. In May 1943, Berlin was declared *Judenrein*. In June 1943, the *Reichsvereinigung* was dissolved and its leadership deported.

EXPORTING NAZI JEWISH POLICY

Once the war began in September 1939, Germany attempted to export its Jewish policy to those countries it occupied, such as Poland, Hungary, and Vichy France, or that fell under its influence, such as Slovakia, Croatia, and Bulgaria. The countries' response to cooperation with German demands regarding the Final Solution varied. Factors that determined support for the murder of European Jewry included the changing political climate, whereby, as in the case of Hungary, the perception of a German defeat altered the government's response to the deportations; the intensity of antisemitism in a country, or the lack thereof; the willingness of the population to view Jews as their fellow nationals rather than as a foreign element; and the willingness of the general population to oppose the persecution and deportation of Jews. An additional factor was the role of the churches. Would clergy remain silent in the light of laws that segregated and persecuted Jews? Would the churches speak out against the deportations, and would the churches, as was the case in Germany, make a distinction between baptized Jews and Jews?

The success of the Final Solution also required the cooperation of the political leadership and bureaucracy, which promulgated decrees that segregated Jews from the rest of society. These steps included the enactment of laws that defined who was a Jew, followed by a census of the Jewish population and the requirement that Jews register their assets for the eventual expropriation of their property and businesses ("Aryanization"). In the stage preceding the roundup of Jews for deportation, the expectation was that Jews would be used for forced labor. The measures were capped with an edict that, for identification purposes, required Jews to wear a Star of David armband, a regulation the Germans insisted on in all countries under the occupation.

Slovakia

Slovakia, under Father Josef Tiso and the right-wing nationalist Hlinka party, was an example of a country where the population supported the Final Solution but also where distinctions were made between Jewish converts and Jews. In August 1940, Eichmann sent his representative, Dieter Wisliceny, to Slovakia to advise the government on Jewish affairs. Under his direction, the Hlinka Guard and Slovak volunteers were reorganized along the lines of the SS and given the responsibility for carrying out anti-Jewish measures. Deportations began in March 1942, and by October more than 75 percent of Slovakia's Jews had been "resettled," most of them being sent to Auschwitz.

Although the racial laws were in effect, some Jews, clinging to any kind of hope, converted to Christianity. The number of these conversions is uncertain, but perhaps as many as several thousand Jews became Christians in an effort to save their lives. Against the background of the deportations and the pressure from the churches to protect the converts, the Slovak parliament passed a law on May 15, 1942, that redefined a Jew as someone who belonged to the Jewish religion or who had been converted after March 14, 1939. Exemptions extended to the families of Jews converted to Christianity prior to this date and to all Jews in mixed marriages. The action of the parliament, however, may have had as much to do with concern for converts as it was an opportunity to save money, inasmuch as the Germans required payment for transporting Jews from their host countries.

Croatia

The record of Croatia under Ante Pavelic, the leader of the USTASA (the Croatian national organization) movement, the Croatian counterpart of the SS, is another example where the population supported the Final Solution. In fact, in a decree issued on June 26, 1941, Pavelic accused the Jews of inciting the population and engaging in black marketeering. He concluded by declaring that "Jews are collectively guilty," and he ordered them "to be imprisoned . . . in concentration camps."[13] By the end of 1941, two-thirds of Croatian Jewry had been taken to one of eight Croatian-built camps, where they were killed immediately upon arrival or soon after. At the end of 1941, Pavelic declared, "The Jews will be liquidated within a very short time."[14] Pavelic kept his word. Croatian Jews were murdered, for the most part, by Croatians with German encouragement.

The direct involvement of the Germans in the killing of Jews began in January 1942, when it appeared that the Croats had tired of killing Jews. It was decided at the Wannsee Conference that the remaining Jews of Croatia would be removed for resettlement. In spring 1942, both sides agreed to remove Croatian Jews to the east. A member of Eichmann's staff was sent to Zagreb to take charge of the deportations, and in August, 9,000 Jews were deported, primarily to Auschwitz.

France

In France, the Vichy government initiated anti-Jewish measures without any noticeable protest from the population or the church. At the time of the government's establishment in 1940, there were approximately 195,000 Jews living in Vichy France. Most were native born, but about 20,000 east European Jews and 30,000 refugee Jews from Germany and Austria sought safety in the unoccupied zone. What was not anticipated, however, was that the Vichy government was determined to implement its own version of the Nazi racial laws. Beginning in October 1940, anti-Jewish legislation was enacted, defining Jews as those with two or more Jewish grandparents as well as those who belonged to the Jewish religion. On the basis of this definition, Jews were forbidden from holding public office, serving in the military, or practicing most middle-class professions. The legislation also was the basis for the internment of foreign Jews. The cooperation of the French legal establishment in this undertaking surpassed any other country in Europe.

In March 1941, the government created the General Commissariat for Jewish Affairs and appointed Xavier Vallat, an antisemite, as its head. The ostensible purpose of the agency was to coordinate anti-Jewish measures throughout the country, but its primary function was to Aryanize Jewish property. In July 1942, an additional law called for a census of the Jews for the purpose of expropriating Jewish property and enterprises. By the end of 1941, the Vichy government established its version of the Jewish Council when it created the Union Générale des Israélites de France (UGIF), which represented the Jewish community in its dealings with the Vichy government. A similar organization was set up in the German-occupied zone by Eichmann's Jewish affairs expert, Theodor Dannecker. After the Wannsee Conference in January 1942, Eichmann and his Jewish "experts" made plans for the deportation of Jews living in France, Belgium, and Holland to the east. Earlier, in May 1941, the transports to the east had commenced with the deportation of 3,200 immigrant Polish Jews, and this was followed in August by an additional 4,300, including 1,300 native French Jews, who were sent to the Drancy transit camp, which served to intern Jews until they were sent to Auschwitz.

The Drancy camp was established in August 1941 in a suburb of Paris. About 70,000 Jews passed through the camp from its founding to Liberation Day in August 1944. In late March 1942, the first transport of west European Jews was sent to Auschwitz. On June 11, 1942, Eichmann met with his representatives to complete the technical plans regarding future deportations and, at this meeting, Dannecker agreed to deport 100,000 French Jews, taken equally from both zones. In July, 12,884 non-French Jews, including women and children, were eagerly rounded up by French police for deportation. Almost 4,000 additional Jews were sent to Sobibor. The total number of Jews sent to their deaths from the Drancy camp was about 65,000, which included 20,000 French Jewish citizens and 15,000 Polish and 6,000 German Jews.

The roundup of Jews bound for the death camps was accompanied by regulations that required them to abide by curfews and, for purposes of identification, to wear the yellow Star of David armbands and badges. In the occupied zone, the UGIF was allocated the task of providing sanitary supplies for the trains departing to the east, as well as caring for the children whose parents had been sent to Drancy. Still, few Jews escaped the death sentence. Of the more than 12,000 non-French Jews, including 4,000 children, the Germans sent to the Velodrome d'Hiver sports stadium in July 1942 prior to their deportation to the east, only 30 adults survived the war; all of the children were gassed.[15]

In July 1942, the Vichy government began to distinguish between French and foreign Jews. French Jews would remain under the control of the Vichy government, but foreign Jews would be handed over to the Germans. In August 1942, 15,000 foreign Jews interned in transit camps were turned over to the Germans for deportation. In November 1942, when the German army occupied all of France, the UGIF encouraged Jews to flee to the Italian occupation zone in southeastern France, where anti-Jewish measures were not implemented. Approximately 30,000 Jews were living in the Italian zone in relative safety until September 1943, when, after the Italian surrender to the Allies, the Germans occupied the area. With the assistance of French collaborators, the German forces hunted down thousands of Jews, who were subsequently deported. Jews were also victims of mass executions as they were singled out for retaliation in response to the accelerated activity of the French underground. All told, the number of Jews who were deported, executed by the Germans, or died in the transit camps was approximately 90,000. This includes 11,402 Jews who were rounded up by the all-too-co-operative French police.

Netherlands

In the Netherlands, the Final Solution was implemented despite the protest of a sizable segment of the population and the churches. On May 14, 1940, the Dutch surrendered to the invading German army, and the Austrian Nazi, Artur Seyss-Inquart, was appointed the chief civilian admin-istrator of the Netherlands. Almost immediately, he suspended the parlia-ment and appointed Dutch Nazis to important government posts.

At the time of its occupation, the Netherlands had a Jewish population of 140,000, representing 1.6 percent of the population; the number included refugees from Germany, Austria, and the Protectorate of Bohemia and Moravia. Prior to the German invasion, the Jews enjoyed full civic equality, and many of their religious and welfare institutions received government subsidies. During the refugee crisis of the 1930s, the country's Jewish community created the Committee for Special Jewish Affairs, which as-sumed responsibility for the care of refugees who emigrated to the Nether-lands from Germany. In 1939 a special camp in the village of Westerbork was built to detain illegal immigrants, and the Committee for Special Jewish Affairs shouldered the responsibility for running the camp. From 1939 to 1940, more than 34,000 Jewish refugees entered the country, and about 15,000 were still there when the Germans invaded the country.

The Jews of the Netherlands greeted the news of the German victory with great trepidation. Approximately 200 Jews committed suicide rather than face the wrath of the Nazis. Although the Germans behaved in a restrained manner during the first months of the occupation, the hiatus did not last. The first anti-Jewish measures, enacted in August 1940, required the registration of Jewish businesses and the listing of Jewish financial assets, the first steps toward "Aryanization." However, when Jewish professors at the universities of Leiden and Delft were dismissed, the students protested, whereupon the Germans closed the universities. In January 1941, Jews were required to register within a specified period of time or face a prison term of five years and possible confiscation of their property. This was followed by the requirement that an "Aryan" oath be taken by all civil servants, which led to the dismissal of Jews from the civil service, the schools, and the universities. The registration decree was of particular importance to the Germans because it provided them with an overview of the distribution of

Jews by city, street, age, gender, and their relationship to the Dutch through intermarriage.

The Dutch population responded to these measures with indifference, perhaps reinforcing the Nazi expectation that the Dutch would eventually share their ideological disposition toward the Jews. These measures and violent incidents between Jews and Dutch Nazis led Seyss-Inquart to demand the creation of a Joodse Raad, or Jewish Council, to preserve order among the Jews and to implement Nazi decrees. Shortly after its founding in February 1941, the Joodse Raad was unable to prevent a violent altercation that occurred in a Jewish café in Amsterdam that involved the Jewish owner and the police. The Nazis at this point decided to teach the Jews a lesson, and on February 22 they blockaded the Jewish quarter of the city and seized 389 young Jewish men, whom they deported initially to Buchenwald and later to Mauthausen. Only one person survived the ordeal. The arrests, the brutal treatment of the Jews, and the deportations angered Amsterdam's municipal workers, who called for a general strike on February 25. The strike won support from all elements of the population. Caught by surprise, the Germans engaged the strikers and suppressed them after three days of confrontation.

Both sides reached certain conclusions in the aftermath of the strike. The Dutch realized that the Germans would not moderate their treatment of the Jews, and the Germans understood that their efforts to spread antisemitism had failed. In the weeks that followed, the Germans hardened their anti-Jewish policy. On March 12 they began the process of "Aryanizing" Jewish property, and in May a decree ordered the confiscation of all Jewish valuables, except personal items such as wedding rings and gold teeth. At the same time, the RSHA set up the Central Office for Jewish Emigration, not unlike the bureaucracy functioning in Berlin and Vienna. In moving toward its objective of removing Jews from the Netherlands, the RSHA placed all Jewish organizations under the authority of the Joodse Raad, and proceeded to issue additional decrees that would segregate the Jews from the rest of the Dutch population: curfews were instituted; Jews were prohibited from traveling; Jews were allowed to use public transportation only with a special permit; Jews were allowed to shop only between the hours of 3:00 P.M. and 5:00 P.M.; Jews were dismissed from positions in public life, including the arts and the stock exchange; and Jews were barred from public parks. In August 1941, the Germans prohibited Jews from attending public and vocational schools. It fell to the Joodse Raad to fill the educational vacuum by opening its own schools. Emulating what already existed in Germany, certain stores were designated as off-limits to Jews, as well as boardinghouses and other venues where Jews and non-Jews met in public. Once the total segregation of the Jews was completed, the Germans turned to the confiscation of Jewish property and then to deportations.

In early 1942 the deportation of Jews to the death camps commenced, with their concentration in Amsterdam, and their transport from there to the Westerbork transit camp. To facilitate the roundups, Jews were required to wear the yellow badges, which the Joodse Raad was ordered to distribute. Many among the Dutch were outraged by this decree, and some began to wear a yellow badge of their own as an act of solidarity with the Jews. When the deportations began in July 1942, an outraged Dutch population reacted. Led by the Dutch churches, they protested the German actions in their Sunday sermons and as a group confronted Seyss-Inquart and demanded that the deportations halt. Eventually the Dutch Reformed church agreed to halt its protest when the Germans agreed to exempt Christians of Jewish origin from the deportations. However, the Catholic archbishop, Johannes de Jong, insisted that his protest telegram to Seyss-Inquart, which condemned the deportations, be read in church. In retaliation for the cleric's action, the Germans arrested 201 Jewish converts to Catholicism, including priests and nuns, and deported them to Auschwitz.

The public protest had no effect on the Germans, who continued to move Jews to Westerbork, and from there to Auschwitz and Sobibor. Although most of Holland's population was hostile to the German occupation and the treatment of the Jews, the SS was aided in the deportations by Dutch collaborators who joined Dutch Nazi paramilitary and military organizations. Historian Henry L. Mason has estimated that between 120,000 and 150,000 persons, or one out of every 70 Dutchmen, was charged after the war with collaboration with the Germans.[16]

The response of Jews to the deportations varied. Some refused to believe that the reports about the extermination camps were more than rumors, while others sought exemptions from the Jewish Council, which was able to issue stamps that represented the German priorities for deportations. Roughly one out of six Jews received stamps, and therefore exemption from deportation, as a result of their association with the Joodse Raad. A number of Jews went into hiding, the best-known example of whom were the Frank family.

The Franks went into hiding on July 9, 1942, but not before Otto Frank had planned the move. Having few illusions about the Nazis, Otto Frank, who had emigrated earlier from Germany, began preparations almost immediately after the Nazi occupation of the Netherlands. In an incremental, methodical manner, the Franks moved their possessions to a vacant annex located at the top of a house on Prinsengracht 263. They remained there until August 4, 1944, when the SD in Amsterdam received an anonymous phone call disclosing the Frank hiding place. When the police arrived and arrested the Franks, they also searched for money and jewelry. In the process of searching for valuables, one of the policemen inadvertently emptied an attaché case with the diary of Anne Frank, the teenaged daughter. After the police left, Miep Gies, one of Otto Frank's employees, returned to the annex and found the diary. The Franks were sent to Westerbork and deported from there to Auschwitz, where Anne's mother, Edith, perished. Anne and her sister, Margot, were sent to Bergen-Belsen at the end of October 1944, where both died from typhus. Otto Frank was the only surviving member of the family.

The last roundup of Jews took place on September 29, 1943, when about 2,000 Jews, including the Joodse Raad leadership, were taken to Westerbork. All told, approximately 110,000 Jews were deported to Auschwitz and Sobibor; about 5,000 survived. Neither Dutch Jewry nor the people of the Netherlands ever developed an effective resistance movement. Thus, the periodic support that the Jews received from their countrymen never effectively obstructed the Nazi objective of making the Netherlands free of Jews. The result was the destruction of 75 percent of Dutch Jewry.

Bulgaria

In Bulgaria, where antisemitism was not as much an issue as in other countries, a distinction was made between native and foreign Jews. Bulgaria also is an example where the population and the churches joined to oppose government plans to deport the Jews. Bulgaria remained neutral following the outbreak of World War II. The situation changed in March 1941 when Germany agreed to Bulgaria's annexation of western Thrace from Greece and Serbian Macedonia from Yugoslavia. Unlike other southeastern European countries, Bulgaria did not have a Jewish problem until its alliance with Nazi Germany. The Jewish population in Bulgaria proper numbered 50,000 and constituted less than 1 percent of a population of 6 million. But German influence in the Balkans during the 1930s brought with it the introduction of antisemitism, as Bulgarian students returning from German universities and emigrés from the Soviet Union spread Nazi propaganda throughout the country. It was not until the appointment of Bogdan Filov as Bulgarian premier in February 1940 that antisemitism became a political issue in Bulgaria. As Bulgarian policy became more pro-German, the influence of antisemitism grew proportionately. On December 24, 1940, the

Bulgarian parliament passed the Law for the Protection of the Nation, which emulated German racial laws regarding Jews, with the exception that the parliament exempted certain converts from the racial definition. This exemption led to an increase in mixed marriages and hundreds of "mercy baptisms." The law also exempted Jews who had been wounded in war or were decorated war veterans.

Bulgaria followed the pattern of many other European countries that followed German policy in its treatment of Jews. German influence led to the decree that forbade Jews to retain Bulgarian-sounding names and the requirement that they use only Jewish first names. But the legislation went much further. A partial list included the barring of Jews from certain types of employment, a prohibition on owning real estate in rural communities, and the requirement that Jews register their property with the government. Jews were also subjected to a curfew. Telephones and radios were removed from their homes and places of business. In September 1943, the government required that the Star of David be worn by all Jews. The Law for the Protection of the Nation was also applied to the 14,000 Jews residing in Thrace and the territory taken from Yugoslavia.

In June 1942, the Bulgarian government moved to solve its Jewish problem by expelling Jews from Bulgaria and confiscating their property. Toward this end, a Commissariat for Jewish Affairs was established in August 1942 under the direction of the Ministry of the Interior. Its purpose was to monitor the implementation of the Law for the Protection of the Nation and to finance the commissariat's activities by placing special fees on Bulgaria's Jews. Jews were, in essence, expected to pay the cost of administering antisemitic regulations. The ultimate objective, however, was to prepare Jews to finance the expense of their deportation to the east. The Commissariat for Jewish Affairs was headed by Alexander Belev, a German-trained lawyer and one of the few Bulgarians who believed in antisemitism. It was Belev who met with SS-Hauptsturmführer Theodor Dannecker, Eichmann's representative in Bulgaria, on February 22, 1943, and secretly agreed to surrender to German jurisdiction the fate of the Jews in Bulgaria proper and the newly acquired territories. Part of this agreement provided as a first step the deportation of 20,000 Jews to German territories in the east. On March 4, approximately 12,000 Jews from Thrace, Macedonia, and eastern Serbia were placed in concentration camps, and by the middle of the month the remaining 11,384 Jews were deported to Treblinka.

News that a camp was being constructed for the purpose of deporting Jews to the east spread through Bulgaria's Jewish community. As the leaders of the Jewish community in Sofia prepared to appeal the deportations, they were joined by an outraged Bulgarian public. The Bulgarian people joined in solidarity with their Jewish fellow citizens and showed their determination to protect them. Bulgarian and Macedonian nationalists sent representatives to Sofia to meet with the minister of the interior, Petur Gabrovski, who under personal threat canceled the deportation order. Gabrovski's action, however, affected only the Jews in Bulgaria proper. There appears to have been little, if any, support for Bulgaria's "foreign Jews," that is, those in Thrace, Macedonia, and eastern Serbia. The Germans continued the pressure to deport the Jews, but public opinion, now joined by the Bulgarian Orthodox church, prevented the government from complying with the demands emanating from Eichmann's representative. In the fall of 1943, the Germans, realizing the futility of forcing their Jewish policy on a reluctant Bulgaria, halted their pressure regarding deportations.

Denmark

In Scandinavia, resistance to the Nazi plans to deport the Jews reached heroic proportions. The record of Sweden and, in particular, Denmark during the Holocaust remains a model of how resistance to the Nazis saved thousands of lives. At the time of the German occupation in April 1940, Denmark had about 8,000 Jews, who constituted 0.2 percent of the population. The number of Jews included 1,500 recent arrivals from Germany, Austria, Bohemia, and Moravia. Jews as a whole were totally integrated into all aspects of Danish political, economic, and social life. Although a Danish Nazi party attempted to stir up anti-Jewish feelings, antisemitism did not gain a foothold in Denmark. With the German occupation, Himmler attempted to pressure the Danes into passing anti-Jewish measures, but they resolutely resisted any coercion on the Jewish question. As a consequence, neither anti-Jewish legislation nor efforts to "Aryanize" Jewish property were attempted by the Germans. At the Wannsee Conference in January 1942, Danish refusal to cooperate with the Germans in the matter of the Jews led to a proposal that the Final Solution of Danish Jewry be deferred until the end of the war. This policy, however, was reversed in spring 1943, when Dr. Werner Best was appointed Reich commissioner for occupied Denmark.

During Best's tenure, the Danish resistance emerged as a force in opposing the German occupation. Spurred on by Allied victories on all of the battlefronts, the resistance engaged in strikes and sabotage, which resulted in Denmark's coming under martial law. The state of emergency gave Best the opportunity to request that the Jews of Denmark be deported.

In early October 1943, the Germans began arresting Jews, which aroused the ire of the Danish population. They alerted Jews to the danger and helped them to hide. In cooperation with the Swedish government, nearly the entire Jewish population was first hidden and then ferried across to Sweden.

This act of solidarity was initially a spontaneous operation on the part of the Danish people but was soon given direction by the Danish resistance. The protest was joined by King Christian X and the heads of the Danish churches, who urged from their pulpits that the Danish people help the Jews. Sweden, in turn, discreetly made it known that it was prepared to take in all Jewish refugees. All but 400 Danish Jews managed to escape the Nazis. Although those who were rounded up by the Nazis were deported to Theresienstadt, the Danish people did not forget them. They sent food parcels and insisted that the Danish government be permitted to inspect the camp. In June 1944, permission was granted, and a Danish delegation accompanied the International Red Cross to inspect Theresienstadt. Although most Jews sent to the camp were eventually deported to Auschwitz, this was not the case with the Danish Jews because of the agitation of tne Danes. Eventually the Danish Jews interned in Theresienstadt were transferred to a camp in Sweden in spring 1945, thanks to the intervention of Swedish Red Cross representative Count Folke Bernadotte. At the conclusion of the war fifty-one Danish Jews had perished, all of them of natural causes at Theresienstadt.

Italy

Italy also falls into the category of those nations whose population resisted German efforts to implement the Final Solution. From Mussolini's seizure of power in October 1922 to the passage of the racial laws in 1938, antisemitism was a marginal phenomenon in Italy. Jews had supported the Fascist Party in large numbers until the mid-1930s, and Mussolini did not share the animus toward the Jews of his Axis partner, Adolf Hitler. In fact, Mussolini at one time had a mistress who was a Jew. However, Hitler exerted pressure on Mussolini, and in 1938 Italy adopted racial laws that adapted German racial theories to Italian conditions. The result was legislation that satisfied no one, least of all the Germans, who viewed the racial laws as a watered-down version of the Nuremberg Laws. Furthermore, the Italian government legislated many exceptions. The laws also angered the Holy See and the population in general. Nevertheless, the racial laws were enforced, and they took their toll on the Jewish community.

In 1939 there were approximately 57,000 Jews in Italy constituting about 1 percent of the population. About 10,000 Jews were refugees from Germany and Austria. Although Jews had attained full civil and political rights in Italy, the survival of the Jewish community was threatened by a growing rate of intermarriage, which crested at 30 percent on the eve of World War II. The anti-Jewish laws that were decreed in November 1938 therefore came as a shock to Italy's Jewish community. Jews were excluded from the civil service, the army, membership in the Fascist Party, and the ownership of enterprises that employed large numbers of Italians. In June 1939, the government barred Jewish professionals from serving clients who were non-Jews. Marriages between Jews and non-Jews were forbidden. In addition, limitations were placed on Jewish landownership, as well as on property in general. Consequently, many Jews lost their wealth, and what had been a prosperous community teetered on the verge of poverty.

Despite the social and economic hardships, Italy's Jews could take solace in the fact that the government resisted all German demands that they be deported, despite Italy's military and economic dependence on Germany. Although Mussolini was locked into the anti-Jewish legislation that shaped his wartime leadership, outside of Italy, especially in the Italian-occupied territories in France, Yugoslavia, and Greece, the protection of the Jews was one way in which Italy could assert its independence from its Axis partner. Combined with humanitarian considerations, the Italian-occupied territories became havens of refuge for Jews. The need to assert Italy's sovereignty also explains why Mussolini refused to deport its citizens of Jewish ancestry, despite the fact that Jews endured great hardship and deprivation. The protection afforded by Mussolini came to an end when the Germans occupied Italy in September 1943. Between September 15, 1943, and January 1944, at least 3,110 Jews were deported from Italy to Auschwitz under the direction of Eichmann's Jewish affairs experts. An additional 4,056 Jews were deported in early 1944 as the Germans systematically began the roundups throughout northern and central Italy. Yet because of the assistance of ordinary Italians, approximately four-fifths of Italian Jewry were saved.

Romania

The exigencies of war played a role in the extent to which the Final Solution was implemented in Romania. On the eve of World War II, Romania was a nation torn by political conflict. King Carol II's rule was threatened by the rise of the Fascist Iron Guard, which was founded in 1927 and was characterized by an extreme antisemitism matched only by the Nazi storm troopers in Germany. Opposed to the parliamentary form of government and meshing Christian mysticism with a cult of death, the Iron Guard was committed to excluding Jews from all aspects of Romanian life, as well as depriving them of their civil rights. Iron Guard propaganda stressed that the Jews were responsible for all of the ills that afflicted Romanian society. During the mid-1930s, the Iron Guard forged ties with the Nazis, stressing the commonality of their beliefs on the Jewish question.

The Romanian government enacted a law on August 8, 1940, that canceled citizenship for most Romanian Jews and prohibited mixed marriages. Jews were accused of aiding the communists and serving the interests of the Soviet Union. Following the installation of the National Legionary State in September 1940, with Ion Antonescu as prime minister and Horia Sima, the leader of the Iron Guard, in a key government position, King Carol II was deposed in a bloodless coup. Although a minority in the government, the Iron Guard controlled several important government agencies.

Life became more precarious for Romania's Jews as the Iron Guard initiated a campaign of terror against them. They legally confiscated Jewish property and moved immediately to displace Jews from the economy. These restrictions were accompanied by the plunder of Jewish property. When Antonescu insisted that law and order be maintained and that Jews be gradually eliminated from the economy, he was faced by the opposition from the Iron Guard. On January 21–23, 1941, the Iron Guard under Sima staged a coup against the Antonescu government, which was accompanied by anti-Jewish riots. The coup failed, in part because Hitler supported Antonescu and placed Nazi units stationed in Romania at his disposal. With German support, the Romanian army controlled the country, and Antonescu ruled as a military dictator.

Romania joined Germany in the invasion of the Soviet Union. This gave the Antonescu regime the excuse to expel Jews from various parts of Romania. Forty thousand Jews were forced out of villages and towns on Antonescu's orders, and their property was confiscated. In the Soviet Union, Romanian army units took part in the killing of Jews in cooperation with *Einsatzgrüppe* D. Thousands of Jews were rounded up by Romanian soldiers and sent off, without bread or water, in crowded cattle cars to no particular destination. Those who did not die as a result of suffocation or hunger were shot.

Much of Antonescu's pro-German policy and willingness to cooperate with the Nazis regarding the Jewish question were based on his expectation that this alliance would gain territory for Romania. But by early 1942, Antonescu had doubts about the ability of Germany to win the war. Added to these considerations were the reports of heavy Romanian losses on the Russian front. Together they forced Antonescu to reconsider his total cooperation with Germany. In summer 1942, Eichmann sent one of his operatives to Bucharest and reached an agreement with the government to commence deportations. Interventions by non-Jews, including the Romanian clergy and the papal nuncio, Archbishop Andrea Cassulo, together with the courageous and unceasing efforts of the leadership of the Jewish community, had their effect. The combination of a deteriorating war situation and the belief that the pope was directly involved in the efforts to protect Romania's Jews led Antonescu to cancel his agreement to deport the country's remaining 292,000 Jews to the Belzec extermination camp.

In March 1943, Ion Antonescu, on a visit to Hitler, found himself pressured to reverse his decision, but he refused. By the end of the year, Antonescu concluded that the solution of Romania's Jewish problem was to allow Jews to emigrate in return for a sizable cash payment. Eichmann was determined to abort Antonescu's plan, and in August 1944, the Germans sank two ships with "illegal immigrants" sailing from Romania to Palestine.

The failure of the Nazis to exterminate the entire Jewish population of Romania does not diminish the large numbers who were murdered by the Romanians and the Germans. In Transnistria only about 50,000 out of 300,000 Bessarabian and Bukovinian Jews survived, and about 50,000 were deported to Siberia during the Soviet occupation, with their ultimate fate still unknown. Most of the others were killed by *Einsatzgrüppe* D and their Romanian auxiliaries. Approximately 300,000 Jews in Romania survived.

Hungary

The last phase in the deportation of Jews occurred in Hungary, with the German occupation of Hungary in March 1944. Between May 15 and July 9, 1944, about 437,402 Jews were deported from Hungary to the death camps. The majority were sent to Auschwitz. The number of Jews in Hungary at the time of the deportations numbered some 762,000, with an additional 100,000 converts to Christianity who nevertheless were considered Jews according to Nazi racial laws.

Although integrated into the cultural life of Hungary, Jews became targets of antisemitism after World War I, when they were associated with the short-lived communist dictatorship of Bela Kun in 1919. The terrible economic conditions and the humiliation of territorial losses following the war led to Kun's fall and Admiral Miklos Horthy's becoming the regent of Hungary in 1920. During the 1920s and 1930s, Horthy's regime was characterized by an official antisemitism. During the early 1930s Hungary and Nazi Germany drew close because the Germans sought to expand their influence in east-central Europe, and Hungary sought markets for its agricultural products at a time when it was suffering from the worldwide depression.

Cooperation with Germany also resulted in the legitimation of the Arrow Cross Party, a pro-Nazi and vehemently antisemitic paramilitary group. Hungary also joined the Nazis in the invasion of Yugoslavia and the war against the Soviet Union. Following the Nazi defeat at Stalingrad, which included heavy Hungarian losses, the Horthy government reconsidered its alliance with the Germans and sought to extricate itself from its ally. In late 1943, the Hungarians sent peace feelers to the West, which the Germans did not attempt to halt as long as Hungary maintained its economic agreements. Horthy also called for the withdrawal of the Hungarian army from the Soviet Union. As it became apparent that the Horthy government was moving closer to changing sides, the Germans decided to move against Hungary. With the Soviet army nearing the Carpathian Mountains, Hitler sent for Horthy in March 1944 and told him of plans to occupy Hungary. On March 19, 1944, German troops occupied Hungary and immediately set up a government loyal to Germany. The Germans also sent various "experts," including Adolf Eichmann, and members of the Jewish Section of the RSHA to orchestrate the Final Solution in Hungary.

Although deportations commenced in 1944 with the German occupation, daily life for Hungarian Jewry had begun to deteriorate much earlier. The first anti-Jewish laws were promulgated by the Horthy government as early as May 1938. One law placed a quota on the number of Jews permitted in private business. In 1939 a more sweeping law barred Jews from important positions in the media and limited their number in the professions. Subsequent legislation prohibited Jews from acquiring Hungarian citizenship through naturalization, marriage, or adoption. Following the annexation of territories in Ruthenia, the Hungarians rounded up some 17,000 stateless Jews and dumped them into German-occupied Ukraine. When the Germans objected to the Hungarian action, 6,000 Jews were returned and used as slave laborers; the other 11,000 were killed by *Einsatz* commandos. From 1942 to the German occupation in 1944, Jews continued to be subject to forced labor and more extensive expropriations, but they were not handed over to the Nazis. In fact, the Hungarian government refused the German demand that Jews be required to wear the yellow Star of David and be deported to Poland. In May 1943, Prime Minister Miklos Kallay, in a public speech, rejected the "resettlement" of the Jews as a "final solution" so long as the Germans refused to respond satisfactorily as to their ultimate destination.

The German occupation of Hungary in March 1944 deposed Prime Minister Kallay and ended whatever protection Hungary's Jews had from being deported. Kallay was replaced by the pro-German Dome Sztojay, who almost immediately issued a wave of anti-Jewish decrees, including the requirement that Jews wear the yellow Star of David. With guidance and assistance from Eichmann and his team of experts, the Hungarians tightened the noose around the necks of the country's Jews. As was the case in other countries under Nazi occupation, the anti-Jewish measures began with decrees that led to the isolation of the Jews. Jews were limited in their ability to travel, and their telephones and radios were confiscated. The yellow badges made them easy targets for the Arrow Cross Party. Next came the expropriation of property as Jews found that their bank accounts, jewelry, and other valuables were subject to confiscation. Jewish-owned businesses, industrial enterprises, and financial establishments also were being prepared for the Hungarian version of Aryanization. Moreover, antisemitism had become profitable as Hungarians plundered Jewish property. The Germans, in fact, were surprised by the number of tips they received from Hungarian informers hoping to benefit from Jewish misfortune.

The concentration of Jews in ghettos was decreed on April 28, 1944. For this purpose, Hungary was divided into five main sectors, with fifty-five ghettos and three concentration camps, all for the purpose of interning 427,000 Jews with the eventual objective of deporting them to the death camps. Along with the creation of the ghettos, Eichmann assembled leaders of the Jewish community and demanded that they establish a Jewish Council that would carry out German decrees in the ghettos, as was the case in Poland. From May 15 to May 24, under Eichmann's supervision, 16,000 Jews were deported to Auschwitz. At the Auschwitz end, in preparation for the large influx of Jews from Hungary, the squads in the gas chambers, crematoriums, and the warehouses where the victims' belonging were stored were reinforced, and the crematorium was kept working twenty-four hours a day.

On April 25, 1944, the eve of the deportations, Joel Brand, a member of the Relief and Rescue Committee of Budapest (Va'ada), established in January 1943 for the purpose of helping Jewish refugees who had escaped from Slovakia and Poland, was summoned by Adolf Eichmann to offer his "Blood for Goods" proposition. Approved by Himmler, the arrangement would have exchanged 1 million Jews for goods, including 10,000 trucks that were promised to be used for civilian purposes or only on the eastern front. The deal would have allowed Jews to leave Hungary and find refuge in any Allied-controlled part of the world except Palestine, where the Germans had promised Hajj Amin al-Husseini, the mufti of Jerusalem, Jews would not be permitted to emigrate. Brand was allowed to go abroad to establish contact with the representatives of world Jewry and the Allies. He received his travel arrangements on May 15, the day the deportations from Hungary began. He set out for Turkey and was eventually detained by the British in Cairo.

His message did reach the western Allies, where it was discussed by both the Soviet Union and Great Britain. On July 13, 1944, the British government's Committee for Refugee Affairs concurred with the Soviet Union and turned down the proposal. It may be that the Soviets understood that the trucks obtained by the Germans in such an exchange would be used against them on the eastern front. The trade also would have violated the Allied declaration of unconditional surrender, which eliminated the possibility of this type of negotiation with the Germans.

Eichmann, who had agreed to suspend deportations until a reply was received, betrayed his promise and continued to transport Jews without interruption to Auschwitz. There is no evidence that Eichmann ever intended to halt the deportation of Jews to Auschwitz even for a brief period of time.

A different type of rescue effort in Hungary was attempted by Rezso Kasztner, a prominent member of the Relief and Rescue Committee of Budapest. The committee was aware of the death camps and was active in smuggling refugees from Poland and Slovakia into Hungary. In the misbelief that the Germans had ransomed Jews for money in Slovakia, the committee attempted to open up similar negotiations with Eichmann's representatives in German-occupied Hungary in 1944. After negotiations with Eichmann and the payment of a fee of $1,000 per person to the SS, a train with 1,684 Jews left Hungary in summer 1944, supposedly bound for Spain or Switzerland. Instead it went to Bergen-Belsen, where the Jews were detained. The train included members of Kasztner's family, as well as some prominent Jews of Budapest. Kasztner believed that this would be the first of many trains that would follow and thus remove the death sentence that hung over the heads of Hungarian Jewry. But subsequent trainloads of Jews did not follow, and Kasztner was accused of giving preference to family and friends. He would later be accused of having created the illusion of rescue by promoting the idea that the trains would take Jews to safety instead of warning them of the deportations, and therefore making the roundup of Jews for transport that much easier for Eichmann.

In July 1944, Himmler gave permission for the SS to negotiate with Kasztner, and subsequently the representative of the Joint Distribution Committee, Saly Mayer, met with the SS at a location near the Swiss border. The result of the first meeting on August 21, 1944, was an order by Himmler to halt the deportations of Jews from Budapest, and 318 Jews from the "Kasztner train" were released and allowed to enter Switzerland. In December, the rest of the Jews detained at Bergen-Belsen were set free and similarly allowed to enter the Swiss state. Given his ideological propensity, the question remains as to why Himmler agreed to negotiate with "the real enemies of Nazism" and allow these small numbers to escape. Yehuda Bauer has argued that Himmler believed that all Jews must be exterminated, but if Germany found itself in an unfavorable military situation, it could temporarily suspend its war against the Jews in order to gain a breathing space. "A basic desire to murder all the Jews does not contravene a readiness to use them, or some of them, as hostages to be exchanged for things that Germany needed in a crisis. . . . There would be plenty of time to return to the murder policy once Germany was on its feet again."[17] The reality was that the Kasztner episode was a momentary interruption in the killing process.

During June and July, an additional 382,000 Jews were cleared from different sections in greater Hungary, and by the end of July, over 434,000 Jews had been sent to Auschwitz. Fearing retribution from the Allies in a war that Germany appeared to be losing and having received protests from Sweden and the free world, Horthy halted the deportations, but his ban on the deportations was a case of too little and too late. Most of Hungary's Jews, except for those in Budapest, had already been liquidated. Eichmann was angered by Horthy's refusal to continue the deportations, which were now being prepared for the Jews of Budapest, and he was determined to continue the transports. On one occasion he bypassed Horthy's orders and transported 2,000 Jews, only to have the transport returned by Hungarian troops. The zealous Eichmann was not deterred and in a second attempt successfully sent the trainload of Jews to Auschwitz.

Between August and October 1944, the condition of Hungary's remaining Jews improved as Horthy was determined to remove his country from the war and halt the persecutions that had brought so much disapproval from the free world. But aided by the Germans, a coup against the Hungarian government took place on October 15–16, 1944, led by Ferenc Szalasi, the leader of the Arrow Cross. Szalasi became prime minister and remained in that office until the Soviet conquest of Hungary in early winter 1945. Horthy, isolated and without political allies, resigned his position and was removed with his family to Germany.

The optimism shared by the Jews of Budapest during the previous months was replaced by trepidation as the Szalasi government resumed deportations. Auschwitz, however, was in the process of being dismantled, and instead of transports leaving the country for the extermination camp, Jews were placed in slave labor battalions in Hungary. Toward the end of 1944, about 160,000 Jews were left in Budapest, where life was made miserable by terror attacks organized by Arrow Cross gangs. The coming of winter added to the suffering as cold and hunger pervaded their ghetto-like existence. By the end of winter, prior to the Russian occupation of Budapest on February 14, 1945, an additional 20,000 Jews had died. The figures are startling when one considers the relatively short time that the Final Solution was carried out in Hungary. Over 450,000 Jews of greater Hungary, or 70 percent, were killed by the Germans. About 140,000 survived in Budapest, and 50,000 to 60,000 Jews survived in the provinces.

Gypsies

The deportation of Jews to the death camps was paralleled by the German effort to exterminate the gypsies of Europe. As in the case of the Jews, Nazi ideology viewed the gypsies as subhuman because of their rootlessness. Gypsies, lacking a country of their own, were perceived as parasites living off the host nations that allowed them to reside within their borders. The irony in regard to this Nazi stereotype is that the gypsies had migrated about 2,000 years ago from northern India, the ostensible home of the "Aryan race," and were therefore of "Aryan" descent.

In fact, most Europeans were suspicious of the gypsies, believing them to be idolatrous, if not engaged in witchcraft. Only in the Balkans was there some toleration for the gypsies. Elsewhere, images of them as thieves and kidnappers of little children spread throughout the rest of Europe. In both Germany and Austria, where gypsies were victims of severe discrimination, numerous regulations that limited their movement and rights were rigorously enforced. Although population data on the gypsies are difficult to assess, many scholars estimate that about 1.5 million lived in Europe on the eve of World War II.[18]

The Nazi persecution of the gypsies mirrored that of the Jews. In September 1933, gypsies were arrested throughout Germany in accordance with the Law against Habitual Criminals. The Nuremberg Laws of 1935 that defined the status of Jews in Germany also included regulations with regard to the gypsies. For example, marriages between gypsies and Germans were forbidden The Research Office for the Science of Inheritance, which in 1937 was renamed the Research Office for Race Hygiene and Population, declared that 90 percent of the approximately 28,000 German *Rom* (gypsies) were *Mischlinge*, and therefore non-Aryans. As part of the Nazi program to eliminate "lives undeserving of living," gypsies were designated as asocials and a threat to public health. Viewed as parasites feeding off the body of the German people, most were sent to Dachau, where many underwent forced sterilization.

After the start of World War II, Heydrich was already calculating the removal of more than 30,000 gypsies from the Reich and, along with Jews and Poles, their deportation to the *Generalgouvernment*. Although only 2,500 were shipped to Poland, it was evident that the severity of Nazi policy toward both the gypsies and the Jews had intensified. In the fall of 1941, Austrian gypsies were sent to the Lodz ghetto, where they were segregated from the Jewish population. When a severe typhus epidemic broke out in the gypsy section, the Germans refused to provide medical assistance. The great bulk of the gypsies of Lodz were eventually sent to the Chelmno extermination camp. There is no record of any survivors.

Although the bulk of the gypsies in both Germany and Austria were considered non-Aryan, there was the matter of "pure" gypsies. In October 1942, Himmler issued a decree that distinguished between *Mischling* gypsies and those considered of pure blood, whereby the latter would be permitted a certain degree of freedom of movement. Ultimately Himmler's directive exempted some 13,000 Sinti and 1,017 Lalleri (the gypsies had divided into the two tribes centuries earlier) from the fate awaiting the great majority of the gypsies. On December 16, 1942, Himmler issued an order that in effect called for the Final Solution of the gypsy problem whereby they would be sent to Auschwitz-Birkenau. Exceptions were made for those "socially adapted" to German life, former Wehrmacht soldiers, and those necessary for wartime labor. However, in each of these categories, those who were exempted were to be sterilized. The Himmler order of December 16 was to seal the fate of Europe's gypsy population.

The first transport of Reich gypsies arrived in Auschwitz in February 1943. Placed in a gypsy "family camp," they suffered incredible hardships, and many died of starvation and disease. Others were used in medical experiments, such as those performed by Josef Mengele. According to Yehuda Bauer, about 13,000 gypsies from Germany and Austria were deported to Auschwitz. Gypsies, however, were targets of the Nazis from the start of the war in September 1939. Between 1939 and 1940, 2,500 were sent to Poland and were killed there. Another 3,000 were sent to camps in Austria, where they perished, and the 5,000 sent to Chelmno were gassed.

Data on the fate of gypsies throughout the rest of Europe are difficult to determine. Bauer estimates that more than 200,000 gypsies were killed in the *Porrajamos* (the gypsy word for the Holocaust), although he cautions that this figure may be an underestimate. Raul Hilberg has estimated the figure to be around 100 million, and gypsy scholar Ian Hancock argues that as many as 750,000 gypsies, or as much as one-third or more of all the gypsies of the world, were killed by the Germans.[19]

In comparing the fate of the gypsies with the Jews, the words of Yehuda Bauer shed light on the distinctions that the Nazis made between the two targeted peoples:

Gypsies were not Jews and therefore there was no need to kill all of them. Those Gypsies who were of "pure blood" or who were not considered dangerous on a racial level could continue to exist, under strict supervision. The *Mischlinge* were . . . doomed to death. The difference between the fate of the Gypsies and that of the Jews is clear. The Jews were slated for total annihilation, whereas, the Gypsies were sentenced to selective mass murder on a vast scale.[20]

THE DEATH CAMPS

The Nazis continued to deport Jews, gypsies, and other "asocials" even after it became apparent that it was only a matter of time before they lost the war. The trains deposited their passengers at the seven major extermination camps located in German-occupied Poland: Chelmno, Belzec, Treblinka, Sobibor, Majdanek, Stutthof, and Auschwitz-Birkenau.

Auschwitz

It was at Auschwitz that the bulk of the deported Jews were killed, and this extermination camp has since become synonymous with the Holocaust.

Jews who arrived at Auschwitz were subjected to a selection, whereby those who appeared strong and healthy were waved to one side and designated for hard labor. The others were sent to the gas chambers. The process of selecting who would live and who would die was placed in the hands of SS doctors such as the infamous Dr. Josef Mengele, whose name has became synonymous with perverse medical experiments at Auschwitz.

Mengele was not alone in performing medical experiments on Jews, gypsies, and other prisoners of interest to the SS doctors. In July 1942, Himmler proposed the sterilization of Jewish women at Auschwitz as a means of advancing the war against the Jews, especially the offspring of mixed marriages. This project was placed under the supervision of SS physician Carl Clauberg, who had performed similar procedures at Ravensbruck. Clauberg, together with Mengele and other SS doctors, established sterilization stations in Block 10 at Auschwitz, where the doctors engaged in their experiments by means of repeated and unprotected X-rays. They selected groups of twins, including children, and dwarfs for their experiments.

Mengele and other Nazi doctors were part of the selection process at Birkenau that met the new arrivals. Told to disembark (*"Raus!"*), the Jews were hurried from the boxcars and ordered to leave their personal belongings behind. They were then forced to stand in one of two lines, the men in one and the women in the other. It was at this point that the selection process took place, with the SS doctors directing the arrivals to one side, for the gas chambers, or to the other, for forced labor. Throughout the process, the deportees did not appear to comprehend the significance of the two lines. Survivors have testified to the emotion of being separated from their families, with mothers and young children going to one side and older children deemed fit for labor going to the other.

Those designated for the gas chambers were ordered to undress and place their clothes on hooks, and to tie their shoes together. To make the deception even more authentic, each person was given a piece of soap and brought to the gas chamber, which was equipped with shower heads. Once inside, the door was sealed, and pellets of Zyklon B were poured into the room from a vent in the roof. As soon as the pellets came into contact with the air, they were converted to gas. Since the gas worked in an upward direction, the first to die were the children, and the last were those strong enough to climb atop the piles of bodies. The SS men responsible for releasing the Zyklon B wore gas masks to protect themselves from the fumes. An advantage of using this gas, from the Nazi perspective, was that it left no odor inside or outside the chamber.

The gassing occurred on the day of the deportees' arrival at Auschwitz, and their corpses were then collected by *Sonderkommandos*, or Jewish prisoners, assigned to the crematoriums, who were responsible for collecting the bodies and bringing them to one of the ovens. Personal belongings of the murdered prisoners were collected and stored in a specially built warehouse—nicknamed "Canada," because the camp inmates associated Canada with wealth—and from there shipped to Germany. Special attention was directed toward salvaging whatever valuables the victims had on their person, including their hair, eyeglasses, and gold teeth, which were routinely extracted from the corpses.

The victims chosen for hard labor were sent to an area of the camp called "the quarantine," where their clothes were taken from them and exchanged for prison-striped garb. Their humiliation continued, with both men and women inmates having their hair shorn. (The hair was sent to Germany, where it was processed as mattress filling.) Many prisoners in the quarantine were so emaciated and weak that they were referred to as *Muselmann*, camp jargon for someone who could not move or react to the environment. Once moved from the quarantine area, the prisoners were sent to different sections of the Auschwitz camp for hard labor.

Perhaps the most dreaded part of the day was the roll call (*Appell*), which occurred in both the morning and the late afternoon, when the prisoners returned from their work. Historian Jozef Busko describes the terror of the *Appell* as one in which the prisoners "were made to stand at attention, motionless, usually sparsely clad, for many hours in the cold, in rain and snow, and whoever stumbled or fell was sent to be gassed."[21] Upon leaving the quarantine, prisoners were registered, and numbers were tattooed on their left arm. Those who were immediately gassed upon arrival at Auschwitz went unregistered.

The number of Jews murdered at Auschwitz-Birkenau is estimated at between 1.1 and 1.3 million. Almost one-quarter of the Jews killed during World War II were murdered there. Of the 405,000 registered prisoners who received numbered tattoos, only about 65,000 survived.

Sobibor

The Sobibor extermination camp was established as part of the *Aktion Reinhard* operation and functioned from May 1942 to October 1943. It was staffed by veterans of the euthanasia program, one of whom was the camp commandant, Franz Stangl. During the seventeen months of its operation, more than 250,000 Jews were killed. As was the case at Auschwitz, railroad tracks led the trains directly into the camp. The selection process took place immediately after the Jews were ordered out of the boxcars. Unlike Auschwitz, the *Aktion Reinhard* camps were constructed solely as extermination camps; there was no possibility of avoiding the gas chambers through labor.

In Sobibor, where carbon monoxide gas was used, the five gas chambers operating in the camp had the capacity to kill 400 people in twenty to thirty minutes. Between 200 and 300 Jews were assigned the task of removing the bodies from the gas chambers and bringing them to burial pits. Toward the end of 1942, the Germans began to burn the corpses in order to hide the evidence of mass killings. A special team of prisoners called the "dentists" were charged with extracting gold from the teeth of the victims before the bodies were placed in the burial pits. In July 1943, Himmler ordered that Sobibor be transformed from an extermination to a concentration camp.

Treblinka

The Treblinka camp began operation in July 1942 and was dismantled following a revolt by Jewish prisoners on August 2, 1943. In the eleven months of its existence, between 800,000 and 1 million people, including more than 870,000 Jews and 2,000 gypsies, were exterminated in the gas chambers and buried in mass graves. As was the case in Auschwitz and Sobibor, Jews from all parts of Axis Europe were brought to the camp by railway cars. To ease the anxiety of the Jews exiting from the boxcars, the Germans built a bogus railway station with a huge clock to create the impression of arriving at a town. Once the selection was made, the Jews were ordered into the area called "deportation square," the men being chased to one set of barracks and women and children to another, where they were made to undress and their hair was shorn. From their barrack, the women and children were driven through a passage lined on both sides by barbed wire that led to the partially concealed gas chambers. The Germans referred to the passage as the hose (*Schlauch*) or the "Way to Heaven" (*Himmelstrasse)*. The passage to the gas chamber was lined by SS men armed with whips and clubs and with dogs, who expedited the walk of the unsuspecting Jews to their deaths.

In late February 1943, Himmler visited the camp and ordered that the bodies of the victims be burned. When mass graves were opened, the bodies were removed and burned on pyres. The ashes and crushed bones were then reburied in the same graves. Himmler was determined to remove all traces of the mass murder that had taken place at Treblinka.

Majdanek

Majdanek, constructed in the winter of 1940–1941, served as a labor camp for Jews, Poles, and Soviet prisoners of war during its first years. In 1942 the first Jews arrived in the camp from Slovakia and the Bohemian Protectorate; by the end of 1943, more than 125,000 had been killed. In all, nearly 500,000 persons from twenty-eight countries passed through Majdanek. Of these, 360,000 died as a result of starvation, disease, beatings, and 28 percent were exterminated in the gas chambers or through other forms of execution.

The gas chambers at Majdanek were modeled after those at Birkenau, although the Germans also used mobile vans and shot prisoners. Leni Yahil has described the sadistic guards at the camp:

The SS men . . . tortured people for their pleasure; they were especially fond of slaughtering infants and children before their mother's eyes. At roll calls, which were held every morning and evening . . . inmates were harassed with particular zeal, for example, by ordering to put on and take off their caps in rhythm. At times, one of the prisoners was ordered to step forward and informed that he had been condemned to death, the sentence being quickly carried out by hanging.[22]

The most notorious act of murder at Majdanek was the mass shooting of 17,000 Jews on November 3, 1943.

DEATH MARCHES

The vast majority of the Jews murdered in the Holocaust were killed in the extermination camps in Poland. But Jews and other victims of Nazi genocide also died as a result of the "death marches." As the Russian forces drew near, the Germans implemented the last stages of the Final Solution: the death marches. In order to protect a still useful labor force, Himmler ordered hundreds of thousands of prisoners, including more than 200,000 Jews, vacated from the camps in the East and marched to concentration camps in Germany. In the five-month period between January and May 1945, more than 250,000 prisoners died due to exposure, starvation, and cruel treatment by their SS guards.

Buchenwald

Buchenwald, located north of Weimar, was founded in July 1937. Until the outbreak of the war, Jews were sent to Buchenwald as part of the Nazi objective to pressure them to leave Germany. In October 1942, Jews held at Buchenwald were transferred to Auschwitz. When the Germans began to dismantle Auschwitz in January 1945, thousands of Jews were force marched to Buchenwald. Several hundred of these evacuees were children who were housed in a special barrack known as Children Bloc 66. Other Jewish prisoners were subjects of medical experiments.

Bergen-Belsen

Bergen-Belsen was established in April 1943 as a detention camp and became a concentration camp in March 1944. The camp, located in Lower Saxony, consisted of a main camp and five satellites, including four that held large numbers of Jewish prisoners. Invariably those who arrived at Bergen-Belsen received no medical attention and minimal food rations. Thousands died in the camp as a result of the terrible conditions. The camp population was approximately 15,000 persons, of whom 8,000 were women.

In the last weeks of the war, tens of thousands of prisoners were evacuated from both the extermination camps and concentration camps, such as Buchenwald, and force marched to Bergen-Belsen. These included 20,000 women prisoners from Auschwitz. The camp was unprepared to handle those who survived the death marches. Its administration did nothing to house the large number of prisoners streaming into the camp. In addition, those incarcerated lacked water and food. The result was a serious outbreak of typhus, which in March 1945 claimed the lives of 18,168 prisoners, including Anne Frank. The total number of deaths from January to April 1945 was 35,000. When the British army liberated the camp on April 15, 1945, there were 60,000 prisoners in the camp who were chronically ill. There were also thousands of unburied bodies strewn all over the camp, a scene captured on film by the horrified British. In the first five days after the liberation of Bergen-Belsen, 14,000 persons died, and an additional 14,000 perished in the following weeks.

CONCLUSION

In German-occupied Europe, the steps that led to the death camps followed an organized plan. Following the sequence first used in Germany, the events leading to the Final Solution began with a legal definition of who was a Jew, followed by the expropriation of Jewish property, Jewish segregation, and eventual deportation. The organization of the plan to murder the Jews was anything but random. It involved the bureaucracies of Germany and the occupied countries. The administrative hand of Adolf Eichmann was present in every country where the Germans were able to deport Jews, and he was aided by collaborationist governments that placed their bureaucracies at his disposal.

The death camps were similarly organized. Little was left to chance. The killing process at Auschwitz and the other extermination camps was run on principles of management that would have rivaled the most efficient factories in terms of productivity. Ideological fervor and a bureaucratic ethos committed to fulfilling its task at all cost combined to make genocide possible even after it was apparent that the war was lost.

By the time the war ended, the Jews of Europe, the Nazis' primary ideological enemy, had suffered proportionally the largest number of casualties among those designated for death in the name of Aryan supremacy. Prior to the initiation of the Final Solution, the Jewish population in Europe stood at approximately 9,797,000 people. The number of Jews annihilated by the Nazis has been estimated at between 5,291,000 and 5,933,900.[23] In addition, the Nazis exterminated another 19,000,000 people considered enemies of Germany's new order in Europe.[24]

NOTES

1. Richard Rubenstein, *The Cunning of History: The Holocaust and the American Future* (New York: Harper Colophon Books, 1975), p. 25.

2. Robert Wistrich, *Who's Who in Nazi Germany* (New York: Bonanza Books, 1982), p. 63.

3. Paul Hilberg, *The Destruction of the European Jews* (New York: Holmes & Meier, 1961), p. 278.

4. Ibid., p. 298.

5. Israel Gutman, "Ghetto," in Gutman, ed., *Encyclopedia of the Holocaust* (New York: Macmillan,) 2:579– 582.

6. Lucy Dawidowicz, *The War against the Jews* (New York: Bantom, 1975), p. 139.

7. Leni Yahil, *The Holocaust* (New York: Oxford, 1990), p. 328.

8. Ibid., p. 329.

9. Ibid., p. 297.

10. Louis P. Lochner, ed., *The Goebbels Diaries* (New York: Popular Library, 1948), entry for March 11, 1943, p. 294.

11. Peter Wyden, *Stella* (New York: Simon & Schuster, 1992), p. 108.

12. Ibid., p. 141.

13. Menachem Shelah, "Croatia," in Gutman, ed., *Encyclopedia of the Holocaust*, 1:325.

14. Ibid., p. 326.

15. Dawidowicz, *War*, p. 362.

16. Henry L. Mason, *The Purge of the Dutch Quislings: Emergency Justice in the Netherlands* (The Hague: Nijhoff, 1952), p. 40.

17. Yehuda Bauer, *Jews for Sale? Nazi-Jewish Negotiations, 1933–1945* (New Haven: Yale University Press, 1994), p. 199.

18. Philip Friedman, *Roads to Extinction: Essays on the Holocaust* (Philadelphia: Jewish Publication Society, 1980), p. 382.

19. Ian Hancock, "Responses to the Romani Holocaust," in Alan S. Rosenbaum, ed., *Is the Holocaust Unique?* (Boulder, Colo.: Westview Press, 1996), p. 44. Hancock claims that the Himmler order of December 16 signaled the fate of Europe's gypsies in the same way that the Wannsee Conference did so for the Jews.

20. Yehudo Bauer, "Gypsies," in Gutman, ed., *Encyclopedia of the Holocaust*, 2:638.

21. Jozef Buszko, "Auschwitz," in Gutman, ed., *Encyclopedia of the Holocaust*, 1:110.

22. Yahil, *Holocaust*, p. 363.

23. Dawidowicz, *War*, pp. 402–403; R. J. Rummel, *Deomocide: Nazi Genocide and Mass Murder* (New Brunswick, N.J.: Transaction Publishers, 1992), pp. 29–30.

24. Rummel, *Deomocide*.

The interior of the Fassenstrasse synagogue in Berlin after its destruction on Kristallnacht. Used by permission of Yad Vashem

SS men "amusing" themselves by cutting off the beard of a Jew in Plock, Poland. Used by permission of Yad Vashem

A crowded street in the Warsaw ghetto. Used by permission of Yad Vashem

Woman selling Star of David armbands in the Warsaw ghetto. Used by permission of Yad Vashem

A Jewish family being deported from Amsterdam. They were allowed to take only what they could carry. Used by permission of Yad Vashem

Disembarkation at Auschwitz, Birkenau. Used by permission of Yad Vashem

The main gate to Auschwitz: "Work Makes You Free."

Typical wooden block in Birkenau. Housed as many as 1,000 prisoners. Used by permission of Steven Paskuly

Crematorium photo taken from a German POW in 1945. Used by permission of Thomas Hollingsworth

Crematory I as it appears today. This is the only gas chamber still standing in Auschwitz. Used by permission of Steven Paskuly

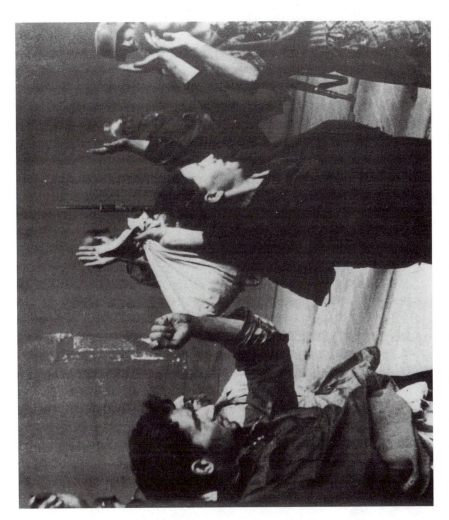

Members of the Jewish Combat Organization after their capture in the Warsaw ghetto. Used by permission of Yad Vashem

A group of Jewish partisans from the Vilna ghetto who took part in the battles for the liberation of the Vilna district. Used by permission of Yad Vashem

Nordhausen, 1945. Used by permission of Richard S. Miller

5

Resistance

In the aftermath of the Holocaust, questions as well as accusations arose as to whether more could have been done to prevent the murder of 6 million Jews. The arguments have ranged from the charge that the *Judenräte* betrayed their fellow Jews by cooperating with the Germans in the deportations process to the perception that Jews allowed themselves to die like sheep to the slaughter. The refrain "never again" was a response to the perceived inability of the Jews to resist their killers. The accusation of failing to resist the Germans, however, has not been limited to the Jews. Pope Pius XII and the Catholic church have been criticized for their silence and lack of moral resistance to the Holocaust. More recently, questions have been raised as to whether the Allies could have done more to prevent millions of Jews from being gassed in Auschwitz.

THE JEWISH COUNCILS

The debate surrounding the *Judenräte* requires an understanding of the situation facing the Jewish Councils in German-occupied Europe. The fortunes of the Jews in the ghettos deteriorated after the Nazi invasion of the Soviet Union in June 1941. The gassing of Jews began at Chelmno in December 1941, and by summer 1942, the death camps had become operational. This turn in Nazi policy toward the Jews put the Jewish Councils in an impossible situation. They were expected to fill the assigned daily quotas for the transports taking Jews to the newly constructed annihilation camps in Poland.

How the councils reacted to this situation has become a subject of controversy among those who have written about the Holocaust. Specifically, to what degree were the Jewish Councils guilty of inadvertent complicity with the destruction of European Jewry? Did they do enough to keep Jews alive? By cooperating with the Nazis, did they make it easier for the perpetrators to send their victims to their deaths? One response that has shaped the debate over the role of the *Judenräte* in the Final Solution has been that of Raul Hilberg, who, in his magisterial work, *The Destruction of European Jewry*, wrote,

The Jewish councils, in the exercise of their historic functions, continued until the end to make desperate attempts to alleviate the suffering and to stop the mass dying in the ghettos. But at the same time, the councils responded to German demands with automatic compliance and invoked German authority to compel the community's obedience. Thus the Jewish leadership both saved and destroyed its people. . . . Some leaders broke under this power; others became intoxicated with it. . . . With the growth of the destructive function of the Judenrate, many Jewish leaders felt an almost irresistible urge to look like their German masters.[1]

Hilberg cites the observations of a visitor to the Krakow ghetto in March 1940, who was impressed with the contrast between the poverty of most Jews and the luxury displayed at the Jewish Council headquarters, which was furnished with beautiful chairs and heavy carpets. In the Lodz ghetto, Hilberg found that Mordecai Chaim Rumkowski, the leader of the Jewish Council in Lodz, printed postage stamps bearing his likeness and referred to the ghetto inhabitants as "my Jews." Rumkowski, in fact, ruled Lodz by the force of his personality. His authority was felt everywhere, and he was able on occasion to outwit the SS. Despite the fact that he was hated by the Jews of Lodz, there was never anyone who could seriously challenge his leadership.

Hannah Arendt, in *Eichmann in Jerusalem*, wrote that without Jewish help in administrative and police work, there would have been chaos and disorder, and this would have made it necessary for the Germans to use their own manpower to collect Jews for transport to the death camps at a time when German soldiers were at a premium because of the war. She concludes her controversial book with these damning words: "To a Jew this role of the Jewish leaders in the destruction of their own people is undoubtedly the darkest chapter of the whole dark story."[2]

The debate is complicated by the ghetto leadership, which, in its response to German decrees, entered into unprecedented areas of moral ambiguity. In at least four ghettos, the councils were led by strong and even dictatorial personalities. In addition to Rumkowski, Moshe Merin, the chairman of the ghetto in Upper Silesia, vigorously enforced the German demand for forced labor. Yet he was aware that Jews who were deemed unfit for work were sent to their deaths and that others were sent to forced labor camps. Thus Merin was able to protect one segment of the ghetto population at the expense of those too weak or ill to work. Often overlooked is that in this concept of "work as a means of rescue," Merin had the support of the rabbis of Bedzin and Sosnowiec. Merin's policy continued even after a third of the ghetto had been sent to Auschwitz by August 1942.

In Vilna, Jacob Gens became the sole representative of the ghetto when the Germans dissolved the *Judenräte* in July 1942. Gens also promoted the idea of "work for life," meaning that as long as Jews engaged in productive work, they had a chance to survive. He believed that cooperation with the Germans was necessary in order to gain time until they were defeated in the war. Gens's most controversial act was to hand over to the Nazis 406 Jews who were old or chronically ill. The Nazis had originally asked for 1,500 children and women who were unemployed, but Gens countered the order and justified his actions by claiming that he wanted to keep the children and women alive for the future of the Jewish people. At the end, when the Nazis began the liquidation of the ghettos in August and September 1943, Gens had the opportunity to escape the fate of his fellow Jews. Instead, he chose to remain because his escape would mean disaster for the remaining Jews in the ghetto. On September 14, 1943, he was summoned to Gestapo headquarters and shot to death.

The head of the Bialystok ghetto, Efraim Barasz, aware of the mass murder of Jews, nevertheless believed that work "would serve as a protective shield and that our main rescue effort has to be based on the establishment of a highly developed industry."[3] Toward this end, Barasz rigidly enforced German directives and issued strong warnings against acts of sabotage. He even took part in the deportation of some of the ghetto population in February 1943 in the course of which 9,000 Jews were driven out and murdered on the spot. Yet despite the severity of Barasz's rule, he maintained close contact with the Polish underground and for a while coordinated his activities with the commander of the Jewish Fighting Organization in Bialystok. Like Gens, Barasz had faith that as long as Jews engaged in productive labor, he could save the ghetto from total liquidation and the Jews from certain death. But this required close cooperation and compliance with German directives.

For Rumkowski, the key to survival was also through productive labor. Under his leadership, 120 factories were established in Lodz, which he supervised with great zeal and organizational ability. Although he cooperated with the German authorities, he attempted at one point to convince them to reduce the number of Jews designated for deportation to the Chelmno death camp. Denied this plea, the Germans made him responsible for deciding who was to be included in future deportations, thus earning himself the hatred of the ghetto population. In early 1944, when the Lodz factories were closed by the Nazis and the killing process shifted from Chelmno to Auschwitz, Rumkowski urged the ghetto inhabitants to obey orders to report for deportation. In August 1944, he and his family were deported to and killed at Auschwitz.

Was Rumkowski a traitor to his own people, or did his policies, like those of Gens, Barasz, and Merin, extend the life span of the ghetto population? Further complicating the assessment of leaders such as Rumkowski is that the Lodz ghetto remained in existence when all the other ghettos in Poland had been liquidated; its 5,000 to 7,000 survivors constituted, in relative terms, the largest number of Holocaust survivors in one ghetto in German-occupied Poland.

It would seem that any judgment concerning the *Judenräte* leadership must consider that the ultimate fate of the Jews was decided not by the Jewish Councils but by the Germans. Once the decision to implement the Final Solution was made in 1941, it was the Nazis who decided the time and place for the implementation of their mission. Formal resistance was an impossibility, but strategies were devised to keep Jews alive as long as possible, with the hope that the Allies would defeat Germany before the entire Jewish population was killed.

One such strategy involved the use of bribery to buy Jewish lives. In Slovakia, Rabbi Michael Dov Weissmandel, a leader of Slovakia's Jewish community, was involved in an effort to save not only the Jews of Slovakia but all of Nazi-occupied Europe as well. In summer 1942, a group of Jewish activists sought to prevent the deportation of Slovak Jewry through the payment of a ransom. The Europa Plan, as it came to be known, was presented to Dieter Wisliceny, Eichmann's representative in Slovakia, whereby he was given between $40,000 and $50,000 to halt the deportation of the Jews. When deportations did in fact stop, the group believed that it was because of the ransom payment. There is no evidence that Wisliceny was responsible for the cessation of the deportations, but the group believed that their strategy had worked. Rabbi Weissmandel concluded that through ransom payments, they could save the lives of the rest of the Jews of Europe. The Working Group was formed, which solicited funds from Jewish organizations in the free world. The solicitation letter, signed by Rabbis Weissmandel and Armin-Abba Frieder, proposed that in exchange for the end of the deportations and extermination of Europe's Jews, world Jewry would pay the Germans $2 million to $3 million. The plan failed, in part because the Allied nations would not allow the transfer of funds to the Axis countries. In August 1943, Wisliceny brought his negotiations with the Working Group to an end, and within a year deportations from Slovakia resumed. The Working Group members blamed the failure of the plan on Jewish organizations for not providing the necessary funds, thus relegating European Jewry to a bleak and uncertain fate.

The Jewish leaders had limited options. The Holocaust could not be foreseen, and when it did become apparent that the liquidation of ghettos and the deportation to the camps meant death for the Jews, different strategies and responses emerged. In Warsaw, for example, Adam Czerniakow, the head of the *Judenräte*, upon learning that the trains were taking Jews to their deaths, resisted the German orders by committing suicide rather than cooperating.

The Nazi objective of annihilating the Jewish people was not evident at the start to either the Jewish leadership or the community. That the Nazis hid their plans from the Jews and engaged in a strategy of disinformation in regard to their objectives reinforced the ignorance that prevailed in the ghettos about Nazi intentions. Finally, as Isaiah Trunk reminds us, regardless of what the Jewish Councils did, the fate of European Jewry was sealed by the Nazis. The Nazi objective of annihilating the Jews of Europe, combined with the impotence of Jewish communities throughout German-occupied Europe, meant that the Jewish people were marked for death regardless of their behavior toward the victimizers.[4] The *Einsatzgrüppen* accompanying the *Wehrmacht* invasion of the Soviet Union murdered between one and 1 million and 1.5 million Jews without recourse to the establishment of Jewish Councils or decisions made by Jewish leaders. The argument remains as to whether a more obstructive resistance to German demands would have prolonged Jewish life in the ghetto, or whether the strategy of rescue through work was the only feasible response in the light of Germany's intentions.

Resistance of a more forceful nature did take place in some ghettos and death camps and among Jews who fled into the forests to join partisan bands. Where possible, Jews resisted the Germans, and given the limitations affecting a people ill fed, beaten, and demoralized by the Germans, the number of those who physically resisted the Nazis is surprising.

Following their conquest of Poland in September 1939, Germans immediately took measures against Poland's Jewish population. Measures enacted in Warsaw deprived Jews of their livelihood and reduced them to penury. Jews in the trades and professions lost their positions, and in November 1939, all Jews were required to wear a white armband with a blue Star of David on it. Under conditions of increasing poverty, tens of thousands of Jews left the city, only to be replaced by an estimated 90,000 Jews who arrived from towns and cities from the western district of Poland, where conditions were even worse than in Warsaw. In November 1940, Germany sealed off the Jewish section of Warsaw.

WARSAW GHETTO UPRISING

The most famous instance of Jewish resistance was the 1943 Warsaw ghetto uprising. An underground resistance movement took shape in the Warsaw ghetto from the beginning of its existence in November 1940. In the months leading up to the revolt, the Germans ruthlessly implemented the roundup of Jews for deportation. Jewish ghetto policemen who failed to round up the daily quota of Jews saw their own families deported. On September 5, 1942, there were approximately 130,000 Jews left in the ghetto, and on that day the SS ordered that all Jews appear at the *Umschlagplatz* for a selection. When the *Aktion* was over, the population of the Warsaw ghetto had been reduced from 380,000 to 70,000. Throughout the months that led up to the September selection, German ghetto firms sought to protect their workers from the *Aktion*. Even after the giant selection of September 5, German factories continued to operate with Jewish labor on several streets, but much of the ghetto remained empty.

The *Aktion* was perpetrated by no more than 50 SS men with the help of some 200 Ukrainian guards and an equal number of Latvians. Until September 5, the fear of reprisals mitigated against resistance as an option. The *Aktion* of September 5 changed all that, albeit too late to save the thousands who would meet their deaths at Treblinka.

In the fall of 1942, the various political parties in the ghetto came together and agreed to resist further deportations with force. By October 1942, a coordinating committee (KK) was established in which the Socialists (Bund), Zionists, and communists agreed to work together in a united front against the Germans. By the middle of the same month, a fighting force, the Jewish Fighting Organization (ZOB), was founded and placed under the command of the military arm of the KK. One group that did not participate in the umbrella organization was the Zionist Betar, or Revisionists, who set up their own fighting organization. Both fighting groups made efforts to contact the Polish underground and to raise money for the purchase of arms.

Shortly before the Warsaw revolt, the two bodies came together under ZOB authority. The ZOB, although based in Warsaw, also established branches in other large ghettos for the purpose of creating cadres of resistance fighters.

When the Nazis decreed another wave of deportations on January 18, 1943, Jews refused to comply with the order. The Germans managed to gather about 1,000 Jews, but this time the group included armed members of the Jewish Fighting Force. Hand-to-hand fighting broke out, and soon the column of deportees dispersed. Although the Germans continued the roundups during the next several days, few Jews responded to the German order to report to the *Umschlagplatz*, although 5,000 to 6,000 Jews were sent on the transports. By January 22, the Nazis ceased the *Aktion*. This was regarded by the ghetto fighters as a German defeat. It was also a defeat for the Jewish Council and the Jewish police, who now lost whatever authority they had over the Jewish population. Most Jews now followed the directions given them by the Jewish resistance.

Himmler, monitoring the outbreaks in the ghetto, ordered its dissolution. The responsibility for the razing of the Warsaw ghetto was given to brigade führer Jurgen Stroop. The final liquidation of the ghetto began on Monday, April 19, 1943, the eve of Passover. The ghetto was surrounded, and three hours later the *Waffen*-SS entered. They were immediately met with concentrated fire and incendiary bombs. Stroop, who had experience combating partisans, kept a record of the ensuing revolt, and his report constitutes the primary documentation of the Jewish resistance in the ghetto. At first, Jewish resistance forced the Germans to withdraw from the ghetto inasmuch as they were surprised by the armed response. In the first few days, the resistance engaged the Germans in street battles, and in retaliation, the Germans adopted the tactic of systematically burning the ghetto, building by building. This strategy forced the Jews to abandon their positions as resistance fighters, and they attempted to use the sewer system to escape from the ghetto. But the Germans countered by blowing up the manholes and lowering smoking candles into sewer passages. As Jews came up for air, they were shot. By April 22, the Germans were in control, the ghetto was burning, and Jews were being killed in increasing numbers. On May 8, Mordechai Anielewicz, the Jewish commander of the resistance, was slain. On May 12, Arthur Zygelboim, a Jewish Bundist labor leader who was a member of the Polish parliament in exile in London, killed himself when word of the liquidation of Warsaw's Jews reached him. Among those slain were his wife, Manya, and his sixteen-year-old son, Tuvia. In a letter he wrote before his suicide, Zygelboim condemned the world's indifference to the mass destruction of Polish Jewry and the defeat of the Warsaw ghetto fighters.

On May 16, Stroop announced that the *Aktion* was complete, and to mark the event, he ordered the burning of Warsaw's Great Synagogue. Although in one dispatch Stroop wrote that "the Jewish quarter of Warsaw no longer exists," Jews continued to hide in bunkers and engage in armed clashes. Stroop's final report noted, "Of the total of 56,065 Jews who were seized, 7,000 were destroyed during the course of the *Grossaktion* inside the former Jewish quarter; in deportation to Treblinka 6,929 were exterminated, which adds up to 13,929 Jews destroyed. In addition to the 56,065, another 5,000 to 6,000 lost their lives in explosions and fires."[5] German losses were reported as sixteen dead and eighty-five wounded. Stroop's figures may have been underestimated, especially in enumerating German casualties, but the importance of the ghetto revolt was not in its numbers but in its reverberations among the remaining Jews of Poland. The Warsaw ghetto revolt became a legend even as the war continued and gave Jews throughout the world the belief that something of great historical significance had occurred in this revolt against the Germans.

LVOV UPRISING

Inspired by the Warsaw ghetto revolt, uprisings followed in the ghettos of Lvov and Bialystok. When the Germans and their Ukrainian auxiliaries moved into Lvov in June 1943 for the final liquidation of the ghetto, they found that the 20,000 remaining Jews were hiding in small shelters modeled on the bunkers in the Warsaw ghetto. Although there was no organized resistance movement in the Lvov ghetto, the Germans nevertheless faced Jewish opposition in the form of hand grenades and Molotov cocktails hurled at them. German and Ukrainian casualties numbered nine dead and twenty wounded. The German response was to blow up and burn houses where Jews were concealed in order to force them to emerge. According to German reports, 3,000 bodies were dragged out from their hiding places.[6] Eventually the Germans liquidated the ghetto after seizing 7,000 Jews, who were sent to the Janowska camp, where they were killed. The *Aktion* was completed on June 2, 1943, with an additional 3,000 Jews meeting their deaths.

BIALYSTOK UPRISING

The lesson of the Warsaw ghetto uprising was not lost on the Germans. When they entered the Bialystok ghetto on August 16, 1943, together with their Ukrainian helpers, they were led by Odilo Globocnik, one of their most experienced commanders, to carry out Himmler's explicit orders to liquidate the ghetto. The Germans ordered the Jewish Council to post notices that the 30,000 Jewish inhabitants of the ghetto were to be moved to Lublin. As tens of thousands of Jews moved to the designation area for deportation, the underground, consisting of communists, the Bund, and Zionist youth movements, launched an attack against the Germans. The fighting lasted for five days, but the Jews were no match for the armored cars, tanks, and the large force the Germans brought to the battle. Having lost the struggle, the leaders of the revolt committed suicide.

RESISTANCE AT EXTERMINATION CAMPS

Jewish resistance was not confined to the ghettos. It took place in all of the extermination camps in Poland. At Auschwitz, aside from acts of heroism by individuals who managed to acquire arms and shoot their captors, escape was the most common form of resistance; 667 Poles, Russians, and Jews escaped the camp, but 270 were later captured and executed. Two Jews, Alfred Wetzler and Walter Rosenberg (Rudolf Vrba), escaped on April 7, 1944, and managed to reach Bratislava, where they recounted all that they had witnessed at Auschwitz to the Jewish community leaders of Slovakia. They estimated that about 1.75 million Jews had been killed by that time at Auschwitz and that the camp authorities were preparing for the murder of the Hungarian Jews who were due to arrive at the camp.

Auschwitz

The best-known act of resistance was the formation of the Auschwitz Fighting Group, which had cadres in Birkenau and Monowitz. Both groups were active in helping prisoners with medicine and food, as well as organizing escapes. This underground group engaged in acts of sabotage and prepared for the revolt that eventually occurred in Birkenau on October 6, 1944.

The revolt happened at the moment when the mass extermination of Hungarian Jewry was coming to an end. The Jewish *Sonderkommandos* (the detail that placed the bodies of those killed in the gas chambers into the crematoriums) realized that their own days were numbered and made contact with members of the Auschwitz underground group, urging them to revolt against their captors. When they were turned down, the *Sonder-*

kommandos launched the revolt on their own. Limited in weapons to explosives, they nevertheless commenced the attack on October 6, 1944, when they blew up Crematorium 3, destroying the installation. Immediately after the rising, the SS crushed the revolt and rounded up and executed the participants. Some of the *Sonderkommandos* managed to keep diaries, which detailed the rising in Auschwitz. The diaries, buried and discovered after the war, constitute a detailed account of the excesses and barbarity in Auschwitz.

Sobibor

The Sobibor camp was located near a forest that tempted prisoners to escape, although the Germans put up a barbed wire fence and planted mines to prevent it. The escapes that were successful brought immediate retaliation from the SS, who would execute dozens of prisoners at a time.

During summer 1943, a secret organization of Jewish prisoners was formed for the purpose of organizing a mass escape from the camp. In mid-September, this underground group was joined by Soviet Jewish prisoners of war, including Lieutentant Aleksandr Pechersky, who was given the command of the organization. The plan was to kill the SS men in the camp, seize weapons from the camp armory, cut the barbed wire, clear the mines, and then fight their way out of the camp. The revolt broke out on October 14, 1943, and was partially successful. Eleven SS men and several Ukrainian auxiliaries were killed, and about 300 prisoners managed to escape. All of the camp's Jews took part in the rising, but many were shot by the Germans, and others were killed by the mines. Of those who escaped, some reached partisan units, but most were tracked by the Germans and executed or killed by antisemitic elements of the Polish partisan movement.

In the aftermath of the uprising, the Germans liquidated Sobibor after executing all of the Jews still in the camp. Plans to transform Sobibor into a concentration camp were abandoned. By the end of 1943, practically all traces of Sobibor vanished as the Germans razed the camp area and planted crops where it had stood. By war's end, about fifty Jews remained alive from among those who had managed to escape during the revolt.

Treblinka

In August 1943, a rebellion led by a Warsaw doctor, Ilya Horonzitzki, and a Jewish officer from the Czech army, Zelo Bloch, broke out at Treblinka. The plan that they devised was similar to the one at Sobibor:

stealing weapons from the SS, seizing control of the camp, and then burning it. Once the attack was accomplished, they would flee to the forests to join the partisans. The rising initially included only fifty to seventy men, but the expectation was that once the revolt began, the rest of the camp's prisoners would join. On August 2, the revolt broke out and met with some initial success. The armory was opened and weapons distributed to members of the resistance. But the Germans became aware of the revolt, and exchanges of gunfire broke out between them and the rebels. Camp buildings were set on fire, and masses of prisoners attempted to storm the fence area. Some were able to escape, but once the Germans recovered from the surprise of the revolt, they apprehended those who had fled. Of the approximately 750 prisoners who escaped, 70 managed to survive the war. After crushing the revolt, the Germans demolished Treblinka, using the labor of the remaining prisoners before killing them.

Buchenwald

In Germany, a resistance movement that included Jews was organized in the Buchenwald camp in 1943. The International Underground Committee, as it was known, engaged in acts of sabotage at the Buchenwald armaments works. Arms and ammunition were also smuggled into the camp by the underground. Beginning in April 1945, the Germans began to evacuate the camp, and of the 28,250 prisoners designated for removal from the main camp, 7,000 to 8,000 were either killed or died by some other means. During the next few days, despite the efforts of the underground to slow the evacuation process, about 25,500 prisoners incarcerated in the Buchenwald main camp and its satellites perished. On April 11, approximately 21,000 prisoners, including 4,000 Jews, were liberated by American forces.

ADDITIONAL EXAMPLES OF RESISTANCE

Emaciated, diseased, and brutally treated, Jews found it difficult to organize resistance but acted defiantly when the opportunity presented itself. These acts of resistance nevertheless did not prevent the murder of millions of Jews in the extermination camps. Still, thousands of Jews escaped the camps and confronted the Nazis in the forests of eastern Europe and the Balkans. Jewish partisan groups fought with the resistance in Yugoslavia, Bulgaria, and Greece, where they were accepted as equals. In western Europe, Jews joined the resistance movements in the German-oc-cupied countries.[7] In France, Jews were participants in the French underground. In Belgium, a Jewish underground organization, Comité de Défense des Juifs (CDJ), which was affiliated with the Belgian resistance movement, was created in response to the deportations.

In summer 1942, the CDJ assaulted an official of the AJB responsible for sending out the lists for deportation. In April 1943, the CDJ attacked a transport from the Mechelen camp headed for Auschwitz, the only instance of an armed attack on a train taking Jews to an extermination camp. The various Belgian resistance movements also included many Jews, and with the help of large numbers of the population, including church institutions and unaffiliated individual Belgians, about 25,000 Jews were hidden from the Germans.

In Germany, where active opposition to Hitler was limited to distributing leaflets and publishing illegal literature, the Herbert Baum band from 1937 to 1942 was the most important Jewish resistance group. In May 1942, they set fire to the anti-Soviet exhibit organized in Berlin by Joseph Goebbels as a means of diverting the German public from knowledge of the casualties suffered by the army on the Russian front and the ongoing food shortages. Baum and the rest of his circle were arrested and tortured; most of them were executed between July 1942 and June 1943.

JEWISH PARTISANS

In the Baltic states, Belorussia, and the western Ukraine, it is estimated that 20,000 to 30,000 Jews joined partisan units in the forests. Perhaps the most famous of the Jewish partisan leaders was Alexander Bielski (1912–1995). Joined by his brothers, the so-called Bielski Brigade, consisting of more than 300 fighters, fought a nonstop guerilla war against the Germans in Belorussia, derailing troop trains, blowing up bridges and electric stations, and committing other acts of sabotage. Unlike other resistance groups, the Bielskis threatened retaliation against villages that gave up Jews to the Germans.

In the Ukraine, Diadia Misha (Uncle Misha) fought the Germans in the forests and villages. In other Soviet regions, the resistance was an appendage of the Soviet army and included Jews who took leadership positions in over 200 partisan detachments but fought under assumed Russian or Ukrainian names.[8] There were also Jews among the paratroopers who came from the Soviet Union to organize partisan warfare in Poland. About 2,000 Jews fought in the Polish partisan movement in the *Generalgouvernement*. Jews also served as commanders in the Polish communist partisan movement. All told, between 1942 and 1944, there were twenty-seven Jewish partisan units fighting against the Germans in Poland and about one thousand who took part in the Warsaw Polish uprising in the summer of 1944.

In general, Jewish partisans put themselves under the authority of the national partisan groups that fought the Germans. The inability of the Jews to organize their own guerrilla movement was due to the absence of support from the surrounding population or a government in exile. Given the prevalent antisemitism in eastern Europe, Jews could never be sure that in approaching a farmer for food or shelter, they would not be betrayed and handed over to the Germans.

It is difficult to evaluate the difference Jewish resistance made in the light of the Holocaust. Where the opportunity presented itself, Jews did fight back. In the light of Raul Hilberg's conclusion that "the reaction pattern of the Jews is characterized by almost complete lack of resistance . . . the Jewish victims, caught in the straightjacket of their history, plunged themselves physically and psychologically into catastrophe," one must consider the observation made by Elie Wiesel in regard to Jewish resistance: "The question is not why all Jews did not fight, but how so many of them did. Tormented, beaten, starved, where did they find the strength—spiritual and physical—to resist."[9] Jews were too few in number to defend themselves against Germany's plan to annihilate them. Jewish resistance was dependent on the willingness of their fellow partisans to enlist in the cause of Jewish survival. Given the endemic antisemitism that characterized much of Europe, it is not surprising that whatever successes were achieved in saving Jewish lives, the numbers were bound to be small. Yet Jews were not entirely alone in the effort to save their brethren. The attempt to murder the Jews of Europe also caused a number of Gentiles to risk their lives to save the lives of the Jews.

RIGHTEOUS GENTILES

Holocaust historian Henry Huttenbach once remarked that the smallest street in the world was the Avenue of the Righteous located outside Yad Vashem, the Holocaust memorial museum, in Jerusalem. The number of Gentiles who intervened on behalf of the Jews, at a time when hiding or assisting a Jew meant severe punishment for the rescuer, is difficult to determine, although it has been estimated that less than half of 1 percent of the total non-Jewish population of German-occupied Europe helped to rescue Jews. In 1989 about 8,000 of the "Righteous Gentiles amongst the Nations," a term of honor used by Yad Vashem, were recognized by Israel with the planting of a tree in each of their names along the avenue on Har ha-Zikkaron (the Yad Vashem Memorial Hill).

Saving Jewish lives took the form of concealing Jews in one's home, such as in the case of Maria Countess von Maltzan, who hid the Jewish writer Hans Hirschel along with other Jews in her small Berlin apartment, or in attics, as in the case of the Anne Frank family. Those who were protected in this manner remained for weeks to years without seeing daylight. Although food was always scarce, it was typically shared by the rescuers with the Jews whom they were hiding. Rescuers who concealed Jews were always alert to the dangers inherent in the frequent searches conducted by the Nazis to uncover those in concealment. Righteous Gentiles were also wary of collaborators who would denounce them to the Nazis for protecting Jews. Although most of these acts of heroism were the deeds of individuals who for religious or humane reasons were moved to place their lives in jeopardy, there were also cases of collective rescue.

In the Dutch village of Nieuwlande, each villager agreed to hide one Jewish family or at least one Jew. All of the 117 inhabitants of the village were eventually recognized as among the "Righteous Gentiles amongst the Nations." In the small Protestant village of Le Chambon-sur-Lignon in southern France, many Jews were hidden in full view of the Vichy government and a nearby division of the SS, thanks to the leadership of the pastor, André Trocme. I have already noted the mass collective effort of the Danes, who rescued 7,000 of Denmark's 8,000 Jews by transferring them in small boats to Sweden. The European section of the American Friends Service Committee (AFSC) distinguished itself in its work on refugee matters. Working in cooperation with the American Jewish Joint Distribution Committee, the Quakers sent representatives to Germany in 1939 to ascertain the condition of both Jews and Christians under Nazi rule. Although the Quakers worked primarily with Christian refugees, their assistance to Jewish refugees in Paris, Marseilles, Lisbon, and Madrid was crucial in saving lives. The Quaker role in feeding and rescuing Jewish children in France was an outstanding example of what other Christian denominations might have accomplished had they shown the same interest as the Society of Friends in helping Jews.

There were also individuals who for humanitarian reasons risked their lives and careers in their efforts to save Jews. Raoul Wallenberg (1912–?), a Swedish diplomat, saved the lives of tens of thousands of Jews in Budapest on the eve of the Nazi deportations. Dr. Aristides De Souza Mendes (1885-1954) was a Portuguese diplomat who risked his career to help Jews when, against orders from his government, he issued nearly 10,000 travel visas to Jews escaping Nazi terror. A similar example of a public official who defied his government's indifference to the plight of the Jews was Paul Gruninger (1891–1972), the former chief of police of the Swiss canton of St. Gallen who was responsible for saving the lives of 2,000 Jewish refugees who crossed the Swiss border from Germany and Austria in 1938–1939.

The efforts of the Japanese consul in Kaunas (Kovno), Lithuania, Sempo Sugihara, saved thousands of Jewish lives. The German invasion of Poland led to a wave of refugees streaming east into neutral Lithuania. Fearing that the Nazis would soon occupy Kaunas, many Jews sought visas to leave Lithuania, but these were almost impossible to obtain. The sympathetic Dutch consul in Kaunas, Jan Zwartendijk, however, signed a document stating that an entry visa was not required for the admission of aliens to the Dutch possessions in the Americas such as Curaçao, Surinam, and Dutch Guiana. The refugees, however, still needed papers indicating their ultimate destination as a prerequisite for leaving Lithuania. They also needed permission to pass through the Soviet Union and Japan. Sugihara was able to use Zwartendijk's document as the legal cover for issuing a transit visa for travel through Japan. The Soviets had made the issuance of such visas conditional for travel by train across Siberia to Vladivostok. The Japanese government, however, refused to allow the issuance of the travel visas, and after repeating his urgent request three times, Sugihara decided to issue the visas despite the dire consequences that both he and his family could expect as a result of his disobedience. Most of the Jews who used the visas ended up in Japan for a few months and spent much of the war in Shanghai. Eventually many of these reached the United States and Palestine, although none made it to Curaçao or any of the other Dutch possessions. Included among those saved by the efforts of both Sugihara and Zwartendijk were 400 talmudic scholars who constituted the faculty and student body of the Mirrer Yeshiva. This talmudic academy was the only yeshiva from eastern Europe to survive the war intact.[10]

Sempo Sugihara is sometimes referred to as the "Japanese Schindler." This comparison is to Oskar Schindler, whose efforts to save nearly 1,200 Jews was celebrated in Steven Spielberg's epic film, *Schindler's List*. Schindler (1908–1974) was one of several German entrepreneurs, including Julius Madritsch and Raimund Titsch, who went to the aid of the Jews interned in the Plaszow labor camp by providing them with food beyond the allotted near starvation rations and protecting them from the brutal whims of Amon Goeth, the camp commandant. Schindler was born to a Catholic family residing in the Sudetenland and arrived in Krakow in late 1939 following the German invasion of Poland. Once established in

Krakow, he took over two firms previously owned by Jews. He now operated the firms, which manufactured enamel kitchenware products, for the German occupation administration. Soon after, he established his own factory on the outskirts of Krakow and employed mainly Jewish workers, thereby protecting them from deportation to Auschwitz.

When the Krakow ghetto was being liquidated in early 1943, many of its Jews were sent to the Plaszow labor camp, administered by Amon Goeth. Schindler and Goeth, also a Catholic, maintained good relations with one another and, thanks to his connections in the Armaments Administration, Schindler was able to arrange with Goeth for about 900 Jewish workers from the Plaszow camp to work in his factory. Some of the workers in Schindler's factory were unfit and unqualified for the tasks that they were assigned, and had this been discovered, they would have been worked to death at the labor camp or deported to Auschwitz. Schindler, for reasons that remain unclear, was determined to protect all of "his Jews," and in 1944, when the Soviet army approached Krakow, he was granted permission to reestablish his firm as an armaments production company in Brunnlitz, located in the Sudetenland, and to take his workers with him. Because the company produced 45-mm shells for rocket casings, it was considered strategic for the German war effort. Schindler therefore was allowed to transfer about 800 Jewish men from the Gross-Rosen camp and 300 Jewish women from Auschwitz. In Brunnlitz, the 1,100 Jews were provided with food, medical care, and shelter, and were allowed to practice their religion. Schindler also launched a rescue operation when he received permission from the Germans to take 100 Jews from the Goleszow camp, who were left stranded and nearly frozen to death in a railway car, to the Brunnlitz factory, where he nourished them back to life. In 1962, Schindler, now almost impoverished and living on the sufferance of those Jews whom he had saved, planted a tree bearing his name in the Garden of the Righteous at Yad Vashem.

In German-occupied Poland, Irena Sendler ("Jolanta"; b. 1916), a member of the Polish Council for Aid to the Jews (Zegota), helped to alleviate the suffering of many Jews. Because she worked for the Social Welfare Department of the Warsaw municipality, she was able to enter the Warsaw ghetto, where she provided Jews with money, medicine, and clothing. When walking the ghetto streets, she wore the yellow Star of David armband as a symbol of solidarity with the Jewish people, as well as not to call attention to her activities. Sendler specialized in smuggling Jewish children out of the ghetto and placing them with non-Jewish families. She oversaw eight apartments where Jews were hiding under her care. In 1943 she was arrested by the Gestapo and incarcerated in the Pawiak prison, where she was brutally tortured. She survived her ordeal and continued to work for the Zegota for the remainder of the German occupation. In 1965 she was recognized by Yad Vashem as a "Righteous Gentile amongst the Nations."

Righteous Gentiles were not only those who hid or protected Jews. There were also those like Jan Karski (1914–) who risked his life to tell the West about the German massacre of the Jews. A member of the Polish underground and a courier of the Polish government in exile, Karski was sent in 1942 on a mission to evaluate the general situation in occupied Poland, as well as to report on the condition of the Jewish population. Twice he slipped into the Warsaw ghetto and met with Jewish leaders, who briefed him on the desperate situation. In November 1942, Karski reached London via Sweden and reported his information to the Polish government. He also met with Winston Churchill and other prominent members of the British establishment. Based on his report, the Polish government in exile called on the Allies to take measures to prevent the murder of European Jewry. Karski next went to the United States, where he met with President Franklin D. Roosevelt, to whom he disclosed the serious plight of Polish Jewry and was given assurances that something would be done. Remaining in the United States, Karski devoted his energies to arousing public opinion against the Nazi atrocities against the Jews. In 1944 he published *The Story of a Secret State*, an account of his witness to the unfolding tragedy of Polish Jewry.

THE FAILURE OF ORGANIZED CHRISTIANITY

The failure of organized Christianity to resist the Nazis is also part of the history of the Holocaust. By 1938, the Protestant clergy in Germany had been purged of all ministers who dissented against the government. In various European countries under German occupation, individual Protestant and Catholic clergy spoke up on behalf of the Jews. In the case of Catholic priests, this may have resulted from signals received from the Vatican that permitted priests to help Jews. The Vatican, however, was not occupied by Germany, and its status as the preeminent moral institution in Europe should have elicited a stronger response to the extermination of the Jews. The record, however, indicates that the papacy refused to confront Germany openly in the period between 1941 and 1945 despite the information it had received regarding the Final Solution.

The papacy's record is complicated by the involvement of the Vatican in helping leading Nazis, including Adolf Eichmann and Josef Mengele, to escape to Latin America at the end of the war. It remains to be answered as to whether the same signals that priests received from the Vatican to rescue some Jews during the war were similarly given on behalf of fleeing Nazis war criminals. Regardless of the motives for his silence, Pius XII's ambivalence in regard to the fate of the Jews groups him, along with the Allies, with those who failed to place a high priority on the rescue of the victims of the Nazi genocidal war against the Jews and other targeted groups.

THE ALLIES

Reports of the mass murder of the Jews came to the attention of the Allies from the World Jewish Congress (WJC). Despite its ambivalent attitude toward Jewish refugees, Switzerland remained neutral throughout the war, and it was there that the WJC had its headquarters. Dr. Gerhart Riegner, the WJC representative in Geneva, was informed by a German source of the planned extermination of the European Jews by means of poison gas and other methods. On August 8, 1942, Riegner sent the following cable to Rabbi Stephen S. Wise, the president of the WJC and a close friend of President Roosevelt, and to Sidney Silverman, a member of the British Parliament:

Received alarming report that in Führer's headquarters plan discussed and under consideration according to which all Jews in countries occupied or controlled Germany numbering 3.5–4 million should after deportation and concentration in the east be exterminated at one blow to resolve once and for all the Jewish question in Europe. Actions reported planned for the autumn; methods under discussion including prussic acid. We transmit information with all necessary reservations as exactitude cannot be confirmed. Informant stated to have close connections with highest German authorities and his reports generally speaking reliable.[11]

After many years, we now know that the informant was Eduard Schulte, a Leipzig businessman, and that his information was not entirely accurate inasmuch as the mass murder of Jews had already begun in June 1941. Nevertheless, Schulte corroborated reports that had previously reached the West regarding the mass murder of Jews.

The U.S. Department of State refused to transmit the Riegner cable to Wise because the information was not substantiated, but he received the cable on August 28, 1942, from Sidney Silverman. Wise passed the information on to Undersecretary of State Sumner Welles, who asked Wise not to make the contents of the cable public until the information was confirmed. Wise agreed but at the same time informed President Roosevelt as well as members of the cabinet and Supreme Court justice Felix Frankfurter of the cable's contents. On November 24, 1942, Wise made public the contents of the Riegner cable, but only after the government was convinced that the news of the mass murder of Jews was true. Subsequently, Wise would be criticized for withholding the information from the public for three crucial months at a time when Jews were being killed daily. Wise, however, had confidence that the Roosevelt administration would respond to the destruction of European Jewry with all the resources available to the U.S. government.

Rabbi Wise's faith in Roosevelt was not warranted. Once the United States entered the war against Germany several days after the Japanese attack on Pearl Harbor, Roosevelt operated amid many political pressures that prevented his taking a more forceful stand in behalf of European Jewry. Those pressures included an antisemitism that did not recede once the United States entered the war against Germany. In fact, it continued to influence many sectors of public life, including the State Department, which feared that an influx of Jewish refugees from Europe would result in the entry of Nazi spies masquerading as persecuted Jews. This was one stated reason for its opposition to the liberalization of the immigration laws. Because of antisemitism in the United States, Roosevelt concluded that the war could not be depicted as one to save the Jews of Europe. Consequently, it was a rare occasion that Roosevelt departed from his use of the phrase "political refugees" to single out the plight of the Jews. For these reasons, the response of the Roosevelt administration to the destruction of European Jewry, at least until 1944, was one of gesture rather than action.

The murder of the Jews was not mentioned at the major conferences held by the Allies at Casablanca, Tehran, or Yalta. When between May and December 1942 the British government found itself under public pressure to do something on behalf of the Jews, the United States responded by joining Great Britain and other Allied nations in a declaration condemning the "bestial policy of cold-blooded extermination" rather than in advocating a concrete strategy against Germany. The declaration, however, was insufficient; the situation of European Jewry deteriorated, and as a consequence, both Great Britain and the United States convened the Bermuda Conference on April 19, 1943.

THE BERMUDA CONFERENCE

The ostensible purpose of the conference was to find a solution to the refugee crisis in order to defuse public protest over the revelations that the Nazis were embarked on a program of systematically liquidating the Jews of Europe. The conference, convened on the initiative of Great Britain, was destined to fail almost from the start as the British insisted that the Jewish character of the crisis be played down. Despite the corroborated information that the Nazis had singled out the Jews for extinction, the British insisted that the issue of the Jews be treated as one of the many groups victimized by the Germans. This manifested itself in the language of the conference, which used the euphemism "political refugees" to disguise the plight of the Jews. Discussion of Palestine as a refuge for Jews was ruled out at the start of the conference, as was negotiating with the Germans with regard to the Jews. In fact, most recommendations for rescue were rejected, and it became clear that the real purpose of the conference was to assuage public opinion without taking specific steps to rescue Jews. When George Backer, a delegate representing the Organization for Rehabilitating through Training (ORT)—an American-Jewish agency created to teach skills to Jews— pointed to the availability of ships that could save the lives of about 125,000 Jews in eastern Europe by transporting them to safe havens, his request was rejected, as was his plea that the Allies make available ships that might have saved the lives of several thousand Jewish children. Historian Henry Feingold has noted that the Bermuda Conference showed that government officials "experienced few qualms in devising strategies to deflect its concern. Both the British and American governments were willing to go to extraordinary lengths to avoid doing what needed to be done."[12]

THE WAR REFUGEE BOARD

The Bermuda Conference ended with an optimistic news bulletin that spoke of the possibility of helping "a substantial number of refugees," but in reality the conference was a failure. It was widely condemned by the American Jewish press and all of those concerned with the plight of Europe's Jews. When concrete action was taken, it was almost forced on the Roosevelt administration.

In fall 1942, when news of the Jewish catastrophe in Europe was filtering back to Washington, Henry Morgenthau, Jr. (1891–1967), the secretary of the treasury and the highest-ranking Jew in the Roosevelt administration, was informed by his subordinates in the Treasury that State Department officials were deliberately withholding information regarding the murder of Europe's Jews. In January 1944, Morgenthau's assistant, Josiah DuBois, Jr., handed him his "Report to the Secretary on the Acquiescence of This Government in the Murder of the Jews." The report documented the "willful failure" of the State Department to pass on information or use its authority to offer aid to the victims of the Nazi extermination campaign. After changing the document's title to "A Personal Report to the President," Morgenthau, together with Benjamin V. Cohen and Samuel Rosenman, two of Roosevelt's advisers who were Jewish, presented the report to the president on January 16, 1944. Perhaps fearful that should this information become public it would be politically devastating for him and the Democratic party, Roosevelt in that same month established, by executive order, the War Refugee Board (WRB).

The creation of the WRB represented a new policy in which the government would take "all measures within its power to rescue the victims of enemy oppression who are in imminent danger of death." Despite the provision that all government agencies were to assist it, the WRB found that the War Department was uncooperative and the State Department was obstructive. The work of the WRB was further handicapped by poor funding and Roosevelt's lack of interest and support. Despite these difficulties, the WRB was involved in the efforts to save Hungarian Jews and was instrumental in pressuring the Hungarian government to stop the deportations of approximately 230,000 Jews from Budapest. It was the WRB that sent Raoul Wallenberg, a Swedish diplomat, to Budapest, and his work there was funded by the agency.

One of the board's most publicized projects was the evacuation of 982 Jewish refugees from Italy to a safe haven in an unused army camp in Oswego, New York, in August 1944. The WRB had hoped to open up additional havens in the United States as an example for other nations to open their doors, but Roosevelt would agree only to the Oswego project due to his fear of an antisemitic backlash against his administration. Although the WRB was established after millions of Jews had already been killed, it nevertheless played a decisive role in saving approximately 200,000 Jews. This was accomplished through such activities as the protection of Jews within Axis Europe through WRB-financed underground activities and diplomatic pressure.

THE CONTROVERSY OVER THE BOMBING OF AUSCHWITZ

Despite some successes of the WRB, the Roosevelt administration and Great Britain have been accused of not utilizing all of the resources at their command to rescue the Jews of Europe from extermination. Aiding Jews was complicated by the Allied policy of unconditional surrender, which mitigated against bribing or negotiating with Germany on behalf of the

Jews. This criticism has been exacerbated by the controversy over the failure of the Allies to bomb Auschwitz. By spring 1944, the Allied governments were aware of the killing operations at Auschwitz. At the same time, the Allied air forces controlled the skies over Europe and, according to author David Wyman, had the range to bomb Auschwitz as well as the railways leading to it.[13] Raids over Auschwitz did not take place despite appeals made by European and American Jewish leaders that this be done on humanitarian grounds. In spring 1944, two escapees from Auschwitz reached Slovakia and informed the Jewish leadership of the mass gassing of Jews. Rabbi Michael Dov Weissmandel sent this information to the West and pleaded, to no avail, that the Allies bomb both the railway lines leading to Auschwitz and the extermination camp.[14]

The policy of the U.S. War Department justified a position of inaction by declaring that such attacks would be an impractical diversion. Instead, the Allies argued that "the most effective relief to victims of enemy persecution is the early defeat of the Axis, an undertaking to which we must devote every resource at our disposal."[15] For the Allies, resisting genocidal behavior took the form of defeating Germany in the war.

David Wyman has argued that the refusal of the War Department to order the bombing of Auschwitz was in part a response to the creation of the WRB. The War Department feared that cooperation with the WRB would necessitate military forces' being diverted to rescue missions, and as a consequence, it unilaterally decided on a policy of noninvolvement in rescue. Wyman points out that this was done despite awareness that the policy was in violation of the president's executive order to cooperate with the WRB, although it is not entirely clear that the president included strategic bombing as part of his directive. Regardless of how it interpreted Roosevelt's executive order, the War Department appears not to have considered the possibility of bombing Auschwitz. When the first bombing requests came to the War Department from the WRB, the department rejected them out of hand without looking into its chance for success. The department never considered the efficacy of such strikes nor did it consult the air force commanders in Italy about the feasibility of such raids. Instead, it used the argument that such strikes would divert military power from essential war operations.[16] The last request for bombing Auschwitz was rejected in November 1944, although these bombings were within the range capability of the U.S. Air Force based in Italy. The air force did bomb German synthetic oil plants, situated within forty-five miles from Auschwitz, and en route to their targets, the aircraft flew along or over key deportation railway lines. On two occasions, between August 20 and September 13, American bombers struck the industrial sites of Auschwitz itself, less than five miles from the four huge gas chamber installations.

A different view of the failure to bomb Auschwitz holds that for such a strike to be successful, it would have required about half of the very best Mosquito fighter-bomber crews or B-25s, and that this would have diverted aircraft from targets that were deemed strategically more important from a military standpoint. Furthermore, according to this argument, diversions of heavy bombers, B-25s, P-38s, or Mosquitos with attendant losses could have been justified only if the probability of success had been higher. At the time, no one could predict how much damage the bombing might have wrought on the gas chambers and crematoriums at Auschwitz. The bombing of Auschwitz, if done for the purpose of eliminating the killing facilities, would have required a mini-campaign in order to ensure success. An additional consequence of such an operation would result in most prisoners who survived the air attack being quickly rounded up and forced to repair the damage caused by the air strikes. Trains destined for Auschwitz would probably have been diverted to other camps, such as Mauthausen in Austria, Belsen, Buchenwald, or any of the other German camps. Finally, the rate of mass killing might have been slowed for a few days or weeks but, "most certainly, it can be said that any low level air raid on Auschwitz-Birkenau would have been a one-shot proposition because the camps would have been easy to defend against precise low attitude strikes."[17] From their own experience, senior air commanders had concluded that attempts to bomb Auschwitz would have diverted resources from vital military and industrial targets and would have resulted in heavy Allied casualties. This argument concludes that the failure to bomb Auschwitz had more to do with the awareness of operational limits than with a lack of concern of what was happening to the Jews or a reluctance to involve the American military establishment in rescue efforts.

THE INTERNATIONAL RED CROSS

The Allies adhered to the policy that the best way to save the Jews of Europe was to defeat Germany as quickly as possible. No special bombing missions were ordered against the largest of the death camps in Poland despite the Allied awareness that millions of Jews were being murdered by the Germans. Immediate help for the Jews therefore had to come from other sources.

One organization that responded in an ambiguous manner to the Nazi genocide was the International Red Cross (ICRC). During the war the primary role of the ICRC, founded in 1863 as a private humanitarian organization, was to link national chapters of the organization in the protection of wounded soldiers and to ensure the correct treatment of prisoners of war. This responsibility had been ratified by fifty nations, including Germany, in Geneva in 1929. Its statutes also gave the ICRC the authority to take humanitarian steps on behalf of political prisoners being held by their own governments. Twice in the 1930s the ICRC sent representatives to visit concentration camps in Hitler's Germany. It was more common, however, for the ICRC to delegate concerns of a humanitarian nature to its national chapters, and therefore it relied on the German Red Cross to visit the internees' place of detention and ensure the passage of their right to correspond with the outside world, as well as to receive parcels allowed to them by the German government.

The start of World War II and the German implementation of the Final Solution created an unprecedented situation for the ICRC. As the Germans replaced a policy of forced emigration with deportations to the east, they made every effort to carry out their activities in secret. Representatives of the Red Cross were rarely witnesses to deportations, and with the exception of two visits, one to Buchenwald and the other to a carefully prepared Theresienstadt, they were never permitted to enter the concentration or death camps until the end of the war. As the ICRC learned of the exterminations, it met to decide on the risks involved in assisting those facing death in the east. Complicating the matter was the recognition that the German Red Cross was not willing to assume the task of determining the fate of deportees, mostly Jews, or even to request permission to provide aid for them. Under these circumstances, the ICRC requested that the Germans grant deportees from France and Belgium, who were sent to concentration camps in the Reich, the same guarantees provided to civilian internees. The German foreign office never responded to this request.

As in the case of the Vatican, the ICRC engaged in quiet diplomacy and never appealed to public opinion in regard to Nazi atrocities. Nor did it single out Jews in its correspondence. Rather, the Jews were included in the general category of prisoners, deportees, and hostages whom the Red Cross believed to be entitled to the same conventions, under international law, that provided protection to military combatants. The ICRC also refused to raise the question of racial discrimination in terms of the Geneva conventions. Therefore it did not protest when the Nazis separated Jewish medical personnel from their Gentile counterparts in order to send them to the eastern front. Finally, as one historian has pointed out, it did not seek—exploiting its initiative or basing itself on the general principles of humanitarian rights—to intervene on behalf of the Jews in general, intervention that might have taken the form of a protest to a competent . . . representative of the German authorities, or of a demand for action from the Allies.[18]

The ICRC failure to voice its indignation regarding the massacre of the Jews may perhaps have been due to its fear that in speaking out on their behalf, it would compromise its work in protecting the millions of prisoners of war on the eastern front, in particular, and its worldwide role of assisting internees of all types, in general; or it may have simply concluded that the rescue or protection of the Jews was an impossible task. This ambivalence regarding a more active stance in helping Jews was modified somewhat at the beginning of 1943, when the ICRC intervened in countries where it believed there was a possibility of aiding Jews. The ICRC sent food, clothes, and medicine to Jews in states that were either allied to or satellites of Germany. In 1941 the ICRC created the Joint Relief Commission of the Red Cross specifically for this purpose, but its objectives were stymied because it never succeeded in obtaining permission from the Allies to pass through the continental blockade. Prepared to provide provisions to the ghettos in the *Generalgouvernement*, its operation was limited to providing small quantities to a limited number of camps in the east and to refugees in the south of France. In November 1944, the ICRC assigned a representative to Bucharest, who subsequently made a tour of the Transnistria area and used the resources of his organization to alleviate the plight of the survivors of the massacres that had taken place there. However, the representative, Charles Kolb, had as his primary mission the task of organizing the emigration of Jews to Palestine by way of the Black Sea and Turkey. In this enterprise, he had the help of the Romanian Red Cross as well as the WRB. However, the Red Cross took care not to violate the provisions of the British White Paper of 1939, which limited the number of Jews allowed into Palestine. The Germans predictably refused to issue exit permits, and Kolb's mission failed.

Perhaps the most successful endeavor of the ICRC in regard to the Jews was its intervention in Hungary in spring 1944. The ICRC had asked the Hungarian government to halt the deportations; for reasons of national self-interest, Hungary agreed. During the period of the suspension of the deportations, the ICRC found shelter for thousands of Jews in Budapest. This effort was joined by Raoul Wallenberg and Swiss diplomat Carl Lutz, who issued thousands of visas and emigration certificates, which protected the Jews from being shipped to the extermination camps when the deportations were resumed.

Although Jewish resistance against the Germans was a difficult undertaking, it was made even more so because of the indifference of the non-Jewish world. Nevertheless, it is incorrect to conclude that Jews did not confront the Germans when the opportunity presented itself. In every part of German-occupied Europe, including the death camps, Jews either confronted the Nazis or participated in the various partisan movements that fought against the enemy. The resistance, however, did not prevent the destruction of most of Europe's Jews, and at the same time, it raised questions about the strategies Jewish leaders adopted in confronting the Germans. The debate over the Jewish Councils initiated by Raul Hilberg and Hannah Arendt will continue to inform the argument over the complicity of the Jews in their own demise. Similarly, future scholarship is certain to provide new insights into the reasons for the failure of the Allies and the Catholic church to do more to save the Jews of Europe.

NOTES

1. Raul Hilberg, *The Destruction of the European Jews* (New York: Holmes & Meier, 1961), p. 146.

2. Hannah Arendt, *Eichmann in Jerusalem* (New York: Viking Press, 1963), pp. 117–118.

3. Israel Gutman, "Efraim Barasz," in Gutman, ed., *Encyclopedia of the Holocaust* (New York: Macmillan, 1990), 1:148–149.

4. Isaiah Trunk, *Judenrat: The Jewish Councils in Eastern Europe under the Nazis* (Lincoln: University of Nebraska Press), p. xvii.

5. *The Jewish Quarter of Warsaw Is No More! The Stroop Report*, trans. and anno. Sybil Milton (New York: Pantheon, 1979), May 16, 1943, May 24, 1943.

6. Hilberg, *Destruction of the European Jews*, p. 327.

7. Yuri Suhl, *They Fought Back: The Story of the Jewish Resistance in Nazi Europe* (New York: Crown, 1967), p. 3.

8. Israel Gutman, "Partisans," in Gutman, ed., *Encyclopedia of the Holocaust*, 3: 1111.

9. Both quotations are found in Suhl, *They Fought Back*, pp. 3–4.

10. Mordecai Paldiel, "Sugihara, Sempo," in Gutman, ed., *Encyclopedia of the Holocaust,* 4:1424. Also see Hillel Levine, *In Search of Sugihar* (New York: Free Press, 1996), pp. 209–260.

11. Yehuda Bauer, "Riegner Cable," in Gutman, ed., *Encyclopedia of the Holocaust*, 3:1275.

12. Henry L. Feingold, "Bermuda Conference," in Gutman, ed., *Encyclopedia of the Holocaust*, 1:205.

13. This is one of the major arguments made in David S. Wyman, *The Abandonment of the Jews: America and the Holocaust, 1941–1945* (New York: Pantheon, 1984). Also see David S. Wyman, "Bombing of Auschwitz," in Gutman, ed., *Encyclopedia of the Holocaust*, 1:119–121.

14. Shlomo Kless, "Michael Dov Weissmandel," in Gutman, ed., *Encyclopedia of the Holocaust*, 4:1639–1641.

15. Wyman, "Bombing," p. 119.

16. David S. Wyman, "War Refugee Board," in Gutman, ed., *Encyclopedia of the Holocoust*, 4:1596.

17. James H. Kitchen III, "The Bombing of Auschwitz Reexamined," in Verne W. Newton, ed., *FDR and the Holocaust* (New York: St. Martin's Press, 1996), pp. 183–217.

18. Jean-Claude Favez, "Red Cross International," in Gutman, ed., *Encyclopedia of the Holocaust*, 3:1230.

Conclusion

When the Soviets liberated Auschwitz in January 1945, they found in the barracks known as "Canada" 348,820 men's suits, 836,255 women's garments, 5,525 pair of women's shoes, 38,000 pairs of men's shoes, and huge quantities of toothbrushes, glasses, false teeth, gold caps and fillings from teeth, and 7 tons of hair. This appropriation of Jewish possessions, including body parts, marked the culmination of a process that began in Germany in the late 1930s, when the Germans expropriated the bank accounts, securities, insurance policies, art collections, and other material objects of value from its Jews. The possessions of the murdered Jews were intended to be used for the German war effort, inasmuch as they were deemed of value by those who administered the Final Solution.

In the spring of 1945, the United States and Great Britain liberated the concentration camps in Germany. The first camp the Allies occupied was Natzweiler in Alsace in April 1945. The shock of viewing thousands of emaciated bodies and "cadaverous survivors" was so overwhelming that General Dwight D. Eisenhower, commander of the Allied invasion of Europe, insisted that as many American soldiers as possible be taken to the camps to witness the evidence of the atrocities that were perpetrated by the Nazis. Eisenhower later wrote of the initial reaction to what he had seen in the camps in his book *Crusade in Europe*:

I have never felt able to describe my emotional reaction when I first came face to face with Nazi brutality. . . . I visited every nook and cranny of the camp (Ohrdruf) because I felt it my duty to be in a position from then on to testify at first hand about these things in case there ever grew up at home the belief or assumption that "the stories of Nazi brutality were just propaganda."[1]

Eisenhower's shock was reinforced by film taken by Allied troops recording the horror found at the various camp sites. Numbed GIs took thousands of photographs when they entered the camp grounds, pictures that have become an indelible record of the enormity of the Nazi horror.

Eisenhower's fear that Nazi atrocities would one day be dismissed as exaggeration or propaganda was addressed by the trial of Nazi war criminals at Nuremberg on October 18, 1945. The court's official designation was the International Military Tribunal (IMT), and its purpose was to try the major Nazi war criminals for crimes against humanity and peace by planning, executing, and organizing crimes, as well as ordering others to do so during World War II. Twenty-two Nazi military leaders were tried at Nuremberg; they included Hermann Goering, Alfred Rosenberg, Hans Frank, Arthur Seyss-Inquart, Julius Streicher, and others accused of war crimes.

The Nuremberg Trial was a historical first, and established the principle that wars of aggression in any form are forbidden. The Nazi leaders were found guilty of engaging in a criminal conspiracy and participation in a criminal organization, the National Socialist Party. The testimony given at Nuremberg presented the world with the full horror of what soon was to be described as the Holocaust.

The judgment at Nuremberg was merely the tip of the iceberg. It became apparent to the Allies that the unprecedented nature of Nazi criminality involved millions of participants and raised questions as to whether it was possible to bring all of the perpetrators to trial. Nevertheless, beginning with Great Britain in the 1950s and continuing in Poland, France, and more recently in Germany, trials of Nazis accused of complicity in the murder of Jews have been an ongoing legacy of the Holocaust. Inasmuch as many of those tried since the first trial at Nuremberg were not first-rung Nazi leaders but the second tier of those who implemented criminal acts, fundamental questions have arisen in regard to the question of personal responsibility. Were many of the perpetrators of war crimes acting under orders from their superiors, and was this sufficient cause to exculpate them from charges of participating in genocide? The judgment at Nuremberg was an emphatic no. Nuremberg established the principle that under international law, individual responsibility exists for those who would obey orders that are deemed war crimes.

Despite the widespread awareness of the horrors of the death camps since the trial of Adolf Eichmann in Israel in 1961, it remains a question as to whether the United States would confront genocide more assertively than it did during the Holocaust. An argument has been made that the United States cannot be the policeman of the world and cannot intervene in disputes that do not threaten its national interest. In the light of past genocide in Cambodia, the treatment of the Kurds in Iraq, the genocidal acts perpetrated in Rwanda between the Hutu and Tutsi tribes, and "ethnic cleansing" in Bosnia, the shadow of the Nuremberg trials continues to resonate. The failure of the International Criminal Tribunal, created by the United Nations with American support, to try Bosnian Serb leader Radovan Karadzic and his general, Ratko Mladic, on charges of war crimes because of political considerations raises questions as to whether the Holocaust, and the principles set forth at Nuremberg, have made genocide any less likely to occur than during World War II.

What, then, has been the legacy of the Holocaust since the end of World War II? In Germany, antsemitism has become a social taboo that can no longer be expressed publicly. Although latent antisemitism still exists in Germany, much of it takes the form of arguments over issues such as reparation payments to Jewish victims of the Nazis and the moral guilt associated with the Holocaust. As for the Nazis' primary victims, the Holocaust has made most Jews strong supporters of Israel. Many Jews believe that had there been a Jewish state, there would not have been a Holocaust. Although most Jews are loyal citizens of the nations that they live in, they nevertheless treasure the existence of Israel as an insurance policy against any possible future genocide directed against the Jewish people. To the degree that Hitler referred to the Jews as a "rootless people," Jewish identity has been strengthened by the presence of the Jewish state.

In the United States, the country with the largest Jewish population, Jews have been active in the fight against prejudice. Recognizing that racism can lead to genocide, many Jews were involved in the civil rights movement following World War II. After the opening of the concentration camps, which was witnessed by thousands of returning American soldiers, the entire country moved in the direction of condemning racism and bigotry. It can be argued that it was as much a result of the exigencies of the cold war as it was a reaction to the Nazi genocide that influenced the historic Supreme Court decision in the *Brown* case in 1954 that overturned segregation and led to the civil rights movement.

The commemoration of the Holocaust in recent years has led to its memorialization in many parts of the United States, including the Holocaust Memorial Museum in Washington, D.C. Ostensibly constructed as a warning against genocide, the Holocaust museum and other public memorials of the Holocaust have led to controversy. Ethnic groups representing the victims of the Nazis have challenged the use of the term "Holocaust" to designate an exclusive Jewish tragedy, thereby creating a misunderstanding of the unconventional nature of the Nazi war against the Jews. If Jews were simply included as one of many victims of Nazi racial ideology, then the unique aspects of Nazi racism would be diminished and would leave future generations unprepared to deal with warning signs of genocide.

From our understanding of Nazi racial ideology, it is clear that Jews were the primary intended victims. Once Nazi racist ideology permeated German society, it legitimized the murderous actions taken against the Jews. The Holocaust was made possible by the convergence of hard-core racial antisemites, who moved Germany in the direction of genocide; a bureaucracy that administered orders "without scorn or bias"; and the application of the techniques of industrial management to mass murder, thus creating factories of death. The Nazis rallied the support and participation of ordinary Germans, as well as those who profited from Jewish victimization. They were called on to engage in the wholesale slaughter of a people who had been demonized by Nazi propaganda. Both Christopher Browning and Daniel Goldhagen have shown that ordinary Germans became killers, as did many in the medical and other professions, not because they were necessarily antisemitic, although that was a factor, but because of complex circumstances, including the willingness to believe that, in murdering Jews, one was defending the fatherland.[2]

It may well be that one of the lessons of the Holocaust is that ordinary people placed in extraordinary circumstances are capable of excessive cruelty. This is not to say that we are all potential Nazis. In 1933, the Nazis were a major political party in Germany. It is unlikely that the Aryan Nation or its Nazi equivalent could ever enter the mainstream of American politics or that the American people would elect a David Duke as president. Nevertheless, the history of Nazi Germany and its special treatment of the Jews warns us about the dangers of antisemitism and racism and their deadly consequences. What occurred to the Jews between 1933 and 1945 can happen to any people if society chooses to ignore the spread of bigotry. In Germany there was no massive agitation that something be done about the Jews. There was neither a demand that the Jews be expelled nor support for violence against them. Yet the majority of Germans accepted the steps taken by the government against the Jews and looked the other way as discriminatory laws evolved into a policy of genocide. To mitigate, trivialize, or diminish the centrality of the special circumstances that led to the murder of European Jewry is to ignore the possibility that they can reoccur with another group replacing Jews as the victim.

NOTES

1. Dwight D. Eisenhower, *Crusade in Europe* (New York: Doubleday, 1948), p. 409.

2. Christopher R. Browning, *Ordinary Men: Reserve Police Battalion 101 and the Final Solution in Poland* (New York: HarperCollins, 1992), and Daniel Jonah Goldhagen, *Hitler's Willing Executioners: Ordinary Germans and the Holocaust* (New York: Knopf, 1996).

Biographies: Major Participants in the Holocaust

Mordecai Anielewicz (1919 or 1920–1943) was the commander of the Warsaw ghetto uprising in April 1943. Born into a poor family in a Warsaw slum, he graduated from the Laor Jewish secondary school and joined the Zionist *Hashomer Hatzair* (German youth group) movement where he excelled as an organizer and youth leader. Following the invasion of Poland, Anielewicz fled from Warsaw and made his way to the southern-most part of Soviet-occupied Poland and tried to cross from there into Romania for the purpose of establishing a route for Jewish youth to reach Palestine. He was arrested by Soviet troops and sent to jail. Upon his release he returned to Warsaw, then occupied by the Germans.

By January 1940, Anielewicz had become an underground leader, with the objective of setting up cells among his *Hashomer Hatzair* comrades. He was active in publishing an underground newspaper as well as making illegal trips outside Warsaw to visit communities and his movement's chapters in rural ghettos. Anielewicz found time to study Hebrew and was particularly interested in Jewish history and economics. He was instrumental in organizing educational and cultural groups that embraced hundreds of young people in the *Hashomer* movement.

After news was reported of the mass murders of Jews following the German invasion of the Soviet Union, Anielewicz concentrated his energies on the creation of a defense force in the ghetto. Efforts to link up with Polish resistance movements who were loyal to the Polish government in exile in London were unsuccessful. At the time of the mass deportation of Jews from the Warsaw ghetto in summer 1942, Anielewicz was in Zaglebie, in the southwestern part of Poland, organizing young *Hashomer* comrades into an armed resistance movement. Upon his return to Warsaw, he found the ghetto reduced in size, with only 60,000 of its 350,000 Jews still left. He also found that the small Jewish Fighting Organization (ZOB) lacked arms, and its membership was depleted as a result of the deportations. At this point Anielewicz moved to the leadership of the resistance movement, embarking on a campaign to reorganize and strengthen the ZOB. Within weeks, he was able to merge most of the existing underground groups with the ZOB and create a council consisting of authorized representatives in support of the resistance group. In November 1942, Anielewicz was appointed commander of the ZOB.

On January 18, 1943, the Germans embarked on the second round of deportations from the Warsaw ghetto. The action took the ZOB leadership by surprise, and they were unable to respond quickly to the situation. But one part of the ghetto ZOB decided to act on its own course of action, with Anielewicz taking command of the battle. The fighters deliberately joined the assembled deportees and at an agreed-on signal attacked the Germans. Most of the fighters, who were members of the *Hashomer Hatzair*, were killed in battle, but Anielewicz was saved by his men. Following the battle, the deportations were halted, and in the next three months, from January to April 1943, the ZOB prepared for the decisive test ahead against the Germans.

On April 19, 1943, on the eve of Passover, the Germans launched the final deportation of the Jews of Warsaw. This action served as the signal for the ghetto uprising; what followed was four weeks of brutal fighting in which the large German military force suffered constant casualties. In the first days of the fighting, Anielewicz was in command of the main fighting forces in the ghetto. The resistance fighters eventually retreated into a bunker at 18 Mila Street. The bunker fell on May 8, and the main body of the ZOB, including Anielewicz, was killed. In his last letter, on April 23, 1943, sent to Yitzhak Zuckerman (a member of the ZOB staff who was on assignment on the Polish side), Anielewicz wrote, "Farewell my friend. Perhaps we shall meet again. The most most important thing is that my life's dream has come true. I have lived to see Jewish resistance in the ghetto in all its greatness and glory."

Theodor Dannecker (1913–1945) was a key aide to Adolf Eichmann in the deportation of Jews from France, Bulgaria, and Italy to Auschwitz. Born in Tubingen, Dannecker was a lawyer by training and joined Eichmann's staff in 1937. In 1940 he was sent by Eichmann's Bureau (IV B4), the Berlin section of the Reich Main Security Office that devoted itself to

Jewish matters, to Paris. There, he supervised the preparation of lists of French Jews who were subsequently arrested and deported to Auschwitz. Dannecker was regarded as the Jewish expert of the Gestapo and claimed credit for proposing the ongoing Jewish deportations of Jews from France to the east. A fanatical Nazi, Dannecker constantly urged the Vichy government to take more active measures against the Jews. Vichy officials were surprised by the vehemence of his hatred for the Jews. Xavier Vallet, the first French commissioner for Jewish questions, described Dannecker as "a fanatical Nazi who went into a trance every time the word Jew was mentioned."

Dannecker's responsibilities in France included conducting a census of the Jews in the occupied zone on September 27, 1940, with the objective of depriving Jews of their civil rights. A similar census was taken in Vichy on June 2, 1941. Dannecker's second objective was to undermine the economic life of the Jewish community by removing them from their jobs and ejecting them from all state institutions. In July 1941, Jews were directed to register their businesses with the government, which then appointed provisional directors over their concerns. Dannecker next focused on the concentration of the Jews. Inasmuch as they could not be placed in ghettos, as was the case in eastern Europe, Dannecker ordered nighttime curfews for Jews and prohibited them from changing their domiciles. His last objective was to create a *Judenräte,* which he succeeded in establishing in January 1941. In March 1942, Dannecker insisted that 5,000 Jews be deported from France immediately, and under his direction, the first transport of Jews from the western countries to Auschwitz was planned. The first trains left on March 27, 1942, with 1,012 Jews aboard, and the balance of the 5,000 were subsequently deported between April and June.

Eichmann recalled Dannecker to Berlin at the end of 1942 for abuse of office, and in January 1943, he was reassigned to Bulgaria. There he concluded a written agreement with Alexander Belev, head of Bulgaria's Commissariat for the Jewish Problem, to deport 20,000 Jews from Bulgaria to Auschwitz. The Belev-Dannecker agreement provided for the deportation of 8,000 Jews from Macedonia, 6,000 from Thrace, and 6,000 from Bulgaria proper. Eventually 11,000 Jews from Macedonia and Thrace were sent to Auschwitz, but the Bulgarian government reneged on the agreement to deport Jews from Bulgaria. In March 1944, Dannecker was sent to Hungary by Eichmann as part of a special sixteen-man team, the Special Operational Commando Hungary. The purpose of the unit was to organize the deportation of the country's almost 800,000 Jews. In October 1944, Eichmann appointed him Jewish commissioner in Italy, where he remained until the end of the war. Dannecker committed suicide in an American prison camp in Bad Tolz on December 10, 1945.

Adolf Eichmann (1906–1962) was born in Solingen to a prosperous middle-class Protestant family, which moved to Linz, Austria, where Eichmann spent his youth. After working in his father's mining enterprise, Eichmann moved on to become a traveling salesman for the Vacuum Oil Company between 1927 and 1933, but after a motorcycle accident, he was dismissed from his job. In 1932 he had joined the Austrian Nazi Party, but when the party was banned in Austria in 1933, the unemployed Eichmann moved to Germany. He joined the SD in 1934 and by 1935 had become responsible for the "Jewish question," specializing in the Zionist movement.

During the latter part of the 1930s, Eichmann emerged as one of the chief planners in devising methods for expediting the departure of Jews from Germany. Taking his new responsibility seriously, Eichmann studied both Yiddish and Hebrew, and in 1937, he visited Palestine to determine the possibility of Jewish migration from Germany to the British Mandate area. He concluded that increased immigration of Jews into Palestine was not in Germany's interest, but he nevertheless worked with Jewish groups that were running *Aliya Bet* ("illegal immigration") into the area. After the German annexation of Austria, Eichmann was sent to organize the emigration of its Jews and promptly set up the Central Office for Jewish Emigration in Vienna. Through the use of intimidation and terror, Eichmann was successful in his efforts and subsequently introduced the system of forced emigration in Prague after the Nazis had gained control of Bohemia and Moravia. In December 1939, he was assigned to the Jewish section of the Reich Main Security Office (RSHA), where he worked on both the Lublin Plan and the Madagascar project.

In December 1939, Eichmann was transferred to *Amt IV* (Gestapo) of the RSHA, where he was given the responsibility for dealing with Jewish affairs. From this position, Eichmann's office became the headquarters for the planning of the Final Solution. In 1941 Eichmann visited Auschwitz, and in the same year he was promoted to the rank of SS lieutenant colonel. He played a prominent role at the Wannsee Conference in January 1942, and Heydrich subsequently entrusted him with the implementation of the Final Solution. Although Eichmann claimed at his trial in Israel in 1961 that he personally had nothing against Jews, he nevertheless carried out his task with bureaucratic industriousness. He would bitterly complain about obstacles that prevented him from fulfilling deportation quotas, and even toward the end of the war, when SS leader Heinrich Himmler ordered a halt to the gassing of the Jews, Eichmann ignored the order and continued to send Jews to the death camps.

Only in Hungary in 1944 did Eichmann leave his desk and take an active role in the deportation process. Eichmann was personally responsible for the deportation of 440,000 Jews from Hungary to Auschwitz. When it no longer was possible to send the Jews by train to the death camp, he organized death marches to Austria, from where Jews were sent to forced labor camps in Germany.

When the war ended, Eichmann went into hiding after his escape from an American internment camp in 1946 and fled to Argentina. In May 1960, he was tracked down and abducted by Israeli agents and brought to trial in Israel. The trial engendered a debate about Eichmann's character. Hannah Arendt argued that Eichmann was a very ordinary and banal individual who was not motivated by antisemitism, but carried out orders he received from his superiors within the framework of the Nazi bureaucracy.[1] Others argued that Eichmann personified the evils of Nazism, an ideology that nurtured the drives and conditions that made possible the execution of the Final Solution. The trial took place between April 2 and August 14, 1961. On December 2, 1961, Eichmann was found guilty and sentenced to death for crimes against the Jewish people and crimes against humanity. He was executed on May 31, 1962.

Hans Frank (1900–1946) was the governor-general of the *Generalgouvernment* in German-occupied Poland from 1939 to 1945. Frank was born in Karlsruhe, the son of an attorney. He graduated from a Munich gymnasium in 1918 and joined a right-wing paramilitary group headed by Ritter von Epp in 1919. In the same year he pursued the study of law at the University of Kiel, received his doctorate in 1924, and passed the bar examination in 1926. A militant nationalist, Frank joined both the SA and the Nazi Party in 1923, and in the same year took part in the beer hall putsch in Munich. In the years prior to Hitler's seizure of power, Frank defended him in his many libel cases and emerged as the star defense counsel for the Nazi Party. In 1929 he became the party's chief attorney and Hitler's personal lawyer. It was in this position that Frank investigated the delicate matter of researching Hitler's genealogy for possible Jewish ancestry.

After Hitler took power, Frank's usefulness to the führer rapidly diminished. He never belonged to Hitler's inner circle, perhaps due to his formal objections at the time of Ernst Röhm's murder in 1934 or perhaps because Hitler despised lawyers. He was, however, given many honorific but powerless positions, including his appointment as minister of justice of Bavaria and, from 1934 to 1941, president of the Academy for German Law. Historians have described Frank as ambitious but also a vacillating and insecure person who had a penchant for brutality.

Appointed governor-general of the *Generalgouvernment* in Poland in 1939, Frank was consistently frustrated by Hitler's style of governance, which encouraged a constant internal struggle for power among the different bureaucracies and jurisdictions, and allowed for himself the role of the indispensable arbiter. In particular, Frank found himself at cross purposes with Heinrich Himmler's SS, and he failed in his attempts to place it under his authority. Frank's brutal nature was displayed toward the Poles, whom he treated as slaves of the Greater Reich. From the old royal palace in Krakow, he authorized the extermination of the Polish intelligentsia and ransacked the country's art treasures for personal gain.

Frank was brutal toward the Jews. In December 1941, he gave a speech in which he called for the extermination of the Jews: "We can't shoot these 3.5 million Jews, and we can't poison them, but we can take steps which, one way or another, will lead to extermination." Yet he was torn between the policy of extermination, which he approved in principle, and his need for Jewish slave labor. As Frank stated in a memorandum to Hitler, "You should not slaughter the cow you want to milk."

Because Frank desired to build his own domain, he was inclined toward a pragmatic policy of economic stabilization, but because of his rivalry with Himmler, he would abruptly support policies of radical brutality and destructiveness. Thus, Frank vacillated between opposing and supporting the influx of Poles and Jews who were expelled from the "incorporated territories." He also veered between approving the rational exploitation of the ghetto economies and the policy that encouraged the starvation and then mass murder of the Jews. Frank, however, appeared to be unaware of the policy in the *Generalgouvernment* as it evolved in Berlin. He saw himself as presiding over a modern "crusader kingdom" that would emulate the drive to the east of the medieval order of Teutonic Knights. Hitler viewed the *Generalgouvernment* as a racial dumping ground, a reservoir for slave labor, and the area in which the Final Solution would eventually take place.

Under these circumstances, it was inevitable that Frank would lose his fight with Himmler. In March 1942, Frank was stripped of all jurisdiction over racial and police matters. These were now to be Himmler's exclusive domain. Hitler allowed Frank to remain governor-general of Poland, a position Hitler regarded as the most unpleasant he could give anyone because Poland was perceived as a backwater area with no possibility of influencing decisions emanating from Berlin. After the fall of the Third Reich, Frank was brought to trial at Nuremberg. By this time, he had become reconciled to the Catholic church and even attacked Hitler as a war criminal. Nevertheless, despite his remorse, he was executed as a war criminal on October 16, 1946.

Odilo Globocnik (1904–1945) was born in Trieste to the family of a lower middle-class Austrian-Croatian family. A builder by trade, he joined the Austrian Nazi Party in 1931 and became a leader of its factory cells in the provinces. In 1934 he joined the SS. Globocnik was imprisoned in 1933 for political offenses but reemerged as the liaison between the Austrian and German National Socialists. In 1934 he joined the SS and became the *Gauleiter* of Vienna in 1938 as a reward for his help in subverting the independence of Austria. He was subsequently dismissed from his position for illegal currency dealings. When World War II broke out in September 1939, he was appointed SS and police chief for the Lublin district. In 1941 Himmler gave him the responsibility for the planning and establishment of police- and SS-fortified strategic provinces for the purpose of the resettlement of ethnic Germans in various parts of Poland. Himmler's idea was to create a class of feudal lords who, like the medieval knights, would assign fiefs of various types to the settlers. Globocnik's responsibility was to create a system of defenses in the form of small towns, which would be situated at the intersections of German communication arteries. Eventually Globocnik's authority clashed with Hans Frank, the governor of the *Generalgouvernment*, and after a bitter jurisdictional struggle, Himmler's fantasy was ended. Later that year, Globocnik was put in charge of all the Operation Reinhard annihilation camps, where he utilized the services of most of the personnel who had participated in the euthanasia program in Germany headed by Christian Wirth.

A virulent antisemite, he answered only to Himmler, who permitted him to organize a special SS unit for the purpose of implementing the Final Solution. The record indicates that he carried out his duties with brutal efficiency, which entailed not only the murder of more than 2 million Polish Jews but also the exploitation of manpower, the seizure of hidden valuables and movable property, and the removal of personal objects from his victims, ranging from spectacles to gold fillings from teeth. The estimated amount of the plunder sent to the German Reichsbank from Operation Reinhard came to 180 million reichsmark. Globocnik was proud of his role in the Final Solution, and on one occasion stated "that if there is ever a generation that does not understand our great task then the whole of National Socialism will have been in vain . . . we had great courage to carry out this great work which is so vital."[2]

In mid-August 1943, Globocnik was dispatched to Bialystok to supervise the liquidation of the ghetto, but by the end of the month, he received an unexpected assignment. Ever greedy, Himmler relieved Globocnik of his position in August 1943 for skimming too liberally from the valuables of his victims and reassigned him and his SS unit to Trieste, where he was made higher SS and police leader for the Adriatic region. In Trieste, Globocnik supervised the liquidation of 2,000 Italian Jews at the San Saba death camp in October 1943. He was captured by British troops at the end of the war and committed suicide in May 1945.

Joseph Goebbels (1897–1945) was born in Rheydt, in the Rhine district, to a poor but pious working-class Catholic family. He was educated in a Catholic school and subsequently went on to earn a doctorate in history and literature at the University of Heidelberg. Born with a clubfoot, he was rejected for military service during World War I. His physical deformity appears to have embittered him, and after he joined the Nazi Party in 1924, he overcompensated for his un-Nordic physical appearance with his ideological zeal and fanaticism, especially when it came to the Jews. Because of his doctorate, Goebbels also feared that he would be regarded as a "bourgeois intellectual," and consequently he displayed a hostility to intellectuals. But Goebbels also had oratorical skills, and he used his demagoguery to appeal to the primitive instincts and fears of the unemployed masses.

In 1926 Goebbels was appointed *Gauleiter* of Berlin and in 1928 was elected to the Reichstag. In a series of articles written in 1932 in the Nazi newspaper, *Der Angriff*, Goebbels called for a pogrom against the Jews, and a wave of anti-Jewish violence followed, which spread mayhem throughout Germany. In the election campaigns from 1930 to 1933, he served as the party's chief of propaganda. With Hitler's accession to power, Goebbels became minister of propaganda and public information. In this capacity, Goebbels helped to create the führer myth and convince the public that Hitler was the savior of Germany from the Jews, profiteers, and Marxists. Goebbels was instrumental in eliminating Jews from all aspects of German life, and on May 10, 1933, he organized the burning of books in Berlin, where works of Jewish, Marxist, and other "subversive" authors were publicly burned in huge bonfires.

Goebbels was a virulent antisemite who relentlessly depicted "the Jew" as an abominable creature and the principal enemy of the German people. This depiction of the Jew would be reinforced when Goebbels authorized the production of the *Eternal Jew* (1940), an incendiary film that equated Jews with rats. It was Goebbels who organized the April 1, 1933, boycott against Jewish enterprises in Germany, *Kristallnacht* pogroms in November 1938, and, later, reductions of Jewish activities and freedom of movement in areas under his jurisdiction. Following the conquest of Poland in 1939, Goebbels organized the first deportations from Berlin in keeping with a promise that he made to Hitler to make the city *Judenrein* (cleansed of Jews). Goebbels was also the first to urge that Jews wear the yellow badge, because German soldiers on leave were incensed that Jews were still strolling freely throughout the Reich. On September 1, 1943, the yellow badge regulation became law within the borders of the Greater Reich.

Goebbels strongly urged that there be no retreat from the Final Solution. He combined verbal warnings that the Jews would be exterminated with careful avoidance of propaganda material that disclosed the methods to be used against the Jews. In a speech given in February 1943, Goebbels called for a total war against the Jews and noted in his diary that when it came to the Jewish question, "we are so deeply mired in it that we have no way out . . . experience shows that a movement and a people that have burned their bridges behind them are more likely to fight without reservation than those who have the option to retreat." Goebbels recognized that in the campaign to annihilate the Jews, Germany had passed the point of no return, and he urged that every effort be made to finish the task.

As the war neared its end, Goebbels emerged as Hitler's most loyal follower. In the aftermath of Hitler's suicide, Goebbels disregarded the führer's order that appointed him as Reich chancellor. Instead, on May 1, 1945, he had his six children poisoned with a lethal injection from an SS doctor and then had himself and his wife, Magda, shot by an SS orderly.

Hermann Goering (1893–1946) was born in Rosenheim to the son of a judge who was a diplomat in the service of Chancellor Otto von Bismarck. During World War I, Goering initially served in the infantry and then was transferred to the air force, where he became a distinguished air ace in the Richthofen Fighter Squadron. Awarded the Iron Cross, he left the military a war hero and soon after was attracted to the fledgling Nazi Party. His aristocratic background and heroic exploits during the war made him a prize recruit for Hitler, who soon after made him the commander of the SA Brownshirts (1922). In 1923 Goering took part in the Munich beer hall putsch and subsequently was forced to flee from Germany. He returned to Germany in 1926 and was elected to the Reichstag in 1927 as a member of the National Socialist German Worker's Party. During the next few years, Goering paved the way for Hitler's acceptance among conservatives, big business, and the military. Following Hitler's appointment as chancellor on January 30, 1933, Goering was made Prussian minister of the interior, commander in chief of the Prussian police and Gestapo, and minister of aviation.

Goering took the lead in exploiting the Reichstag fire (February 1933), which many historians believe he engineered. Together with Heinrich Himmler, Goering was responsible for organizing the early concentration camps for political opponents. In 1934 he played a major role in the purge of the SA and shortly after was appointed commander in chief of the German air force. In January 1935 he was promoted to the position of Reichsmarschall and in 1936 was placed in charge of the German Four Year Plan, which gave him virtual dictatorial control over the entire economy. In this position, he created the Hermann Goering Works in 1937, a huge industrial combine that employed about 700,000 workers. When the German armies invaded Poland on September 1, 1939, Hitler appointed him as his successor.

Goering was a flamboyant personality who loved the trappings of power and used the advantages of his various official positions to live ostentatiously. He lived in a palace in Berlin, where he enjoyed a life of debauchery. During World War II, he was responsible for the theft of artworks from collections throughout German-occupied Europe. Nevertheless, Goering remained a popular figure in Germany and was regarded by the masses as honest, warm, and more accessible than Hitler.

Not as fanatic as either Hitler or Himmler in regard to their obsession with Jews, Goering was nevertheless a vicious antisemite. He was responsible for the confiscation of Jewish property in 1937, and, following *Kristallnacht*, it was Goering who fined the Jewish community a billion reichsmarks and ordered the elimination of the Jews from the German economy. Soon after, Hitler placed him in charge of the Jewish question, and in January 1939, he established the Central Office for Jewish Emigration for the purpose of "encouraging" Jews to leave Germany. Coinciding with the German invasion of Poland on September 1, 1939, Hitler designated Goering as his successor. After the invasion of Poland, Goering was active in the expulsion of Jews from the western part of Poland. During the same year he set up the Main Trusteeship Office East, which administered confiscated Jewish property. In May 1941, Goering banned the emigration of Jews from all occupied territories, including France, in view of the "doubtless imminent final solution," and in July he officially authorized Heydrich to set in motion the preparations for the Final Solution.

At war's end, Goering was arrested by the Allies and put on trial by the International Military Tribunal at the Nuremberg Trials in October 1945. He was sentenced to death, but committed suicide in his prison cell on October 15, 1946.

Reinhard Heydrich (1904–1942) the head of the Reich Main Security (RSHA), and the primary implementor of the Final Solution, was strongly influenced in his youth by the same type of antisemitic *völkisch* ideas that attracted Adolf Hitler. Heydrich was born to a well-to-do family in Halle on March 7, 1904. His father was a music teacher and the founder of the Halle Conservatory of Music. His mother was a pianist, and Heydrich was trained as a violinist, a passion that continued throughout his life. In his youth, Heydrich was constantly teased because of his Catholicism and false rumors of possible Jewish ancestry in his family in a town with a large Protestant population.

Too young to serve in the war, Heydrich joined the *Freikorps* in 1919 and was influenced by comrades who were *völkisch* nationalists. In March 1922, he joined the *Reichmarine* under Wilhelm Canaris, and it was this experience that nurtured his interest in intelligence work. By 1926 Heydrich had risen to the rank of second lieutenant but subsequently was accused of having sexual relations with the unmarried daughter of a shipyard director. Because he refused to marry the woman, he was forced to resign from the navy in 1931. In the same year, he joined the Nazi Party, where he attracted Himmler's attention and subsequently rose rapidly through the ranks. Tall, blond-haired, and blue-eyed, Heydrich epitomized the Aryan ideal. Ruthless and calculating, he made himself indispensable to Himmler. It was Himmler who authorized Heydrich to create the *Sicherheitsdienst* or SS Security Service (SD), an intelligence-gathering organization. But like Hitler, Heydrich was wracked by uncertainty caused by his suspected half-Jewish origins. This insecurity and his efforts to avoid being blackmailed perhaps explains why, as head of SD, he compiled dossiers on his rivals and colleagues, as well as enemies of the state. In 1933 the question of his Jewish ancestry was put to rest after a discussion with Hitler, who concluded that the rumor was untrue. Nevertheless, the matter of his ancestry continued to haunt him until his death in 1942.

Heydrich, nicknamed the "Blond Beast," was known for his arrogance as well as his devious methods, which included extortion and terror against his opponents. In his position as head of the RSHA, which combined the SD, Gestapo, Criminal Police, and foreign intelligence services into one centralized organization, Heydrich perfected the techniques of secret police power and was second only to Himmler in generating fear among his rivals in the Nazi hierarchy. In the year before the invasion of Poland, Heydrich had managed to concentrate authority regarding Jewish affairs in his office. Following the annexation of Austria, he sent Adolf Eichmann to Vienna to organize the Center for Jewish Emigration and was so highly impressed with Eichmann's success that he created a similar organization in Berlin. Following the conquest of Poland in 1939, Heydrich's hand was present in every aspect of the Reich's Jewish policy. From the organization of the ghettos to the creation of the Jewish Councils, to the mass deportations of Jews from the annexed parts of Poland, Heydrich was deeply involved in the planning and implementation of the Nazi war against the Jews. Following the invasion of the Soviet Union, it was Heydrich's *Einsatzgrüppen*, which had already killed thousands of Poles and Jews, that was sent to murder the millions of Jews of Russia. It is not surprising that once the Final Solution was decided on during the summer of 1941, Himmler would entrust Reinhard Heydrich with the responsibility for carrying out this murderous enterprise. Toward this end, Heydrich convened the Wannsee Conference on January 20, 1942, which brought together fifteen top Nazi officials for the purpose of coordinating a "general plan . . . for carrying out the desired final solution of the Jewish question."

Ultimately Heydrich's arrogance proved his undoing. He would travel in an open car, with no escorts or protection, through the city streets of occupied Czechoslovakia, where he served as deputy Reich protector of Bohemia and Moravia. On May 27, 1942, his car was attacked by Czechs trained in England who were brought to Czechoslovakia for the purpose of assassinating him. Heydrich was shot and died a few days later on June 4, 1942, from blood poisoning brought on by his gunshot wounds.

Heinrich Himmler (1900–1945) was, next to Hitler, the most powerful individual in Nazi Germany. He was born in Munich on October 7, 1900, to a middle-class Catholic family. During World War I, he served in the

Eleventh Bavarian Regiment as an officer cadet but did not see action at the front. After the war, he received a degree in agriculture from the Munich Technical High School and worked as a salesman for a fertilizer manufacturing firm. In 1923 he joined the Nazi Party and participated in the beer hall putsch alongside his mentor, Ernst Röhm. In 1925 he joined the Schutzstaffel (SS), and in 1926 Himmler became assistant propaganda leader of the Nazi Party. In 1929 he rose to head of the SS.

As Reich leader of the SS, chief of the Gestapo, and head of the *Waffen*-SS, Himmler presided over an SS state built on terror in both the Reich and the occupied territories. In his capacity as Reichsführer-SS, he established the first concentration camp at Dachau in 1933, which he used to terrorize all opponents of the regime as well as his personal enemies. Himmler was obsessed with race and the occult, and he believed in the racial superiority of the Aryan people. His concern for racial purity led him to found the *Lebensborn* movement, a project that encouraged the SS to produce more babies, either legitimately or illegitimately, and toward this end he established *Lebensborn* homes for both wed and unwed mothers. Conversely, Himmler's racism focused on the Jews and Slavs, whom he believed to be subhumans. The invasion of Poland, and later the Soviet Union, gave him the opportunity to remove both groups so that pure-blood Aryans could be resettled on their soil. In October 1939, Himmler was given absolute authority over much of the newly annexed part of Poland, which led to a rivalry with Hans Frank, the governor-general of the *Generalgouvernment*. But with this added responsibility, he subsequently built the extermination camps. In camps such as Auschwitz, Himmler used his authority to exploit Jews and Slavs as slave laborers and to sanction medical experiments on "asocial individuals."

The Final Solution was for Himmler the culmination of his life's work. Of the many groups whom Himmler classified as subhuman or racially inferior, he placed the Jews at the top. He believed that the elimination of the Jews was necessary if the Aryan people were ever to attain racial supremacy. The Final Solution represented a racial armageddon whereby the destruction of the Jews would result in the triumph of the Aryan race and the restoration of Germany's lost Eden-like innocence.

Himmler does not appear to have been a sadist. In fact, he had severe reactions to the killings he witnessed in his inspection tours of the shooting sites in the Soviet Union. He also seems to have been driven by a sense of orderliness and an uncanny sense of organization. Under Himmler, for example, Dachau became a model of systematic management, and the antithesis of the early "wild" Nazi camps. Under his direction, impersonal, systematized terror replaced the random brutality of the earlier period. Theodore Eicke, the camp's commandant, was instructed by Himmler to eliminate all arbitrary punishment and replace it with impersonal anonymous retribution. This manifested itself in the issuance of camp regulations calling for strictly graded punishments for offending prisoners. In planning the Final Solution, Himmler approached his task with efficiency and dispatch and rarely deviated from the objective of murdering Europe's Jews. Indeed, it was because of his unswerving commitment to implement the Final Solution, that historian Richard Breitman, in his biography of Himmler, referred to him as "the architect of genocide."[3]

Himmler increasingly suffered from psychosomatic illnesses following the German collapse on the Russian front and lost much of his influence among Hitler's inner circle. When it was discovered that Himmler was negotiating with the Swedish count Folke Bernadotte to surrender to the Allies and had ordered a cessation of the mass murder of Jews, Hitler stripped him of all offices and ordered his arrest. Himmler was subsequently captured by the Allies in 1945 and committed suicide on May 23, 1945.

Adolf Hitler (1889–1945) was born on April 20, 1889, in Braunau, located at the border between Austria and Bavaria. Alois, Adolf's father, was a civil servant who gave his son the chance to acquire a good education. Despite the opportunity, young Adolf never attained his potential as a student and ultimately left the *Realschule* because of poor grades. This failure was the first of several during Hitler's adolescent years. Consequently, he developed a contempt for people with advanced education and in particular resented people with diplomas and doctorates. Hitler, however, did exhibit an interest in architecture and painting. He had illusions about his abilities and vowed that one day he would rebuild the city of Linz, where his mother had moved the family after Alois's death.

Hitler had a strained relationship with his father. Alois was hard, unsympathetic, and short tempered. There is also some evidence that he frequently physically disciplined his son. Young Adolf was closer to his mother, who died in 1907 after a long bout with cancer. The family doctor, Eduard Bloch, was a Jew, and there is speculation that Hitler's antisemitism subconsciously derived from blaming Dr. Bloch for his mother's death. Yet the facts do not support such an interpretation. Hitler continued to keep in touch with Bloch and later made possible his departure from Germany in 1938 to Switzerland. The issue of the origins of Hitler's antisemitism cannot be resolved with certainty. In his autobiographical *Mein Kampf* (1925), Hitler tells us that he discovered his hatred of Jews in the years he spent in Vienna between 1909 and 1913; the ultra-Orthodox Jews, with their long black caftans and long, curly sideburns, particulary repelled him.

Suspicions about his own possible Jewish ancestry may also have contributed to Adolf Hitler's antisemitism. He was aware of the possibility that his grandfather (Alois's father) may have been a Jew. In fact, Hitler's genealogy remains unclear, but this much is known. In 1837 Maria Anna Schicklgruber gave birth to an illegitimate child, who was known by the name of Alois. In 1842 Johann Georg Hiedler married Maria but did not bother to legitimize the child, who continued to be known by his mother's maiden name. Alois was later brought up in the house of his uncle, Johann Nepomuk Hiedler, who in 1876 took steps to legitimize Alois. From 1877 on, Alois called himself Hitler. Young Adolf was not known by any other surname until his political opponents in the 1920s unearthed the long-forgotten village scandal and without justification attempted to insinuate that Adolf Hitler's real grandfather was a Jew. In 1931 Hitler countered such charges with an investigation by the *Schutzstaffel* (SS or Protection Squad) which concluded that the family for whom Maria Schicklgruber worked (Trummelsclager), and by one of whose sons she became pregnant, was not Jewish or of Jewish descent.

Although in *Mein Kampf* Hitler exonerates his father from instilling in him negative feelings about Jews, there is little reason to believe that Alois was a liberal or tolerant of Jews. Closer to the truth is that the negative feelings about Jews permeated the entire environment of Hitler's youth. His father was a follower of George Ritter von Schonerer's antisemitic pan-German movement and presumably shared in the growing antisemitic sentiment that characterized Vienna during the last third of the nineteenth century. Adolf Hitler's antisemitism, according to his friend August Kubizek, was fully developed by age sixteen. By Kubizek's account, Hitler was fond of one of his history teachers at the technical school, Dr. Leopold Potsch, an ardent nationalist and antisemite who made a great impression on him. Hitler, according to Kubizek, was also exposed to other teachers at the technical school who were similarly antisemitic and openly avowed their hatred of Jews in front of their pupils.

In Vienna, Hitler immersed himself in the racist pamphlets of Lanz von Liebenfels, Guido von List, Theodore Fritsch, and the antisemitic writings of Richard Wagner. By the time Hitler arrived in Vienna in 1909, he was already a confirmed antisemite.

Adolf Hitler's years in Vienna strengthened his antisemitism as a result of his exposure to *völkisch* nationalism and the anti-Jewish currents that permeated the city on the eve of World War I. Antisemitism appealed to Hitler especially during this time of personal failure. Frustrated by his inability to pass the drawing examination at the Academy of Applied Arts in 1909, young Hitler felt shock and disappointment that his opportunity to pursue a career as an architect had been aborted. Hitler would refer to the news as an "abrupt blow." Soon anger replaced disappointment, and he blamed his failure on the four of seven Jewish examiners who graded his drawings. Hitler sent a letter of protest to the academy director in which he threatened "that the Jews will pay for this." This response by the twenty-year-old Hitler indicates that he already harbored hatred against Jews, which intensified as he became more involved in antisemitic circles.

Richard Wagner's music enthralled Hitler. The body of Wagner's work unleashed a world of primitive and powerful emotions. For some, Wagner's music is pure bombast, but for Hitler, the music appealed to the depths of his personality. The passionate nature of Wagner's music was both a mystical and religious experience for Hitler. The combination of melody that appealed to his sense of the heroic and Wagner's antisemitism allowed Hitler to believe that his war against the Jews was replicating the themes that characterized Wagner's written works and music. For Hitler, the conflict between Siegfried and Alberich in the Ring operas became the symbol of the German struggle to overcome the influence of the Jews on the eve of World War I.

Hitler enlisted in the German army upon the outbreak of World War I in August 1914. The irony of Hitler's act was that he had fled Vienna in May 1913 in order to avoid induction in the Austro-Hungarian army. His refusal to serve in his native Austria's army had little to do with fear of military service but with his resentment of serving an empire that, to his mind, tolerated racial groups such as Jews at the expense of the German popula-tion. World War I ended Hitler's aimless life. He joined the List Regiment, where he found a home and was generally accepted by his comrades, although an outsider. Hitler's antisemitism, however, remained unabated despite the fact that the Jewish regimental adjutant, Hugo Gutmann, rec-ommended him for one of the two Iron Crosses that he received for bravery under fire.

Hitler joined the Nationalist Socialist Worker's Party in 1919 and became its chairman in July 1921, presumably because of his extraordinary oratori-cal ability. During the years of the Weimar Republic, Hitler was able to bring together the various strands of antisemitic feelings within German society and called for the resolution of the "Jewish problem" as the precondition for the redemption of Germany. Following his imprisonment in the failed

Munich (beer hall) putsch in 1923, Hitler dictated *Mein Kampf* (My Struggle), and upon his release from Landsberg prison in 1925, after serving only nine months of a five-year sentence, he reestablished the National Socialist Party.

From 1925 to the Nazi seizure of power in 1933, Hitler used constitutional means to gain power in order to destroy the Weimar Republic. After several political crises that followed the economic depression beginning in 1929, Hitler was appointed chancellor on January 30, 1933. Following the Reichstag fire of February 27, basic civil rights in Germany were suspended, and after elections were held on March 5, parliamentary rule was abolished by the passage of the Enabling Act. By the end of March, Hitler had established a dictatorship in Germany.

Hitler was an unusual executive. He encouraged his subordinates to win his approval by competing against one another. Those who were most successful in the fight for bureaucratic survival, like Goering and Himmler, wound up in charge of vast empires. Hitler, however, was always at the top of the bureaucratic hierarchy, and his subordinates came to him to resolve the numerous jurisdictional disputes that emerged among his ambitious underlings. In regard to the Jewish question, he allowed subordinates, such as Himmler and Frank, to engage in jurisdictional rivalry over Jewish policy, which he ultimately settled.

Although no single document exists with Hitler's signature calling for the implementation of the Final Solution, our understanding of Hitler's administrative style suggests that such an order could have been given orally or that the policy had already been agreed on as a by-product of Hitler's speeches attacking Jewish influence in the democratic countries on the eve of World War II. Historians agree about Hitler's responsibility for the decision to implement the Final Solution, and that Himmler's execution of the Final Solution was in accord with Hitler's wishes.

As the war turned against Germany, Hitler retreated to an underground bunker in Berlin in January 1945. When the Soviets advanced on Berlin, Hitler made out his last will and testament, in which he blamed the Jews for Germany's defeat and exhorted the nation to keep the blood pure. He then married his mistress, Eva Braun, and committed suicide with her on April 30, 1945.

Rudolf Hoess (1900–1947) was born in Baden-Baden to a family of pious Catholics. After his father's death in 1915, Hoess, although under age at fifteen, joined the German army and became at the age of seventeen the youngest noncommissioned German officer in the armed forces. He also was awarded the Iron Cross, First and Second Classes, for bravery. After the war, Hoess joined the *Freikorps* in East Prussia, then in the Baltic states, and later participated in battles against the French occupation forces in the Ruhr and the Poles in Upper Silesia in 1921. In November 1922, he joined the Nazi Party, and in the following year he was arrested and sentenced to a ten-year prison term for participating in the murder of a German teacher who had collaborated with the French during the Ruhr occupation. Hoess was pardoned under the Amnesty Law of July 14, 1928, having served less than half his sentence. For the next six years, Hoess worked for the Artamanen Society, a nationalist-*völkisch* group that advocated work on the land and settlement in the east, on Polish territory.

In June 1934, Himmler, a leader of the Artamanen Society, invited Hoess to join the SS. From 1934 until May 1938, Hoess held various administrative positions in the Dachau concentration camp. In 1938 he was transferred to the camp at Sachsenhausen and promoted to the rank of SS captain. In May 1940, he was assigned to Auschwitz and became the founder of the camp as well as its first commandant. At Auschwitz, Hoess proved to be a tireless bureaucrat in the implementation of the extermination process. He never personally attended the selections for the gas chambers or mass executions. Rather, he dutifully carried out Himmler's orders and ascertained that the extermination process functioned smoothly. Hoess appears not to have been a sadist. A family man who loved animals, he treated mass murder as a purely administrative procedure. As Robert Wistrich has observed, Hoess was concerned with "the practical difficulties of carrying out his assignment with maximum efficiency . . . questions involving the precise adherence to timetables, the size of transports, the types of ovens and methods of gassing."[4]

In December 1943, Hoess was made chief of the SS Economic-Administrative Main Office (WVHA) but was sent back to Auschwitz to direct the extermination of the Jews of Hungary. Called *Aktion Hoess*, he presided over the annihilation of 43,000 Jews, and in recognition of his outstanding service in the concentration camps, he was awarded War Crosses, Classes I and II, with swords. After the war, Hoess was arrested by the American military police and handed over to Polish authorities, in keeping with the agreement on the extradition of war criminals. In his Krakow cell in 1946 and 1947, he wrote his autobiography, which was published in English in 1960 as *Commandant of Auschwitz: The Autobiography of Rudolph Hoess*, and included his account of how the Final Solution was put into effect in Auschwitz. Hoess also revealed how he was able to oversee the murder of millions of innocent people without feelings of guilt. He recounted a childhood in which he was raised with a strong sense of duty and defended his compulsion to obey orders and surrender all personal independence as proof of his own morality and sense of decency: "I am completely normal. Even while I was carrying out the task of extermination I lived a normal life and so on." Subsequently, the Warsaw supreme court sentenced him to death, and he was hanged in Auschwitz on April 16, 1947.

Josef Mengele (1911–1978), the holder of both a doctorate in philosophy from the University of Munich in 1935 and an M.D. in 1936, was born in Gunzberg, Bavaria, into an upper-class Bavarian family that owned a business selling farm equipment. He was educated in the gymnasia, rejected religion in favor of *völkisch* racial ideas, and displayed a disposition for military and nationalistic ideas. From 1931 to 1934 he was a member of the *Stahlhelm*, an extreme antisemitic organization, and joined the Nazi Party in 1937 and the SS in 1938. In 1934 he became a research fellow and staff member of the Institute of Hereditary Biology and Race Research, where he studied under Otmar von Verschuer, one of Germany's foremost geneticists and racial hygienists, and he specialized in the study of twins and racial pedigrees. Mengele became a favorite of Verschuer, who encouraged his career and secured his appointment to Auschwitz. Verschuer was also able to provide funds for Mengele's research at the death camp. Mengele repaid his benefactor by periodically sending him preserved body parts from Auschwitz.

In 1940 Mengele joined the *Waffen*-SS medical corps and served as a medical officer in France and Russia. He served with great distinction on the eastern front, receiving the Iron Cross, First and Second Class. He was appointed chief doctor at Auschwitz in 1943 and remained in that position until its evacuation in January 1945. Most Auschwitz survivors recall Mengele as a dapper and immaculately dressed officer who met the new arrivals, as they were herded from the boxcars, whistling tunes from Wagnerian operas. During the *Selektion* process, which he appeared to enjoy, Mengele would point his cane at each person and order him or her to the right or the left.

Mengele was especially active in the *Selektion* of the Hungarian Jews who arrived in Auschwitz in 1944. Because of his research interests, Mengele monitored the *Selektionen* with the objective of finding suitable victims for his experiments. In the course of these *Selektionen*, most Jews were sent to the gas chambers and the rest sent to forced labor. Jews and gypsies served as guinea pigs for his pseudoscientific experiments on infants, young twins, dwarfs, giants, hunchbacks, and other malformed people who piqued his interest. On the other hand, recent arrivals at Auschwitz were immediately sent to their deaths if they showed any sort of physical deformity that might aid him in his "scientific" work. In fact, there was a special dissection ward in Auschwitz where autopsies of murdered camp inmates were performed. Perhaps the most infamous of his experiments were those carried on in the notorious Block 10 on twins, where he hoped to find a method of producing a race of blue-eyed Aryans, thus fulfilling a primary objective of Nazi racial scientists. In order to ensure the validity of his test results, Mengele treated the twins to a more nourishing diet with the inadvertent consequence of allowing a certain number to survive. Other experiments included the excision of the genital organs of the prisoners and the injection of harmful fluids into the veins of the victims. Known as the "Angel of Death," Mengele often showed kindness to his victims before dispatching them to their deaths. Yet for the sake of his dream of breeding a higher form of human being, he was able to torture and murder with a good conscience. When Auschwitz was evacuated, he was transferred to Mauthausen, and when that camp was liberated on May 5, 1945, he escaped to Buenos Aires. Eventually he was reported to have drowned in Brazil in December 1978, although his death remained an issue of controversy for several years after.

Otto Öhlendorf (1907–1951) was head of *Amt* III (Security Service) of the Reich Main Security Office (RSHA), and *Einsatzgrüppe* D commander in the southern Ukraine in 1941–1942. Öhlendorf was born in the Hanover district, the son of a peasant. He went on to study law at the University of Leipzig and Gottingen, graduating in 1933. While still a student, he joined the Nazi Party in 1925 and the SS in 1926. In the early 1930s he was a lecturer at several economic institutions, including the Institute of World Economy at the University of Kiel. Öhlendorf was a specialist in the theories of National Socialism and Italian fascism. He joined the SD (Security Service) in 1936, and became chief of the SD Inland section in the RSHA in 1939. However, he considered his party activities as a sideline of his career. The intellectually minded Öhlendorf was more interested in economics and political theory. Heydrich resented subordinates with divided loyalties and viewed Öhlendorf as too independent. As a consequence, he was determined to teach Öhlendorf a lesson. Inasmuch as the "executive measures" that were to be taken in the Soviet Union were the kinds of responsibility that required complete and undivided attention, Heydrich assigned Öhlendorf to a command post in the *Einsatzgrüppen*.

When Himmler organized the *Einsatzgrüppen* for service in the Soviet Union, Öhlendorf was appointed commander of the D unit in June 1941. By June 1942, Öhlendorf's unit had moved along the Black Sea coast, through the Crimea and Ciscaucasia, killing more than 90,000 men, women, and children—mostly Jews. Unlike other group commanders, Öhlendorf ordered that his men shoot their victims at the same time in order to avoid direct personal responsibility for their actions, inasmuch as he feared that individual killings would have immense psychological repercussions for the executioners. At his trial at Nuremberg, he defended the mass shooting of Jews in places such as Nikolaiev, Kherson, Podalia, and the Crimea as historically necessary to realize the policy of *lebensraum* in the east. Asked whether Jewish children also had to be murdered, Öhlendorf replied that it was unavoidable "because the children were people who would grow up, and surely, being the children of parents who had been killed, they would constitute a danger no smaller than that of their parents." An unrepentant Öhlendorf stated that history would regard his killing units as no worse than those responsible for dropping the atomic bomb on Hiroshima.

For his service in the Soviet Union, Öhlendorf was awarded the Military Service Cross, Class 1, with swords. In November 1943, he was appointed deputy director general and chief of the foreign trade sections in the Reich Ministry of Economic Affairs, in addition to his SD position. A year later, he was promoted to the rank of SS lieutenant-general and figured prominently in Himmler's circle of advisers. In the closing days of the war, Öhlendorf advised Himmler to surrender to the Allies in order to vindicate the SS against the calumnies spread by its enemies. After the war, Öhlendorf was the chief defendant in the Nuremberg Military Tribunals' Case 9—the *Einsatzgrüppen* case. His judges described him as a Jekyll-and-Hyde character, some of whose acts were beyond belief. Sentenced to death in April 1948, he spent three and a half years in prison before being hanged, along with three other *Einsatzgrüppen* commanders, in Landsberg prison on June 8, 1951.

Pope Pius XII (1876–1958) Upon his death in 1939, Pope Pius XI was succeeded by Cardinal Eugenio Pacelli, who became Pope Pius XII. Pacelli had been the papal nuncio to Bavaria in 1917 and later served in Berlin. In 1930 he became cardinal secretary of state and negotiated the Concordat or Papal treaty with Hitler in 1933. His papacy encompassed the period of World War II and the Nazi murder of European Jewry. His record in regard to the latter has become a subject of controversy among historians of the Holocaust. Much of the criticism of Pius XII's tenure comes from his failure to condemn publicly the German extermination campaign against the Jews and his reluctance to voice moral outrage against the Nazi genocide. Rather, Pius XII engaged in diplomacy in an attempt to protect Catholic interests in Germany and in other countries where the church was under attack. In Slovakia, Hungary, and Romania, where the church had some leverage, the Vatican condemned antisemitic legislation, and in other parts of Europe, individual Catholic priests aided Jews when possible. In Slovakia, Romania, and Hungary, Pius XII condemned the deportation of Jews, and here these efforts contributed to saving a minority of the Jews. Less successful were the Vatican's efforts to secure entry visas for Jews to Catholic countries in Latin America.

Pope Pius XII appeared to believe in the efficacy of diplomacy, and in order to be an effective mediator, he refused to condemn the Nazis publicly. It has been argued that perhaps the Vatican failed to comprehend the enormity of the Final Solution. Yet there is evidence that the pope was made aware of the Nazi plan to exterminate the Jews and that the papacy was among the first bodies in the world to receive information about the massacre of the Jews.[5] Furthermore, the Vatican was the best informed of all neutrals since it had priests throughout Europe who both witnessed actions taken against Jews and, one can assume, heard confessions from many of the perpetrators who were Catholic. Despite this information, the Vatican took little action that might compromise its position. When Isaac Herzog, the chief rabbi of Palestine, approached the Vatican to intervene in Spain in order to protect refugees in danger of being returned to Germany, the Holy See failed to intervene. Similarly, the Vatican refused to endorse a plan that would have transferred about 6,000 Jewish children from Bulgaria to Palestine because of the papacy's reservations about Zionism. For the same reason, it also refused to support other Zionist plans to rescue Jews and find a haven for them in Palestine. In Vichy France, the government asked the Vatican if it would object to the promulgation of anti-Jewish laws, and the response was that although the church repudiated racism, it did not repudiate every measure against the Jews. In September 1942, the British government requested that the Vatican condemn the Nazi treatment of inhabitants of the occupied territories and of the persecution of the Jews. When it refused, it drew the following response from the British authorities: "A policy of silence in regard to such offenses against the conscience of the world must necessarily involve a renunciation of moral leadership and a consequent atrophy of the influence and authority of the Vatican."[6]

The failure of the pope to speak out on behalf of the Jews as well as other victims of Nazi oppression should be measured against the fact that where it was possible and did not place the Vatican in harm's way, the Catholic church did act. In many monasteries and churches in Italy, Jews were saved from deportation. The availability of church institutions to protect Jews probably could have resulted only from signals that such efforts would not be hindered by the Vatican. There is also evidence that the pope protested officially, if only privately, where he felt that he had some influence, as in Hungary where the pope himself cabled the regent, Miklos Horthy, asking him to reverse Hungarian policy concerning the Jews.

Despite the decimation of the Catholic clergy and the suppression of Catholic organizations in Poland, the Catholic church did organize a number of rescue attempts to save Jewish children. These examples aside, the record of the Vatican during the Holocaust was ambiguous. By not raising his voice publicly, Pius XII failed to exert the moral leadership that one had come to expect from the papacy. For this reason, his tenure as pope will remain controversial in the history of the Holocaust, if not in the overall record of World War II. Regardless of the motives for his silence, Pius XII's ambivalence in regard to the fate of the Jews and gypsies groups him, along with the Allies, with those who failed to place a high priority on the rescue of the victims of the Nazi genocidal war against the Jews and other targeted groups.

Oswald Pohl (1892–1951) was head of Germany's Economic-Administrative Main Office (WVHA), which had jurisdiction over all work projects for concentration camp inmates. Pohl was in charge of the economic side of the Nazi extermination program with responsibility for collecting the valuables seized from gassed Jewish inmates.

He was born in Duisberg, and after serving in World War I as a navy paymaster, he joined the Nazi Party in 1922, became an SA leader in 1926, and joined the SS in 1929, where he served in the administrative office of the SS main office. Pohl caught Himmler's attention because of his organizational ability, and in 1934 he was made chief administrative officer in the Reich Main Security Office (RSHA), which at the time was concerned with construction matters, including the construction of SS installations in concentration camps. In 1939 Pohl was promoted to the rank of ministerial director of the Ministry of the Interior, where he rapidly developed SS economic enterprises as a result of his connections with specialists from German industry. By 1940 Pohl was in charge of all SS concerns in the concentration camps and the labor camps, where he set up a chain of SS enterprises. All of his responsibilities were combined in 1942 into the WVHA, and Pohl's leadership made him one of the most powerful members in the SS hierarchy.

One of Himmler's objectives during the implementation of the Final Solution was to make the SS financially independent. Under Pohl's direction, the administration of the killing centers acquired an economic accent as the personal possessions of the murdered Jews—such as hair, clothing, gold tooth fillings, wedding rings, and other jewelry—were sent back to Germany to be turned into cash or otherwise used commercially. The gold loot was melted down and sent in the form of ingots to a special SS account in the Reichsbank. The transfer of the property to the German bank was handled by Pohl's office, and according to his testimony, the bank received seventy-six or seventy-seven truckloads of valuables. Other personal possessions, such as watches and fountain pens, were distributed by the thousands to the SS and elite army units or were given to wounded soldiers as Christmas gifts. On occasion, clothing taken from the murdered Jews was turned over to the state's Winter Aid Project (funds used to help the needy during the winter season). Pohl justified his actions by referring to the plundered property as "goods that derived from theft, the receipt of stolen goods, and concealed property," thus implying that it had all been taken from the Jews by right, since they had acquired it by underhanded or illegal means. By the end of 1942, Pohl had emerged as the dominant figure in the German concentration camp system by virtue of annexing some camps outright and controlling others by installing officials responsible to the WVHA.

At the end of the war, Pohl went into hiding, disguised as a farmhand. He was arrested in May 1946 and at his trial admitted that the existence of the death camps had been no secret in Germany. He declared that "in the case of textile and valuables, everyone down to the lowest clerk knew what went on in the concentration camps."[7] Pohl was sentenced to death by an American military tribunal on November 3, 1947, and after spending three and a half years in the Landsburg prison, he was hanged on June 8, 1951.

Emanuel Ringelblum (1900–1944) was a historian and the founder of *Oneg Shabbat* ("Sabbath delight"), a secret archive in the Warsaw ghetto that documented the unfolding events that transpired in the ghetto. Ringelblum was born in Buczacz, eastern Galicia, into a middle-class merchant family. In 1927 he received his doctorate from the University of Warsaw for his thesis on the history of the Jews of Warsaw in the Middle Ages. Ringelblum was an outstanding scholar who had already published 126 scholarly articles on the eve of the German invasion of Poland. During the German occupation of Poland, Ringelblum was involved in many areas of activity in the Warsaw ghetto, which included his participation in the underground, with emphasis on its cultural sector, the establishment of the *Oneg Shabbat* Archive, and maintaining a daily log of Jewish life in Warsaw from the beginning of the German occupation of Poland until his arrest on March 7, 1944.

Ringelblum was also active in running a network of soup kitchens for the ever-increasing impoverished ghetto population, and he organized and promoted committees made up of volunteers with no previous public activity experience. Ringelblum made the soup kitchens, in which tens of thousands of soup portions were dispensed daily, into clubs under the auspices of the underground.

His outstanding achievement was the secret *Oneg Shabbat* Archive, which he started in the first months of the war. Ringelblum and his colleagues collected testimony and reports from Jews who arrived in the ghetto from other parts of German-occupied Europe. Ringelblum was aware of the unprecedented nature of the events surrounding him, and he believed that "it was important that future historians have available to them accurate records of the events taking place."[8] During the final weeks of the ghetto's existence, Ringelblum and his colleagues collected every available document and piece of evidence that related to the deportations to the death camps and passed them on to the Polish underground, which transmitted the information to London. Because of Ringelblum's work, the Allies first learned about the Chelmno extermination camp and came into possession of a detailed report on the deportation of 300,000 Jews from Warsaw. The *Oneg Shabbat* Archive, also known as the Ringelblum Archive, is the most extensive documented source on Jews under the Nazi regime. Ringelblum's writings have been published in Yiddish, Polish, English (*Notes from the Warsaw Ghetto,* 1958), Italian, French, German, and Japanese.

Ringelblum became an advocate of armed resistance, and the archive was placed under the aegis of the Jewish Fighting Organization (ZOB). In March 1943, he accepted an invitation from his Polish colleagues and left the ghetto together with his family, and went into hiding among the Poles. On the eve of the Warsaw ghetto revolt, he returned the moment of the uprising. We do not know what happened to him during the fighting, but in

July 1943, he was found in the Trawniki labor camp. Friends helped him to escape and took him to Warsaw, where he and his family went into hiding. On March 7, 1944, the hideaway was discovered, and he was taken to Warsaw's Pawiak prison, where he and his family were shot to death.

Franz Stangl (1908–1971) was commandant of both the Sobibor (1942) and Treblinka (1942–1943) extermination camps in occupied Poland. Stangl was born in Altmunster, Austria, the son of a nightwatchman who had been a soldier in the Hapsburg Dragoons and who brutalized him throughout his childhood. After training as a master weaver, Stangl joined the Austrian police in 1931. His talent for organization attracted the attention of his superiors, who promoted him to the position of criminal investigating officer. In 1936 he joined the then illegal Nazi Party. In November 1940, Stangl became police superintendent of the Euthanasia Institute at the Hartheim castle near Linz, where the mentally and physically disabled were transferred for extermination. After being sent to Lublin to serve under Lieutenant-General Odilo Globocnik in March 1942, Stangl became commandant of Sobibor, which became operational in May 1942.

During his brief stay at Sobibor, which lasted until September, Stangl supervised the liquidation of 100,000 Jews. But it was at Treblinka that Stangl displayed his talent for organization. He was an efficient and dedicated organizer of mass murder. In less than a year there, he supervised the mass killing of at least 900,000 Jews. His work at Treblinka caught the attention of his superiors in Berlin, who commended him as the "best camp commander in Poland." Stangl was an unforgettable presence at Treblinka. He would greet the new arrivals dressed in white riding clothes and always spoke politely and kindly to them. His friendly demeanor was a ruse. Stangl regarded his victims as cargo to be dispatched. In an interview with the journalist Gitta Sereny near the end of his life, he related that he viewed the Jews as a "huge mass . . . they were naked, packed together, running, being driven by whips." Yet Stangl claimed that his dedication to the extermination process had nothing to do with ideology or his hatred of Jews: "They were weak; they allowed everything to happen, to be done to them. They were people with whom there was no common ground, no communication—that is how contempt is born. I could never understand how they just gave in as they did."[9]

After the revolt in Treblinka on August 2, 1943, Stangl and most of his staff were transferred to Trieste, where, aside from a brief stay at the San Sabba extermination camp, he was employed in organizing antipartisan measures against Yugoslav partisans for Odilo Globocnik. In 1945 Stangl was captured by the U.S. Army and interned as a member of the SS, his earlier record in the extermination camps not being known at the time. In the summer of 1947, he was handed over to the Austrians and transferred to an open civilian prison in Linz in connection with his involvement in the euthanasia program at the Hartheim castle. In May 1948, about to be charged, he escaped and made his way to Rome.

With assistance from Bishop Alois Hudal, Stangl obtained a Red Cross pass, money, and a job as an engineer in Damascus, Syria. In 1951, Stangl and his family moved on to Brazil, where Stangl worked at the Volkswagen factory. In 1967 his presence in Brazil was uncovered by Nazi hunter Simon Wiesenthal, and he was arrested and extradited to West Germany. He was tried for co-responsibility in the murder of 999,000 Jews at Treblinka and sentenced to life imprisonment on October 22, 1970. He died in prison on June 28, 1971.

Christian Wirth (1885–1944) was born in Oberbalzheim, Wurttemberg. During World War I, he earned the Imperial Military Cross, one of Imperial Germany's highest decorations, for bravery on the western front. He lived a life of relative obscurity during the Weimar years and reemerged as a police officer in the early 1930s. Wirth was known for his brutal interrogations, which ultimately resulted in his arraignment before the Wurttemberg court. Nevertheless, by 1939 Wirth had attained the rank of *Kriminalkommissar* in the Stuttgart criminal police. In the same year Wirth was sent to Grafeneckpsychiatric clinic for "euthanasia duties." Wirth was next transferred to Brandenburg-an-der-Havel, a former prison that had become a euthanasia center, where he became its administrative head. At the end of 1939, Wirth carried out the first known gassing experiments on Germans certified as incurably insane. It was at the Brandenburg center that Wirth perfected the method of disguising the gas chambers as showerrooms.

Wirth's reputation in supervising the gassing of incurables in the euthanasia program at Brandenburg caught the attention of his SS superiors. In 1941 he was sent to eastern Europe on a confidential mission, which subsequently led to his assignment in Lublin, where he set up a new euthanasia center, the first outside Germany. By the end of 1941, he was assigned the task of initiating the extermination of Jews at Chelmno. During the next eighteen months, in coordination with Odilo Globocnik, Wirth supervised the murder of more than 1.7 million Jews in the *Aktion Reinhard* death camps. Brutal and sadistic, Wirth was referred to as the "savage Christian" and boasted of the system of terror he brought to the extermination camps. Wirth prided himself on the efficiency of the method of gassing, which he borrowed from his experiences at Brandenburg. Wirth also claimed to have introduced the use of Jewish *Sonderkommandos*, or units of Jewish prisoners who were assigned to the gas chambers and crematoriums for the purpose of burying their own people, but his primary contribution to the extermination process was the development of new gassing techniques at Belzec, which were viewed as an improvement over those at Chelmno. With the addition of gas chambers at Majdanek in the autumn of 1942, Wirth became the most notorious of the Nazi exterminators.

In May 1942, under Wirth's direction, the Sobibor extermination camp began operations, and at the end of eighteen months, more than 250,000 Jews had been gassed. During the same month, the Treblinka extermination camp was constructed and utilized techniques for gassing already operational at Sobibor and Belzec. This was Wirth's largest camp and was equipped with thirty gas chambers, which ultimately led to the annihilation of about 850,000 Jews. Following the liquidation of the Belzec camp in the autumn of 1943, Wirth was promoted to SS-Sturmbannführer and sent to Trieste, where his task was to expedite the deportation of Jews. He was killed by Yugoslav partisans while on a journey to Fiume on May 26, 1944. There is a theory, however, that he was the victim of a Jewish partisan squad organized to hunt down Nazi mass murderers.

Raoul Wallenberg (1912–?), a Swedish diplomat, saved the lives of tens of thousands of Jews in Budapest on the eve of the Nazi deportations to Auschwitz. Wallenberg was born into a wealthy Swedish family. His relatives included diplomats, military officers, and bankers. Born after his father's death, who was an officer in the Swedish navy, Wallenberg grew up in the home of his stepfather, Frederick von Dardell, and was strongly influenced by his grandfather, Gustav Wallenberg, a professional diplomat. Wallenberg studied architecture in the United States at the University of Michigan, but then took up banking and international trade. Business brought him to Haifa in 1936, where he made many contacts with the leaders of the Jewish Agency. During World War II, he was recruited by the Swedish Foreign Ministery upon the recommendation of the World Jewish Congress and the American War Refugee Board, and he was sent to Budapest in July 1944, instructed to help protect the 200,000 Jews residing in the city. At the time of his arrival, approximately 437,000 Hungarian

Jews had already been deported to Auschwitz. His arrival also coincided with the cessation of the deportations as a result of international pressure, including the intervention of King Gustav V of Sweden. Prior to Wallenberg's arrival, the Swedish embassy had discussed the possibility of granting provisional Swedish passports to Hungarian Jews with connections with Swedish citizens, and several hundred of these "protective passports" had been issued. With the coup of October 15, which brought the Arrow Cross Party, a Hungarian fascist party, to power, the relative quiet of the previous months came to an end. The Jews of Budapest now faced the prospect of Eichmann's resuming the deportations as well as attacks from the Arrow Cross Party. Wallenberg, the legation attaché, sprang into action. Over the course of three months, he issued thousands of protective passports, which the Hungarian and German authorities reluctantly honored. Wallenberg's courage and heroism was displayed in his response to the death marches of thousands of Jews Eichmann had organized. As the Jews were being force marched to the Austrian border, Wallenberg followed the convoy and secured the release of those with protective passports. He was even able to board a train and secure the release of Jews who were being sent to Auschwitz.

Wallenberg countered the murderous threat posed by the Arrow Cross Party by setting up special hostels, which were able to accommodate about 15,000 Jews. Working with other legations that issued their own protective passports, Wallenberg established thirty-one protected houses. Together they formed the "international ghetto," a separate entity from Budapest's main ghetto. He also established a number of centers for children, which he placed under the protection of the Red Cross and thereby saved about 8,000 Jewish children. When the Soviets occupied Budapest, Wallenberg went to their headquarters and attempted to negotiate the safety of the city's Jews. The Soviets, however, were suspicious of the Swedish mission and accused its staff of spying for the Germans. On January 17, 1945, Wallenberg was taken away by an armed Soviet guard and never heard of again. In 1981 the United States made Raoul Wallenberg an honorary citizen, and together with his family, it continues to press the Russian government for information regarding his fate.

Dieter Wisliceny (1911–1948), as a member of Eichmann's bureau (1V-B4), was responsible for the mass deportations of Jews from Slovakia, Greece, and Hungary. Wisliceny was born in Regularken, the son of a landowner. As a youth, he displayed an interest in religion but failed as a theology student. He worked briefly as a clerk in a construction firm and was unemployed when he joined the Nazi Party in 1931. He entered both the SS and the SD in 1934. At one time he was Eichmann's superior in the SS but became his deputy during World War II. In 1940 he acted as the adviser on Jewish affairs to the Slovak government, but because of his opportunism and his concern for money, he soon acquired a reputation in Slovakia for accepting bribes.

During the deportations from Slovakia in the summer of 1942, Wisliceny was bribed by the Bratislava-based Jewish Relief Committee to delay the deportation of Slovak Jews. He also entered into negotiations in the ill-fated Europa Plan, initiated by Rabbi Michael Dov Weissmandel, to save the remaining Jews in Europe for a ransom of $2 million to $3 million, to be paid by Jewish organizations abroad. Wisliceny accepted a bribe of approximately $50,000 as a first installment, although there was never an intention to halt the deportations.

In 1943 and 1944, Wisliceny headed the Special Commando for Jewish Affairs in Salonika, where he introduced the definition of a Jew in accordance with the Nuremberg Laws. He ordered the wearing of the yellow badges and subsequently issued a directive that ordered Jewish doctors and lawyers to mount stars on their offices and required Jewish tenants to identify their apartments. Wisliceny's directives were in preparation for the deportations, inasmuch as his assignment in Greece was to see to it that all Jews were deported as quickly as possible. To that end, he insisted on the cooperation of the Jewish leadership, which circulated his directives throughout the community. Wisliceny's mission in Salonika was ultimately a success inasmuch as he was instrumental in the annihilation of Greek Jewry.

In March 1944, he joined Eichmann in Hungary to organize the deportation of Hungarian Jewry. Wisliceny, who preferred to have himself addressed as "Baron" by Hungarian Jews, was a liaison in the "blood-for-goods" negotiations with Joel Brand, in which Eichmann offered to save the lives of 1 million Jews in exchange for goods, including 10,000 trucks.

After the war, Wisliceny served as a witness at the Nuremberg Trial and gave vivid descriptions of the implementation of the Final Solution. Wisliceny is the source of the alleged comment made by Eichmann that "he would 'leap into his grave laughing,' because the feeling that he had five million people on his conscience was to him 'a source of extraordinary satisfaction.'" He was extradited to Czechoslovakia, and while awaiting his trial in the Bratislava, he wrote several important affidavits on the Final Solution, including his role in the Europa Plan, the bargaining over Jewish lives in Hungary, and Eichmann's role in the murder of European Jewry. The latter affidavit was used at the Eichmann trial in Jerusalem in 1961. Condemned to death, Wisliceny was executed in February 1948 for complicity in mass murder.

NOTES

1. Hannah Arendt, *Eichmann in Jerusalem* (New York: Viking, 1963).

2. Raul Hilberg, "Not Much Will," *The Destruction of European Jews* (Chicago: Quadrangle Books, 1961), p. 266.

3. Richard Breitman, *The Architect of Genocide* (New York: Knopf, 1991).

4. Robert Wistrich, *Who's Who in Nazi Germany* (New York: Bonanza Books, 1982), p. 154.

5. John S. Conway, "Christian Churches," in Israel Gutman, ed., *Encyclopedia of the Holocaust* (New York: Macmillan, 1990), 1:292, 293.

6. Sergio Minerbi, "Pius XII," in Gutman, ed., *Encyclopedia of the Holocaust*, 3: 1136–1137.

7. Wistrich, *Who's Who in Nazi Germany*, p. 235.

8. Israel Gutman, "Ringelblum, Emanuel," in Israel Gutman, ed., *The Encyclopedia of the Holocaust* (New York: Macmillan, 1990), 3:1284.

9. Wistrich, *Who's Who in Nazi Germany*, p. 296.

Primary Documents of the Holocaust

THE NUREMBERG LAWS (SEPTEMBER 15, 1935): THE REICH CITIZENSHIP LAW

Following the Nazi seizure of power in 1933, Hitler moved in the direction of curbing endemic violence against the Jews. This turn may have resulted from the fear that continued violence and negative world reaction might jeopardize Germany hosting the Olympic games, which were scheduled to be held in Berlin in 1936. In a series of measures that began in 1933, the Nazis incrementally and legally eroded the position of the Jews in Germany. Despite the discriminatory legislation, Jews still retained their citizenship, except for those who were naturalized after September 1918. But in the spring and summer of 1935 anti-Jewish rioting erupted in Germany. The Nuremberg Laws were passed in response to the rioting and the need to clarify the status of the Jews in Germany. The matter of defining the Jews had also become urgent because the Nazi Party lacked a consensus on antisemitic policy. The constitutional laws that were promulgated at the Nazi Party Congress at Nuremberg in September 1935 rescinded the emancipation provisions that the Jews had enjoyed since the unification of Germany in 1871. The Reich Citizenship Law was subsequently complemented by thirteen additional ordinances issued from November 1935 to July 1943 that effectively excluded Jews from Germany.

Document 1
THE NUREMBERG LAWS (SEPTEMBER 15, 1935)
THE REICH CITIZENSHIP LAW

. . . Paragraph 2. (1) A Reich citizen [*Reichsbuerger*] is only the state member [*Staatsangehoeriger*] who is of German or cognate blood, and who shows through his conduct that he is both desirous and fit to serve in faith the German people and Reich. . . . (3) The Reich citizen is the only holder of full political rights in accordance with the provisions of the laws.

NOTE

In effect, the Jews were by virtue of this law and its various amendments deprived of citizenship and all civil and political rights.

Source: Bernard Dov Weinryb, *Jewish Emancipation Under Attack* (New York: American Jewish Committee, 1942), p. 46. Reprinted by permission of the American Jewish Committee.

THE NUREMBERG LAWS (SEPTEMBER 15, 1935): LAW FOR THE PROTECTION OF GERMAN BLOOD AND HONOR

Also enacted by the Nazi Party Congress at Nuremberg in September 1935, the Law for the Protection of German Blood and Honor prohibited marriages and extramarital intercourse between Jews and Germans, the employment of German maids under the age of forty-five in Jewish households, and the raising by the Jews of the German flag. The impetus for the legislation came from the Reich Medical Association, which urged a law that would prevent *Rassenschande* ("race defilement"), therefore protecting German blood. The Nazis attempted to export the provisions of the Nuremberg Laws through-out German-occupied Europe, with mixed success.

Document 2
THE NUREMBERG LAWS (SEPTEMBER 15, 1935)
LAW FOR THE PROTECTION OF GERMAN BLOOD AND HONOR

Imbued with the conviction that the purity of the German blood is the prerequisite for the future existence of the German People, and animated with the unbending will to ensure the existence of the German nation for all the future, the Reichstag has unanimously adopted the following law, which is hereby proclaimed.

Paragraph 1. (1) Marriages between Jews and state members [*Staatsangho-erige*] of German or cognate blood are forbidden. Marriages concluded despite this law are invalid, even if they are concluded abroad in order to circumvent this law. (2) Only the State Attorney may initiate the annulment suit.

Paragraph 2. Extramarital relations between Jews and state members of German or cognate blood are prohibited.

Paragraph 3. Jews must not engage female domestic help in their households among state members of German or cognate blood, who are under forty-five years [of age].

Paragraph 4. (1) The display of the Reich and national flag and the showing of the national colors by Jews is prohibited. (2) However, the display of the Jewish colors is permitted to them. The exercise of this right is placed under the protection of the state.

Paragraph 5. (1) Whosoever acts in violation of this prohibition of Paragraph 1, will be punished with penal servitude. (2) Whosoever acts in violation of Paragraph 2, will be punished with either imprisonment or penal servitude. (3) Whosoever acts in violations of Paragraph 3 or Paragraph 4, will be punished by imprisonment up to one year, with a fine or with either of these penalties. . . .

Paragraph 7. This law goes into effect on the day following promulgation, except for Paragraph 3 which shall go into force on January 1, 1936.

Source: Bernard Dov Weinryb, *Jewish Emancipation Under Attack* (New York: American Jewish Committee, 1942), p. 45. Reprinted by permission of the American Jewish Committee.

RIOTS OF *KRISTALLNACHT*: HEYDRICH'S INSTRUCTIONS, NOVEMBER 10, 1938

Reinhold Heydrich, as head of the SD (the security service), was in charge of all police action that occurred during *Kristallnacht* (Night of the Broken Glass). The pogrom was precipitated by the assassination of the third secretary of the German embassy in Paris, Ernst vom Rath, by a seventeen-year-old Jewish youth, Herschel Grynzpan, in revenge for Germany's deportation of his parents who were left stranded in a no-man's-land near the German-Polish border. The document is irrefu- table evidence that the pogrom was not a popular demonstration against the Jews in retaliation for the assassination but a carefully orchestrated plan by the SD and SS in cooperation with other police forces in Germany and Austria. The thoroughness of the instructions would indicate that the government was waiting for an excuse to move against the Jewish community and that the assassination presented the opportunity to use violence against the Jews in order to force them to leave the country.

Document 3
RIOTS OF *KRISTALLNACHT*
HEYDRICH'S INSTRUCTIONS, NOVEMBER 10, 1938

Secret
Copy of Most Urgent telegram from Munich, of November 10, 1938, 1:20 A.M.

To:
All Headquarters and Stations of the State Police
All Districts and Sub-districts of the SD

Urgent! For immediate attention of Chief or his deputy!

Re: *Measures against Jews tonight* following the attempt on the life of Secretary of the Legation vom Rath in Paris, demonstrations against the Jews are to be expected in all parts of the Reich in the course of the coming night, November 9/10, 1938. The instructions below are to be applied in dealing with these events:

1. The Chiefs of the State Police, or their deputies, must immediately upon receipt of this telegram contact, by telephone, the political leaders in their areas—*Gauleiter* or *Kreisleiter*—who have jurisdiction in their districts and arrange a joint meeting with the inspector or commander of the Order Police to discuss the arrangements for the demonstrations. At these discussions the political leaders will be informed that the German Police has received instructions, detailed below, from the *Reichsführer* SS and the Chief of the German Police, with which the political leadership is requested to coordinate its own measures:

   a) Only such measures are to be taken as do not endanger German lives or property (i.e., synagogues are to be burned down only where there is no danger of fire in neighboring buildings).

   b) Places of business and apartments belonging to Jews may be destroyed but not looted. The police are instructed to supervise the observance of this order and to arrest looters.

   c) In commercial streets particular care is to be taken that non-Jewish businesses are completely protected against damage.

   d) Foreign citizens—even if they are Jews—are not to be molested.

2. On the assumption that the guidelines detailed under para. 1 are observed, the demonstrations are not to be prevented by the Police, which is only to supervise the observance of the guidelines.

3. On receipt of this telegram Police will seize all archives to be found in all synagogues and offices of the Jewish communities so as to prevent their destruction during the demonstrations. This refers only to material of historical value, not to contemporary tax records, etc. The archives are to be handed over to the locally responsible officers of the SD.

4. The control of the measures of the Security Police concerning the demonstrations against the Jews is vested in the organs of the State Police, unless inspectors of the Security Police have given their own instructions. Officials of the Criminal Police, members of the SD, of the Reserves and the SS in general may be used to carry out the measures taken by the Security Police.

5. As soon as the course of events during the night permits the release of the officials required, as many Jews in all districts—especially the rich—as can be accommodated in existing prisons are to be arrested. For the time being only healthy male Jews, who are not too old, are to be detained. After the detentions have been carried out the appropriate concentration camps are to be contacted immediately for the prompt accommodation of the Jews in the camps. Special care is to be taken that the Jews arrested in accordance with these instructions are not ill-treated. . . .

signed Heydrich
SS *Gruppenführer*

Source: *Documents on the Holocaust, Selected Sources on the Destruction of the Jews of Germany and Austria, Poland, and the Soviet Union.* Edited by Yitzhak Arad, Yisrael Gutman, and Abraham Margaliot. Jerusalem, Yad Vashem, 1981, pp. 102–104. Reprinted by permission of Yad Vashem.

DECREE REGARDING ATONEMENT FINE OF JEWISH STATE SUBJECTS, NOVEMBER 12, 1938

On November 9–10, 1938, a pogrom took place throughout Germany and Austria, precipitated by the assassination of the third secretary of the German embassy in Paris, Ernst vom Rath, by a seventeen-year-old Jewish youth, Herschel Grynzpan, in revenge for Germany's deporta- tion of his parents, who were left stranded in a no-man's-land near the German-Polish border. In retaliation for the assassination, Joseph Goebbels organized a riot against the Jews that resulted in the looting and burning of Jewish property and the destruction of 267 synagogues. This frenzy, known as *Kristallnacht* (Crystal Night or Night of the

Broken Glass), witnessed the murder of thirty-six Jews in addition to assaults and the arrest of 30,000 Jews, who were thrown into concen-tration camps. Both Himmler and Goering were caught by surprise by Goebbels's initiative, and when the damage to Jewish property was assessed, they were outraged to learn that the figure German insur-ance companies were obliged to pay the Jewish owners came to 25 million reichsmarks. This sum would have bankrupted the insurance companies, and it was under these circumstances that Goering con-vened Nazi officials to determine punitive damages against the Jewish community. The decree that followed fined the Jewish community 1 billion reichsmarks for the assasination of vom Rath, forced Jewish store owners to pay for the repair of their property, and nullified their claims against the insurance companies.

Document 4
H. W. GOERING
DECREE REGARDING ATONEMENT FINE OF JEWISH STATE SUBJECTS, NOVEMBER 12, 1938

The hostile attitude of Jewry toward the German nation and Reich, an attitude which does not even shrink from cowardly murder, demands determined resistance and severe punishment.

On the basis of the Decree of October 18, 1936 for the Execution of the Four Year Plan, I therefore order the following:

Paragraph 1. The payment of an atonement of one billion Reichsmarks to the German Reich is imposed on a all Jewish subjects of the State.

Paragraph 2. The Reich Minister of Finance in cooperation with the competent Reich ministers shall issue the regulations for the execution of this decree.

Source: Bernard Dov Weinryb, *Jewish Emancipation under Attack* (New York: American Jewish Committee, 1942), p. 53. Reprinted by permission of the American Jewish Committee.

REGULATION FOR THE ELIMINATION OF THE JEWS FROM THE ECONOMIC LIFE OF GERMANY, NOVEMBER 12, 1938

Following *Kristallnacht*, the German government took the opportunity to drive Jews from all aspects of the German economy. Goering, as head of the German Four Year Plan instituted in 1936, was responsible for making the German economy fit for war and self-sufficient for the purpose of allowing Germany to withstand a blockade in time of war. The effort to increase self-sufficiency had an effect on the *Reich's* antisemitic policy inasmuch as Hitler wanted the whole of Jewry liable for all damage allegedly inflicted by individual Jews upon the German economy. The 1 billion reichsmark fine on the Jewish community in the aftermath of *Kristallnacht* was the first step in that direction. The November 12 regulation served to prevent needed capital from falling into the hands of the Jews and to discourage them from thinking they had a future in Germany.

Document 5
REGULATION FOR THE ELIMINATION OF THE JEWS FROM THE ECONOMIC LIFE OF GERMANY, NOVEMBER 12, 1938

On the basis of the regulation for the implementation of the Four Year Plan of October 18, 1936 (*Reichsgestzblzatt*, I, p. 887), the following is decreed:

1

1) From January 1, 1939, Jews (5 of the First Regulation to the Reich Citizenship Law of November 14, 1935, *Reichsgestzblzatt*, I, p. 1333) are forbidden to operate retail stores, mail-order houses, or sales agencies, or to carry on a trade [craft] independently.

2) They are further forbidden, from the same day on, to offer for sale goods or services, to advertise these, or to accept orders at markets for all sorts, fairs or exhibitions.

3) Jewish trade enterprises (Third Regulation to the Reich Citizenship Law of June 14, 1938—*Reichsgestzblzatt*, I, p. 627) which violate this decree will be closed by police.

2

1) From January 1, 1939, a Jew can no longer be the head of an enterprise within the meaning of the Law of January 20, 1934, for the Regulation of National Work (*Reichsgestzblzatt*, I, p. 45).

2) Where a Jew is employed in an executive position in a commercial enterprise he may be given notice to leave in six weeks. At the expiration of the term of the notice all claims of the employee based on his contract, especially those concerning pension and compensation rights, become invalid.

3

1) A Jew cannot be a member of a cooperative.

2) The membership of Jews in cooperative expires on December 31, 1938. No special notice is required.

4

The Reich Minister of Economy, in coordination with the Ministers concerned, is empowered to publish regulations for the implementation of this decree. He may permit exceptions under the Law if these are required as the result of the transfer of a Jewish enterprise to non-Jewish ownership, for the liquidation of a Jewish enterprise or, in special cases, to ensure essential supplies.

Berlin, November 12, 1938

Plenipotentiary for the Four Year Plan
Göring
Field Marshal General

Source: *Documents on the Holocaust, Selected Sources on the Destruction of the Jews of Germany and Austria, Poland, and the Soviet Union.* Edited by Yitzhak Arad, Yisrael Gutman, and Abraham Margaliot. Jerusalem: Yad Vashem, 1981, pp. 115–116. Reprinted by permission of Yad Vashem.

GHETTO DECREED FOR BERLIN, DECEMBER 5, 1938

Following the events of *Kristallnacht*, the German government issued decrees that made life almost unbearable for Jews. Behind these measures was the objective to force Jews to leave Germany; if they remained, they would live in a restricted environment. As of December 3, 1938, Jews were no longer free to move about as they liked. Under the *Judenbann* ("ban on Jews"), they were forbidden to enter government buildings and use public bathhouses and swimming pools. On December 5, 1938, Jews were evacuated from residences in the prestigious sections of Berlin on the pretext that plans were being made to rebuild the city. This document indicates how circumscribed life for German Jews had become. The ghetto decree was followed by the requirement that Jews register with the Jewish community housing advisory office, which was given wide authority regarding the housing of Berlin's Jews. When Berlin's Jewish ghetto was being readied for liquidation, the data accumulated by that office were a major source for drawing up the lists of Jews to be deported to the death camps.

Document 6
GHETTO DECREED FOR BERLIN, DECEMBER 5, 1938

On the basis of the Police Decree Regarding the Appearance of the Jews in Public of November 28, 1938, the following is decreed for the police district of Berlin.

Paragraph 1. Streets, squares, parks, and buildings, from which the Jews are to be banned, are to be closed to Jewish subjects of the State and stateless Jews, both pedestrians and drivers.

Paragraph 2. Jewish subjects of the State and stateless Jews who at the time when this decree goes into effect still live within a district banned to the Jews, must have a local police permit for crossing the banned area.

By July 1, 1939, permits for Jews living within the banned area will no longer be issued.

Paragraph 3. Jewish subjects of the State and stateless Jews who are summoned by an office within the banned area, must obtain a local police permit for twelve hours.

Paragraph 4. The ban of Jews in Berlin comprises the following districts: (1) All theatres, cinemas, cabarets, public concert and lecture halls, museums, amusement places, the halls of the Fair, including the Fair grounds and broadcasting station on the Messedamm, the Deutschlandhalle and the Sport Palace, the Reich Sport Field, all athletic fields including ice skating rinks; (2) All public and private bathing places. . . .

Source: Bernard Dov Weinryb, *Jewish Emancipation under Attack* (New York: American Jewish Committee, 1942), p. 56. Reprinted by permission of the American Jewish Committee.

CALL TO RESISTANCE BY THE JEWISH FIGHTING ORGANIZATION IN THE WARSAW GHETTO, JANUARY 1943

In July 1942 as the Germans prepared to round up Jews from the Warsaw ghetto for deportation to the death camps, the various ghetto underground organizations merged into the Jewish Fighting Organization (ZOB) under the command of Mordecai Anielewicz. The first wave of deportations resulted in 300,000 Jews being sent to Treblinka. As the Germans launched the second wave of deportations on January 18, 1943, the ZOB responded and infiltrated the column that was on its way to the railway depot that would board Jews for Treblinka. The ZOB stepped out of the column and engaged the Germans in hand-to-hand fighting. The column of Jews dispersed, and news of the fight

quickly spread throughout the ghetto. Although the Germans contin -
ued to round up Jews for deportation, after the events of January 18,
few Jews responded to the German order to report. The Germans
temporarily halted the *Aktion* after a few days, and this was regarded
by the Jews as a German defeat. The call for resistance by the ZOB is
evidence that when the opportunity presented itself, Jews fought back
against the German oppressors.

Document 7
CALL TO RESISTANCE BY THE JEWISH FIGHTING ORGANIZATION IN THE WARSAW GHETTO, JANUARY 1943

To the Jewish Masses in the Ghetto

On January 22, 1943, six months will have passed since the deportations
from Warsaw began. We all remember well the days of terror during which
300,000 of our brothers and sisters were cruelly put to death in the death
camp of Treblinka. Six months have passed of life in constant fear of death,
not knowing what the next day may bring. We have received information
from all sides about the destruction of the Jews in the Government-General,
in Germany, in the occupied territories. When we listen to this bitter news
we wait for our own hour to come, every day and every moment. Today we
must understand that the Nazi murderers have let us live only because they
want to make use of our capacity to work to our last drop of blood and sweat,
to our last breath. We are slaves. And when the slaves are no longer
profitable, they are killed. Everyone among us must understand that, and
everyone among us must remember it always.

During the past few weeks certain people have spread stories about letters
that were said to have been received from Jews deported from Warsaw, who
were said to be in labor camps near Minsk or Bobruisk. *Jews in your masses,
do not believe these tales. They are spread by Jews who are working for the
Gestapo.* The blood-stained murderers have a particular aim in doing this:
to reassure the Jewish population in order that later the next deportation can
be carried out without difficulty, with a minimum of force and without
losses to the Germans. They want the Jews not to prepare hiding-places and
not to resist. Jews, do not repeat these lying tales.

Do not help the [Nazi] agents. The Gestapo's dastardly people will get their
just deserts. *Jews in your masses,* the hour is near. You must be prepared to
resist, not to give yourselves up like sheep to slaughter. *Not even one Jew must
go to the train. People who cannot resist actively must offer passive resistance,*

that is, by hiding. We have now received information from Lvov that the Jewish Police there itself carried out the deportation of 3,000 Jews. Such things will not happen again in Warsaw. The killing of Lejkin proves it. Now our slogan must be: *Let everyone be ready to die like a man!*

Source: *Documents on the Holocaust, Selected Sources on the Destruction of the Jews of Germany and Austria, Poland, and the Soviet Union.* Edited by Yitzhak Arad, Yisrael Gutman, and Abraham Margaliot. Jerusalem: Yad Vashem, 1981, pp. 301–302. Reprinted by permission of Yad Vashem.

BERMUDA CONFERENCE JOINT COMMUNIQUÉ

The Bermuda Conference was convened by the United States and Great Britain on April 19, 1943, for the purpose of finding a solution to the wartime refugee crisis. The impetus for the conference came from Great Britain, which sought to defuse public protest as revelations concerning the Nazi liquidation of the Jews became general knowledge. Little came out of the conference except to extend the mandate of the Inter-Governmental Committee on Refugees, which had been created at the Evian Conference in 1938 to organize emigration and settlement of refugees from Nazi persecution. The failure of the conference even to mention Palestine as a possible sanctuary for the Jewish victims attests to the indifference of both Great Britain and the United States to solving the ongoing tragedy that had befallen the Jews of Europe. Despite an aroused public in both countries, the governments were willing to go to great lengths to avoid doing what needed to be done. The failure of the Bermuda Conference reveals the atmosphere and lack of intentions surrounding the rescue of the Jews.

Document 8
BERMUDA CONFERENCE JOINT COMMUNIQUÉ

The United States and United Kingdom delegates examined the refugee problem in all its aspects including the position of those potential refugees who are still in the grip of the Axis powers without any immediate prospect of escape. Nothing was excluded from their analysis and everything that held out any possibility, however remote, of a solution of the problem was carefully discussed. From the outset it was realized that any recommendation that the delegates could make to their governments must pass two tests: Would any recommendation submitted interfere with or delay the war effort of the United Nations and was the recommendation capable of the accomplishment under war conditions? The delegates at Bermuda felt bound to reject certain proposals which were not capable of meeting these tests. The delegates were able to agree on a number of concrete recommendations which they are jointly submitting to their governments and which, it is felt, will pass the tests set forth above and will lead to the relief of a substantial number of refugees of all races and nationalities. Since the recommendations necessarily concern governments other than those represented at the Bermuda conference and involve military considerations, they must remain confidential. It may be said, however, that in the course of discussion the refugee problem was broken down into its main elements. Questions of shipping, food, and supply were fully investigated. The delegates also agreed on recommendations regarding the form of intergovernmental organization which was best fitted, in their opinion, to handle the problem in the future. This organization would have to be flexible enough to permit it to consider without prejudice any new factors that might come to its attention. In each of these fields the delegates were able to submit agreed proposals for consideration of their respective governments.

Source: Department of State Bulletin, May 1, 1943.

EXTRACT FROM WRITTEN EVIDENCE OF RUDOLPH HOESS, COMMANDER OF THE AUSCHWITZ EXTERMINATION CAMP

Rudolph Hoess was the commandant of Auschwitz between 1940 and 1943. During his tenure he introduced Zyklon B as the preferred method of killing the Jews and other victims who were brought to the death camp. In his autobiography, *Kommandant in Auschwitz* (which first appeared in Germany in 1958), Hoess details the instruction he received from Himmler to implement the Final Solution. This excerpt from his autobiography is an important part of the evidence documenting the reasons for and the implementation of the killing process at Auschwitz. In the autobiography, Hoess characterized himself as someone who had a strong compulsion to obey orders. The extract includes the order to annihilate the Jews that Hoess so dutifully carried out.

Document 9
EXTRACT FROM WRITTEN EVIDENCE OF RUDOLPH HOESS, COMMANDER OF THE AUSCHWITZ EXTERMINATION CAMP

In the summer of 1941, I cannot remember the exact date, I was suddenly summoned to the *Reichsführer* SS [Heinrich Himmler], directly by his adjutant's office. Contrary to his usual custom, Himmler received me without his adjutant being present and said in effect:

"The Führer has ordered that the Jewish question be solved once and for all and that we, the SS, are to implement that order.

"The existing extermination centers in the East are not in a position to carry out the large *Aktionen* which are anticipated. I have therefore ear-marked Auschwitz for this purpose, both because of its good position as regards communications and because the area can easily be isolated and camouflaged. At first I thought of calling in a senior officer for this job, but I changed my mind in order to avoid difficulties concerning the terms of reference. I have now decided to entrust this task to you. It is difficult and onerous and calls for complete devotion notwithstanding the difficulties that may arise. You will learn further details from *Sturmbannführer* Eich-mann of the Reich Security Main Office who will call on you in the immediate future.

"The departments concerned will be notified by me in due course. You will treat this order as absolutely secret, even from your superiors. After you talk with Eichmann you will immediately forward to me the plans for the projected installations.

"The Jews are the sworn enemies of the German people and must be eradicated. Every Jew that we can lay our hands on is to be destroyed now during the war, without exception. If we cannot now obliterate the biological basis of Jewry, the Jews will one day destroy the German people."

On receiving these grave instructions, I returned forthwith to Auschwitz, without reporting to my superior at Oranienburg.

Shortly afterwards Eichmann came to Auschwitz and disclosed to me the plans for the operations as they affected the various countries concerned. I cannot remember the exact order in which they were to take place. First was to come the eastern part of Upper Silesia and the neighboring parts of Polish territory under German rule, then, depending on the situation, simultane-ously Jews from Germany and Czechoslovakia, and finally the Jews from the West: France, Belgium and Holland. He also told me the approximate number of transports that might be expected, but I can no longer remember these.

We discussed the ways and means of effecting the extermination. This could only be done by gassing, since it would have been absolutely impossible to dispose by shooting of the large numbers of people that were expected, and it would have placed too heavy a burden on the SS men who had to carry it out, especially because of the women and children among the victims.

Eichmann told me about the method of killing people with exhaust gases in lorries, which had previously been used in the East. But there was no question of being able to use this for these mass transports that were due to arrive in Auschwitz. Killing with showers of carbon monoxide while bathing as was done with mental patients in some places in the Reich, would necessitate too many buildings and it was also very doubtful whether the supply of gas for such a vast number of people would be available. We left the matter unresolved. Eichmann decided to try and find a gas which was in ready supply and which would not entail special installations for its use, and to inform me when he had done so. We inspected the area in order to choose a likely spot. We decided that a peasant farmstead situated in the north-west corner of what later became the third building sector at Birkenau would be the most suitable. It was isolated and screened by woods and hedges, and it was also not far from the railway. The bodies could be placed in long, deep pits dug in the nearby meadows. We had not at that time thought of burning the corpses. We calculated that after gas-proofing the premises then available, it would be possible to kill about 800 people simultaneously with a suitable gas. These figures were borne out later in practice.

Eichmann could not then give me the starting date for the operation because everything was still in the preliminary stages and the *Reichsführer* SS had not yet issued the necessary orders.

Eichmann returned to Berlin to report our conversation to the *Reichsführer* SS.

A few days later I sent to the *Reichsführer* SS by courier a detailed location plan and description of the installation. I have never received an acknowledgment or a decision on my report. Eichmann told me later that the *Reichsführer* SS was in agreement with my proposals. . . .

Source: Documents on the Holocaust, Selected Sources on the Destruction of the Jews of Germany and Austria, Poland, and the Soviet Union. Edited by Yitzhak Arad, Yisrael Gutman, and Abraham Margaliot, Jerusalem: Yad Vashem, 1981, pp. 350–353. Reprinted by permission of Yad Vashem.

FROM HITLER'S TESTAMENT

As the Red Army approached Berlin, Hitler resolved that if he did not survive, neither would Germany. While hiding in his bunker in Berlin, Hitler married his mistress, Eva Braun, on April 29, 1945, and then wrote his final political testament in which he blamed the Jews for the failure of Germany to win the war. Hitler's last words remained consistent with past speeches and writings in which he singled out the Jews as the primary enemy of the German people. Although a written order from Hitler authorizing the Final Solution has not yet surfaced, the language of the testament leaves no doubt that he was the prime mover behind the Final Solution. Until the moment he committed suicide on April 29, 1945, Hitler urged the Aryan peoples to "fight mercilessly against the poisoners of all the peoples of the world."

Document 10
FROM HITLER'S TESTAMENT

Adolf Hitler

My Political Testament

More than thirty years have passed since I contributed my modest strength in 1914 as a volunteer in the First World War, which was forced upon the Reich.

In these three decades only love and loyalty to my people have guided me in my thinking, my actions and my life. They gave me the strength to make the difficult decisions, such as have never before confronted mortal man. I have used up my time, my working strength and my health in these three decades.

It is untrue that I or anybody else in Germany wanted war in 1939. . . .

But nor have I left any doubt that if the nations of Europe are once more to be treated only as collections of stocks and shares of these international conspirators in money and finance, then those who carry the real guilt for this murderous struggle, this people will also be held responsible: the Jews! I have further left no one in doubt that this time it will not be only millions of children of Europeans of the Aryan peoples who will starve to death, not only millions of grown men who will suffer death, and not only hundreds of thousands of women and children who will be burned and bombed to death in the cities, without those who are really responsible also having to atone for their crime, even if by more humane means. . . .

But before everything else I call upon the leadership of the nation and those who follow it to observe the racial laws most carefully, to fight mercilessly against the poisoners of all the peoples of the world, international Jewry.

Set down in Berlin, April 29, 1945, 4.00 o'clock

Adolf Hitler

Witnesses:

Dr. Joseph Goebbels
Martin Bormann

Wilhelm Burgdorf
Hans Krebs

Source: Documents on the Holocaust, Selected Sources on the Destruction of the Jews of Germany and Austria, Poland, and the Soviet Union. Edited by Yitzhak Arad, Yisrael Gutman, and Abraham Margaliot. Jerusalem: Yad Vashem, 1981, pp. 162–163. Reprinted by permission of Yad Vashem.

APPENDIXES

Appendix I
Estimated Number of Victims Killed in Nazi
Concentration and Extermination Camps

Camp	Type of Camp	Location	Number
Auschwitz-Birkenau	Extermination	Upper Silesia, Poland	1,600,000
Belzec	Extermination	Lublin district, Poland	600,000
Bergen-Belsen	Concentration	Lower Salong, Germany	35,000–50,000
Buchenwald	Concentration	north of Weimar, Germany	43,000
Chelmno (Ger., Kulmohof)	Extermination	west of Lodz, Poland	320,000
Dachau	Concentration	northwest of Munich, Germany	31,500
Gross-Rosen	Concentration	Lower Silesia, Poland	40,000
Majdanek	Extermination	suburb of Lublin, Poland	360,000
Sachenhausen	Concentration	outside of Berlin, Germany	30,000
Sobibor	Extermination	eastern section of Lublin, Poland	250,000
Stutthof	Concentration	east of Danzig (Gdansk), Poland	65,000
Treblinka	Extermination	northeast section of *Generalgouvernment*	870,000

Appendix II
Estimated Jewish Losses in the Holocaust

Country	Initial Jewish Population	Minimum Loss	Maximum Loss
Austria	185,000	50,000	50,000
Belgium	65,700	28,900	28,900
Bohemia and Moravia	118,310	78,150	78,150
Bulgaria	50,000	0	0
Denmark	7,800	60	60
Estonia	4,500	1,500	2,000
Finland	2,000	7	7
France	350,000	77,320	77,320
Germany	566,000	134,500	141,500
Greece	77,380	60,000	67,000
Hungary	825,000	550,000	569,000
Italy	44,500	7,680	7,680
Latvia	91,500	70,000	71,500
Lithuania	168,000	140,000	143,000
Luxembourg	3,500	1,950	1,950
Netherlands	140,000	100,000	100,000
Norway	1,700	762	762
Poland	3,300,000	2,900,000	3,000,000
Romania	609,000	271,000	287,000
Slovakia	88,950	68,000	71,000
Soviet Union	3,020,000	1,000,000	1,100,000
Yugoslavia	78,000	56,200	63,300
Total	9,796,840	5,596,029	5,860,129
Rounded	9,797,000	5,596,000	5,860,000

Source: From Appendix, "Estimated Jewish Losses in the Holocaust" compiled by Yehuda Bauer and Robert Rozett. Reprinted with permission of Macmillan Library Reference USA, a Simon & Schuster Macmillan Company from *Encyclopedia of the Holocaust,* Israel Gutman, Editor in Chief. Vol. 4, p. 1799. Copyright © by Macmillan Publishing Company.

Glossary of Selected Terms

Aktion: Any German military action for political or racial purposes. Most commonly used to describe the German liquidation of the ghettos for the purpose of deporting Jews to the death camps.

Aktion Reinhard: Code name for the extermination of the Jews in the *Generalgouvernment*. The Treblinka, Sobibor, and Belzec extermination camps were constructed for this purpose. The operation was named in memory of Reich Main Security Office chief Reinhard Heydrich, who was assassinated in Prague on May 27, 1942.

Aktion T4: The German euthanasia program launched following the outbreak of World War II. The headquarters of the operation was located on Tiergarten Strasse 4 in Berlin. The euthanasia program was responsible for the killing of more than 100,000 "lives not worth living," including mentally retarded men, women and children, as well as others designated as "asocials."

Allies: The primary countries that fought against Germany in World War II—the United States, Great Britain, and the Soviet Union—as well as resistance groups such as the French and Poles who had their headquarters in England.

Anschluss: The annexation of Austria by the Nazis on March 13, 1938, and its incorporation as a province (Ostmark) into the German Reich.

Antisemitism: A term coined by Wilhelm Marr in 1879 to distinguish between traditional anti-Jewish hatred based on religion to a more inclusive definition based on race.

Appells: The most feared part of the day for inmates of the slave labor camps. Inmates were forced to stand for hours at attention while prisoners were counted and inspected for possible illness. Sometimes special roll calls were announced for the purpose of inmates' witnessing the meting out of punishments, beatings, or executions.

"Arbeit Macht Frei" ("Work Makes Free"): Slogan found above the gates of Auschwitz I and Dachau.

Arrow Cross Party: The antisemitic and pro-Nazi Hungarian political party.

Aryan: An Indo-European language group whose spoken tongue was derived from Sanskrit. Aryans were viewed by the Nazis as a superior race.

Aryanization: The forcible expropriation of Jewish businesses and private property by the German authorities in Germany, and later in German-occupied Europe.

Auschwitz I: The main camp at Auschwitz that employed slave labor.

Auschwitz II: Birkenau, the extermination camp.

Auschwitz III: The Buna-Monowitz camp that used slave labor for the production of synthetic rubber for the I. G. Farben corporation.

Axis: Nazi Germany and its allies: Italy, Japan, Hungary, and other countries under German influence.

Babi Yar: A ravine near Kiev where in 1941 the Nazis, with the support of Ukrainian auxiliaries, shot and buried over 100,000 Jews in one mass grave.

Badge, Yellow: Germany insisted that Jews wear the yellow Star of David in order to distinguish them from the rest of the population. First introduced in Lublin, Poland in November 1939, it later was required of Jews in the occupied countries.

Beer Hall Putsch: In 1923 Hitler failed to overthrow the government of Bavaria as the first step in the Nazi objective of overthrowing the Weimar Republic. This took place in a famous beer hall in Munich, Bürgerbräukeller. Hitler was tried and sentenced to nine years in prison but served only five months.

Bermuda Conference: The conference convened by the United States and Great Britain on April 19, 1943, for the purpose of finding a solution to the wartime refugee problem. The meeting was a failure inasmuch as none of the countries present were willing to bend their immigration laws to take in refugees, and there was an insistence that the Jewish character of the crisis be played down.

Blood Libel: Medieval belief that Jews murder Christian children to obtain their blood for the baking of unleavened bread on Passover. The Germans encouraged the spread of this libel in order to fan antisemitism in Germany and the occupied countries.

Bolshevism: Refers to the communist dictatorship established by Lenin in Russia in October 1917. The Nazis claimed that the bolshevik revolution was the work of the Jews and propagandized that bolshevism was "a Jewish invention."

Buchenwald: Located in central Germany, one of the three original German concentration camps, opened in 1933.

"Canada": The area in Auschwitz where the Jewish victims' baggage and other personal property was stored. The term was used by inmates who believed Canada was a country of great wealth.

Concentration Camps: A group of political "rehabilitation" and labor camps that the Nazis introduced in 1933 within Germany.

Crematorium: A furnace built in the death camps for the purpose of cremating bodies after death by gassing, disease, or starvation.

Dachau: The first of the Nazi concentration camps located outside Munich. The camp, known for its cruelty, opened in March 1933 and interned a variety of prisoners, including socialists, communists, Jews, gypsies, homosexuals, and others viewed as enemies of the Third Reich. The number of inmates reached a peak of 17,000 during World War II.

Death Marches: Toward the end of World War II, the Germans forced concentration camp inmates to march to different locations as they retreated from the Allied armies. The inmates were generally Jews, and the marches were characterized by much cruelty and many deaths.

Degesch: The German firm that distributed the Zyklon B used to exterminate Jews in Auschwitz.

Deportation: The resettlement of Jews from Nazi-occupied countries to the labor or death camps.

Economic and Administrative Main Office (WVHA): The office headed by Oswald Pohl responsible for all work projects in the concentration camps, as well as the camp inspectorate. The WVHA saw to it that the valuables seized from gassed Jewish inmates (clothing, hair, bracelets, wedding rings, etc.) were sent back to Germany for use in the war effort.

Einsatzgrüppen: Literally "action squads." These were the mobile units of the SS and SD that accompanied the German army in Poland in September 1939 and the Soviet Union in June 1941. The four squads sent into the Soviet Union were ordered to kill political opponents, and in the process they perpetrated mass murder, mostly against Jews.

Enabling Act (Law for Terminating the Suffering of People and Reich): In reaction to the Reichstag fire in February 1933, the German government passed the law on March 23, 1933, on which Hitler's dictatorship was based from 1933 until 1945. The law enabled the chancellor to pass laws that bypassed the constitution without the consent of the Reichstag.

Endlosung: German euphemism for the "Final Solution of the Jewish Question," or the objective of annihilating the Jews of Europe.

Euthanasia Program: In the fall of 1939, Hitler officially authorized the "mercy" killing of the "incurably sick." The operation, known as the T-4 program, consisted of six euthanasia installations, where the patients were gassed in rooms camouflaged as shower chambers. It has been estimated that close to 100,000 people were killed in this manner. Hitler suspended the program in the fall of 1941 because of widespread protest in Germany. Many of the personnel from the program were used in the killing operations in the extermination camps.

Evian Conference: The conference convened in July 1938 in Evian, France, to deal with the problem of Jewish refugees' attempting to escape the extreme persecution that followed in the wake of Germany's annexation of Austria. Convened by the United States and including representatives of the western democracies, the conference failed to solve the crisis inasmuch as none of the participating countries were willing to liberalize their immigration laws in order to absorb the refugees or to find places of refuge for the victims of Nazi persecution.

"Farther East": German euphemism for the gas chambers at Auschwitz.

"Final Solution": Nazi code name for the destruction of European Jewry.

Freikorps: Paramilitary groups formed by German officers following the defeat in World War I. Their primary objective was to defend Germany from the communist revolution at home. Dissolved in 1921.

Gauleiter: Nazi Party head in the main territorial unit (*Gau*) in the Reich.

Generalgouvernment: The administrative unit of that part of occupied Poland not annexed to Germany following its conquest in September 1939. It contained the districts of Galicia, Krakow, Lublin, Radom, and Warsaw.

Genocide: The deliberate policy of a state to destroy an entire racial, political, or cultural group of people. The term was first used by Raphael Lemkin in 1944 to describe Nazi violence toward the Jews and the Poles.

Gestapo: Together with the criminal police, the Gestapo constituted the secret state police. The primary function of the Gestapo was to identify enemies of the Reich, put them in "protective custody," use any means necessary to extract information, and send them to prison or concentration camps.

Ghetto: The German revival of the seventeenth-century system that relegated Jews to a designated area of a city where they were forbidden to leave without a pass. The term derives from the Italian word for an iron foundry, the location of the first Jewish ghetto.

Haavara ("Transfer Agreement"): Controversial agreement signed between the German government and the German Zionist Federation and Anglo-Palestine Bank in August 1933, that allowed for the emigration of Jews and the transfer of their capital to Palestine in the form of German goods.

Hlinka Guard: The antisemitic and Nazi-influenced militia of the Slovak People's Party in Slovakia.

Holocaust: Derives from the Greek and signifies a "burnt offering" or sacrifice to God. Generally used to describe the German policy of physically annihilating the Jews of Europe.

Iron Guard: The antisemitic Romanian fascist movement.

Judenfrei: Literally "free of Jews." The Nazi term for areas that had been cleansed of Jews through deportation to the extermination camps.

Judenräte: Council of Jewish leaders established by the Nazis in the ghettos for the purpose of implementing their orders in German occupied Europe.

Judenrein: Literally "cleansed of Jews." The Nazis used the term interchangeably with *Judenfrei*.

Kapo: Trustee or overseer supervisor of inmate laborers in the concentration camps. Sometimes used to describe any prisoner who was given an assignment and collaborated with the Nazis.

Kristallnacht ("Night of the Broken Glass"): State-organized pogrom against Jews in Germany and Austria on November 9–10, 1938.

Lebensborn ("Fountain of Life"): Established by Heinrich Himmler in 1936, primarily to facilitate the adoption of "racially appropriate" children by childless SS couples and to encourage the birth of "racially sound" offspring.

Lebensraum ("Living Space"): The ideological principle behind Nazi foreign policy that entailed the conquest of territories for the purpose of resettling millions of ethnic Germans in the east.

Madagascar Plan: German plan formulated in the spring of 1940 for the expulsion of Europe's Jews and their resettlement on the French island off the southeastern coast of Africa. The plan was abandoned that autumn.

Mein Kampf (*My Struggle*): Hitler's autobiography written in Landsberg prison in 1924 and published in two volumes (July 1925 and December 1926). The book expounds on Hitler's antisemitism and ideology.

Mischlinge: Nazi term for persons having one or two Jewish grandparents.

Mit Brennender Sorge ("With Burning Concern"): Encyclical issued by Pope Pius XI on March 14, 1937, assailing the racist nature of the Nazi government.

Muselmann: Concentration camp term for an emaciated inmate on the verge of death from starvation and exhaustion.

NSDAP: National Socialist Worker's Party. The Nazi Party.

Nuremberg Laws: Two laws that removed Jewish citizenship in Germany and defined the Jews racially. The laws were proclaimed at the annual party meeting in Nuremberg on September 15, 1935.

Nuremberg Trial: Following the end of World War II, twenty-two major Nazi leaders were put on trial in Nuremberg in 1945 and 1946 for crimes against humanity. They were tried by the International Military Tribunal, which included the United States, Great Britain, and the Soviet Union.

Oneg Shabbat ("Sabbath Delight"): Code name for a secret archive in the Warsaw ghetto under German occupation detailing the events that shaped ghetto life. The most important source for the history of the ghetto from October 1939 to its liquidation in 1943.

Partisans: Refers to the anti-Nazi underground fighters in German-occupied eastern Europe.

Reich Central Office for Jewish Emigration: Headed by Adolf Eichmann, the agency was concerned with matters relating to Jewish emigration until October 1941, when further Jewish emigration was prohibited.

Reich Security Main Office: The main security agency, formed on September 22, 1939, from the merger of the SD and the state secret police. Headed by Reinhard Heydrich until his assassination in 1942.

Reichswehr: The name of the German army from 1919 until 1935, when it became the *Wehrmacht.*

Resettlement: German euphemism for deportation to the death camps.

Righteous among the Nations: The name given to non-Jews, by Yad Vashem in Israel, to those who risked their lives to save Jews during the Holocaust.

SA (Storm Troopers): Founded in 1921, the SA, sometimes referred to as the Brownshirts, was the shock troops of the Nazi party.

Schwarze Korps, Das: The official SS newspaper.

SD: The Security Service founded in 1932 under the leadership of Reinhard Heydrich. In 1939 it was merged into the Reich Security Main Office.

Selektion: The term referring to Jewish deportees who arrived at the death camps where the apparently able-bodied were selected for forced labor and those who appeared unfit for labor were sent to their death. Also refers to the selection of Jews in the ghetto who were marked for deportation to the death camps.

Shoah: Hebrew term for the Holocaust.

SIPO (Security Police): The Gestapo, the criminal police, and the border police. Fused with the SD when Heydrich became head of the Reich Main Security Office.

Social Darwinism: The application of Darwinian biological theory to society. Hitler was a strong believer in that aspect of Social Darwinism that popularized the theory of survival of the fittest.

Sonderbehandlung ("Special Treatment"): Euphemism for the extermination of European Jewry. The term was also used by *Einsatzgrüppen* commanders in the Soviet Union in their reports to Berlin, which detailed their mass murder of Jews.

Sonderkommando (Special Squad): SS or *Einsatzgrüppe* detachments. Also refers to the Jewish units in the extermination camps who removed the bodies of those gassed and buried them or placed them in the crematoriums.

SS (Protection Squad): Originally formed as Hitler's personal guard in 1925, it emerged under Heinrich Himmler's leadership, starting in 1929, into the most feared element in the Nazi Party. It was the SS that assumed the responsibility to implement the Final Solution.

Stürmer, Der (*The Attacker*): The antisemitic weekly Nazi newspaper edited by Julius Streicher.

Swastika: Ancient symbol originating in India. The Nazis appropriated the swastika as a symbol of Aryan supremacy.

Thule Society: Founded in 1918 by Rudolph von Sebattendorf, a society dedicated to German nationalism, the occult, and the promotion of antisemitism. Its members included Dietrich Eckert, Alfred Rosenberg, Hans Frank, and Rudolph Hoess. The society funded the fledgling National Socialist Worker's Party, and many of its members eventually joined the Nazi Party.

Umschlagplatz: The area near the railway tracks in Warsaw where Jews were assembled for deportation to the death camps.

Ustasa: Croatian nationalist and antisemitic organization that came into power in April 1941 with the creation of the Croatian state. Responsible for the murder of Serbs, Jews, and gypsies.

Vichy: The capital of unoccupied France and the headquarters of the government led by Marshal Philippe Pétain. The government collaborated with the Germans and, without much prodding, cooperated in the deportation of French Jews to Auschwitz. The Germans occupied Vichy in November 1942.

Völkisch: Refers to pre–World War I German nationalists whose antisemitism was grounded in racist theory.

Völkischer Beobachter (*People's Observer*): Main newspaper of the Nazi Party.

Völksgemeinschaft: "Folk community" or the Aryan national community of the German people.

Waffen-SS: Militarized units of the SS.

Wannsee Conference: Meeting called by Reinhard Heydrich on January 20, 1942, at Wannsee, a suburb of Berlin. The purpose of the meeting was to coordinate the Final Solution with other government agencies.

War Refugee Board: The board established by order of President Franklin Delano Roosevelt in January 1944 for the purpose of rescuing Jews from German-occupied Europe.

Warthegau: The western Polish district annexed to Germany after September 1939.

Wehrmacht: The combined German armed forces.

Yad Vashem: The Holocaust memorial museum in Jerusalem.

ZOB: Polish acronym for the Jewish Fighting Organization in the Warsaw ghetto.

Zyklon B: Hydrogen cyanide or prussic acid pesticide distributed by the Degesh Company. The chemical was first used in the euthanasia program and later used to gas Jews in Auschwitz.

Annotated Bibliography

Arad, Yitzhak. *The Pictorial History of the Holocaust*. New York: Macmillan, 1993.
The story of the Holocaust told in graphic detail through photographs.

Arendt, Hannah. *Eichmann in Jerusalem*. New York: Viking, 1963. Controversial
thesis that the Jewish Councils made it easier for the Germans to deport
Jews to the death camps. Also stresses the ordinariness or banality of those
Nazis, like Eichmann, in the implementation of the Final Solution.

Bauer, Yehuda, and Nili Keren. *A History of the Holocaust*. New York: Franklin
Watts, 1982. An excellent history of the Holocaust that takes into account
other disciplinary approaches to the subject.

———. *Jews for Sale? Nazi-Jewish Negotiations, 1933–1945*. New Haven: Yale
University Press, 1994. Focuses on attempts by Jews and others to
negotiate with the Nazis for the release of Jews in exchange for money,
goods, or political advantages.

Breitman, Richard. *The Architect of Genocide: Himmler and the Final Solution*.
New York: Knopf, 1991. Less a biography than an account of the central
role Heinrich Himmler played in the destruction of European Jewry.

Breitman, Richard, and Allen Kraut. *American Refugee Policy and European
Jewry: 1933–1945*. Bloomington: Indiana Press, 1987. Balanced assessment of the response of the United States to the German persecution and
annihilation of the Jews.

Browning, Christopher. *Fateful Months: Essays on the Emergence of the Final
Solution*. New York: Holmes & Meier, 1985.

———. *Ordinary Men: Reserve Police Battalion 101 and the Final Solution in
Poland*. New York: HarperCollins, 1992. Tracks the history of ordinary
German police reservists and finds that their participation in the killing of

Jews was as much a result of peer pressure as it was of ideological indoctrination.

————. *The Path to Genocide.* New York: Cambridge University Press, 1992. Both of Browning's books document the steps that led to the Final Soution. His argument leans toward the functionalist school that holds that the Holocaust was planned prior to the German invasion of the Soviet Union in 1941.

Bullock, Alan. *Hitler: A Study in Tyranny.* New York: Harper & Row, 1962. Classic political biography of Adolf Hitler.

Burleigh, Michael. *Death and Deliverance: "Euthanasia" in Germany: 1900–1945.* New York: Cambridge University Press,1994. The first thorough investigation of the Nazi euthanasia program. Includes interesting sketches of some of the more important advocates of the program.

Burleigh, Michael, and Wolgang Wippermann. *The Racial German State: 1933–1945.* New York: Cambridge University Press, 1991. Traces the Nazi efforts to restructure German society along racial lines.

Dawidowicz, Lucy. *The War against the Jews, 1933–1945.* New York: Bantam, 1975. A history of the Holocaust arguing that the seeds of the Holocaust were planted as early as the writing of Hitler's *Mein Kampf.*

Dwork, Deborah, and Robert Jan van Pelt. *Auschwitz: 1270 to the Present.* New York, Norton, 1996. The definitive history of the death camp, with many drawings and photographs of Auschwitz.

Edelheit, Abraham J., and Hershel Edelheit. *History of the Holocaust: A Handbook and Dictionary.* Boulder, Colo.: Westview, 1994. Indispensable source on the Holocaust.

Feingold, Henry L. *Bearing Witness: How America and Its Jews Responded to the Holocaust.* New York: Syracuse University Press, 1995. Argues that the constraints of the American political system in the 1930s and 1940s and the extraordinary events of the time made it impossible for the Roosevelt adminstration and American Jews to react differently in response to the plight of European Jewry.

————. *The Politics of Rescue.* New Brunswick: Rutgers University Press, 1970. Accuses not only the Roosevelt administration of irresponsibility in regard to refugee policy but also blames the president's advisers of Jewish extraction of being fearful of an antisemitic backlash if the administration called for the liberalization of the immigration laws.

Fest, Joachim. *Hitler.* Translated by Richard and Clara Winston. New York: Harcourt Brace Jovanovich, 1973. Argues that Hitler was an enormously astute politician who hypnotized Germans and foreigners alike with the scope of his objectives. Absorbingly readable.

Fleming, Gerald. *Hitler and the Final Solution.* Los Angeles: University of California Press, 1982. Influential book emphasizing the "intentionalist" (those historians who believe that Hitler's plan to annihilate the Jews of

Europe was his intention from the moment he became the leader of Germany) argument in regard to the origins of the Holocaust.

Fogelman, Eva. *Conscience and Courage: Rescuers of Jews during the Holocaust.* New York: Anchor Books, 1994. Tells the story of non-Jews who, at great risk, helped Jews escape the Nazis.

Frank, Anne. *The Diary of a Young Girl.* New York: Doubleday, 1995. The classic account of a young girl and her family in hiding from the Nazis.

Friedlander, Henry. *The Origins of Nazi Genocide: From Euthanasia to the Final Solution.* Chapel Hill: University of North Carolina Press, 1995. A comprehensive history of the German euthanasia program within the context of the Nazi plan to exterminate different categories of the racially and physically unfit.

Friedlander, Saul. *Nazi Germany and the Jews: The Years of Persecution, 1933–1939.* New York: HarperCollins, 1997. Argues that Nazi Germany was propelled by a redemptive antisemitism that required the elimination of the Jews if Germany was to redeem its racial purity as a nation.

Friedman, Saul, ed. *Holocaust Literature: A Handbook of Critical, Historical, and Literary Writings.* Westport, Conn.: Greenwood Press, 1993. Excellent compilation of essays on Holocaust bibliography and related topics.

Friedrich, Otto. *The Kingdom of Auschwitz.* New York: Harper Perennial, 1982. An excellent general history of the death camp. Recommended for a student audience.

Gilbert, Martin. *Atlas of the Holocaust.* New York: Pergamon Press, 1988. Includes 316 fully annotated maps that trace the evolution of the Nazi efforts to annihilate the Jews of Europe.

————. *Auschwitz and the Allies.* New York: Holt, Rinehart, and Winston, 1981. A critical examination into the failure of the Allies to bomb Auschwitz.

————. *Final Journey: The Fate of the Jews in Nazi Europe.* New York: Mayflower Books, 1979. Examines the lives of the Jews who died in the Holocaust.

————. *The Holocaust: A History of the Jews of Europe during the Second World War.* New York: Holt, Rinehart & Winston, 1985. Geared to general readers.

Goldhagen, Daniel Jonah. *Hitler's Willing Executioners: Ordinary Germans and the Holocaust.* New York: Knopf, 1996. Controversial book that argues that the Holocaust was a "national project" of the Germans. The author stresses the prevalence of an "eliminationist antisemitism" in Germany that legitimized the murder of European Jews.

Gordon, Sarah. *Hitler, Germans, and the Jewish Question.* Princeton, N.J.: Princeton University Press, 1984. Influential book that examines German-Jewish relations between 1870 and 1945. In particular, Gordon discusses the role that antisemitism played in the rise of the Nazis and in Hitler's electoral successes.

Gutman, Israel. *Encyclopedia of the Holocaust.* 4 vols. New York: Macmillan, 1990. Comprehensive and detailed work. Indispensable for research on the Holocaust.

Hallie, Philip. *Lest Innocent Blood Be Shed.* New York: Harper Colophon Books, 1979. The classic story of the village of Le Chambon and how its villagers protected Jews from the Nazis.

Hilberg, Raul. *The Destruction of the European Jews.* 3 vols. New York: Holmes & Meier, 1985.

————. *The Destruction of the European Jews.* Chicago: Quadrangle Books, 1961. The indispensable classic work on the bureaucratic means employed by the Germans to annihilate the Jews of Europe.

Hitler, Adolf. *Mein Kampf.* Translated by Ralph Manheim. Boston: Houghton Mifflin, 1943. Hitler's autobiography written in Landsberg prison in 1924 and published in 1925.

Katz, Steven T. *The Holocaust in Historical Context.* Vol. 1 (New York: Oxford University Press, 1994. Argues that the Holocaust was a unique historical event. The book compares the Holocaust with other historical acts of genocide.

Keneally, Thomas. *Schindler's List.* New York: Simon & Schuster, 1982. Excellent study of the German industrialist who saved Jewish lives. The Steven Spielberg film was based on this book.

Klarsfeld, Serge. *French Children of the Holocaust: A Memorial.* New York: New York University Press, 1996. Heartbreaking history and chronology with 2,500 photos of French children deported by both the Vichy government and the Germans to the death camps.

Lagnado, Lucette Matalon, and Sheila Cohn Dekel. *Children of the Flames: Dr. Josef Mengele and the Untold Story of the Twins of Auschwitz.* New York: William Morrow, 1991. Mengele's experiments on twins, as told by two of his surviving victims.

Laqueur, Walter. *The Terrible Secret: Suppression of the Truth about Hitler's "Final Solution."* New York: Penguin, 1982. Details the efforts of the Allies to suppress information about the Final Solution from the public.

Levine, Hillel. *In Search of Sugihara.* New York: Free Press, 1996. Detailed account of the Japanese diplomat who risked his career in order to provide exit visas for Jews in Lithuania fleeing the Germans.

Lifton, Robert J. *The Nazi Doctors: Medical Killing and the Psychology of Genocide.* New York: Basic Books, 1986. Raises the question as to how healers become killers. A history of how the German medical profession actively participated in the Holocaust.

Marrus, Michael. *The Holocaust in History.* Hanover, N.H.: University of New England Press, 1987. Scholarly account of the place of the Holocaust in European history.

Marrus, Michael, and Robert O. Paxton. *Vichy France and the Jews*. New York: Schocken Books, 1981. The best account in English of German and Vichy policy in France.

Morley, John F. *Vatican Diplomacy and the Jews during the Holocaust, 1939–1943*. New York: Ktav Publishing House, 1980. Bitter indictment of Pius XII's inaction in regard to the persecution of the Jews.

Morse, Arthur D. *While Six Million Died: A Chronicle of American Apathy*. New York: Random House, 1967. The first major work on the Holocaust documenting the failure of the United States to implement a policy of rescue.

Mosse, George L. *Toward the Final Solution: A History of European Racism*. New York: Harper & Row, 1978. Indispensable study of the influence of nineteenth-century *völkisch* antisemitic ideas on the Nazis.

Niewyk, Donald L. *The Jews in Weimar Germany*. Baton Rouge: Louisiana State Press, 1980. Analyzes the nature and extent of Jewish assimilation in pre-Nazi Germany and Jewish responses to the rise of Nazi antisemitism.

Paskuly Steven, ed. *Death Dealer: The Memoirs of the SS Kommandant at Auschwitz by Rudolf Hoess*. New York: Da Capo Press, 1992. The first English translation of a senior Nazi officer's account of the Final Solution.

Poliakov, Leon. *The Aryan Myth*. Translated by Edmund Howard. New York: New American Library, 1977. Indispensable study tracing the history of the Aryan myth.

————. *The History of Anti-Semitism*. Translated by Richard Howard. New York: Schocken, 1974. Good introduction to the history of antisemitism from ancient times to the Nazis.

Proctor, Robert N. *Racial Hygiene: Medicine under the Nazis*. Cambridge, Mass.: Harvard University Press, 1988. Details how the German scientific community legitimized Nazi racial theory.

Reitlinger, Gerald. *The Final Solution: The Attempt to Exterminate the Jews of Europe*. New York: Beechhurst, 1953. Despite new research since this pioneer work was written, it still ranks among the best overall histories of the Holocaust.

Rubenstein, Richard L. *The Cunning of History: The Holocaust and the American Future*. New York: Harper Colophon Books, 1975. Views Auschwitz as the culmination of a tradition stretching back to the beginning of slavery in Western culture.

Schleunes, Karl A. *The Twisted Road to Auschwitz*. Chicago: University of Illinois Press, 1990. Makes the argument of the functionalists, who contend that the Holocaust was a reaction to circumstances brought about by World War II.

Trunk, Isaiah. *Judenrat: The Jewish Councils in Eastern Europe under Nazi Occupation*. Lincoln: University of Nebraska Press, 1996. The definitive work on the Jewish Councils and a rebuttal to the Arendt thesis that the

Jewish Councils inadvertently aided the demise of the Jews by cooperating with Germans.

Wasserstein, Bernard. *Britain and the Jews' Europe*. London: Clarendon Press, 1979. Documents the attempt of British officials on all levels to sabotage rescue efforts. Only Winston Churchill emerges as sympathetic to the plight of the Jews.

Weiss, John. *Ideology of Death: Why the Holocaust Happened in Germany*. Chicago: Ivan R. Dee, 1996. Traces the evolution of an exterminationist ideology in German history that culminated in radical Nazis who advocated a violent solution to Germany's "Jewish problem."

Wiesel, Elie. *Night*. New York: Avon Books, 1969. Classic work on the Nobel prize–winner's experiences in the Holocaust.

Wistrich, Robert. *Who's Who in Nazi Germany*. New York: Bonanza Books, 1982.

Wyman, David. *The Abandonment of the Jews, 1941–1945*. New York: Pantheon Books, 1984. Influential book that condemns the Allies for their indifference to the plight of European Jewry during the Holocaust, which culminated in their refusal to bomb Auschwitz.

————. *Paper Walls: America and the Refugee Crisis*. Amherst: University of Massachusetts Press, 1968. Argues that although the American people were sympathetic to Hitler's victims, they nevertheless refused to support changes in restrictive immigration laws.

————, ed. *The World Reacts to the Holocaust*. Baltimore: Johns Hopkins Press, 1996. Essays chronicling the impact of the Holocaust on world history and examining how countries around the world have responded to the Holocaust since 1945.

Yahil, Leni. *The Holocaust: The Fate of European Jews*. New York: Oxford University Press, 1990. Perhaps the most authoritative and comprehensive history of the Holocaust. Based on exhaustive research, Yahil rejects the argument that Hitler had no plan for the extermination of the Jews and that Jews went peacefully to the slaughter.

Zuccotti, Susan. *The Italians and the Holocaust: Persecution, Rescue, and Survival*. New York: Basic Books, 1987. Award-winning book that skillfully links personal testimonies with research in advancing our understanding as to why 85 percent of Italy's Jews survived the Holocaust.

Index

About the Author

JACK R. FISCHEL is Chair of the history department at Millersville University in Pennsylvania. He is co-editor of *Jewish American History and Culture: An Encyclopedia* (1992), which received the Association of Jewish Libraries award as the outstanding Judaica reference book. Co-editor of *Holocaust Studies Annual* and currently working on *A Historical Dictionary of the Holocaust*, he has also contributed articles and reviews on the Holocaust to many publications.